THE
FORGOTTEN
HIGHLANDER

THE
FORGOTTEN
HIGHLANDER

MY INCREDIBLE STORY OF SURVIVAL
DURING THE WAR IN THE FAR EAST

ALISTAIR URQUHART

Little, Brown

I dedicate this book to the memory of my mother,
Gertrude Lamont Urquhart

LITTLE, BROWN

First published in Great Britain in 2010 by Little, Brown
Reprinted 2010 (three times)

A CIP catalogue record for this book
is available from the British Library.

ISBN 978-1-4087-0212-3

Typeset in Sabon by M Rules
Printed and bound in Great Britain by
Clays Ltd, St Ives plc

Papers used by Little, Brown are natural, renewable and
recyclable products sourced from well-managed forests and certified
in accordance with the rules of the Forest Stewardship Council.

Mixed Sources
Product group from well-managed
forests and other controlled sources
www.fsc.org Cert no. SGS-COC-004081
© 1996 Forest Stewardship Council

FSC

Little, Brown
An imprint of
Little, Brown Book Group
100 Victoria Embankment
London EC4Y 0DY

An Hachette UK Company
www.hachette.co.uk

www.littlebrown.co.uk

Contents

Singapore and the Thai-Malay Peninsula, during the Second World War

BURMA

LAOS

SIAM
(THAILAND)

FRENCH
INDO CHINA

South China
Sea

Rangoon

Death Railway
Hellfire Pass and Kanyu I, II and III camps
Chungkai Camp
Bridge on the River Kwai

River Kwai

Tamarkan
Ban Pong
Bangkok

CAMBODIA

VIETNAM

Andaman
Sea

Gulf of
Siam

0   100   200   300
Miles

Kota Bharu (Japanese landings)

Strait of Malacca

(MALAYSIA)

Kuala
Lumpur

Port Dickson

SUMATRA

Singapore

Singapore

Fort
Canning

Selarang
Camp

Changi

River Valley Road
Camp

Blakang Mati
(Sentosa)

Introduction

As one of the last survivors of my battalion of the Gordon Highlanders, the majority of whom were either killed or captured by the Japanese Imperial Army in Singapore, I know that I am a lucky man.

I was lucky to survive capture in Singapore and to come out of the jungle alive after 750 days as a slave on the 'Death Railway' and the bridge over the river Kwai. Surviving my ordeal in the hellship *Kachidoki Maru* and, after we were torpedoed, five days adrift alone in the South China Sea, perhaps stretched my luck. So too my close shave with the atomic bomb, when I was struck by the blast of the A-bomb dropped on Nagasaki.

My story may be remarkable but for over sixty years I have remained silent about my sufferings at the hands of the Japanese. So many of us former prisoners of war did, and all for the same reasons. We did not wish to upset our wives and families, and ourselves, with unsettling tales of unimaginable torments. The memories that made us dread the nightmares which came with sleep were just too horrific. And on our liberation we all signed undertakings to the British government that we would not talk about the war crimes we witnessed or reveal what we saw in the atomic wasteland of Nagasaki.

Now I am breaking my silence to bear witness to the systematic torture and murder of tens of thousands of allied prisoners. After the death of my wife, Mary, I wrote down a personal record of everything that had happened to me as a prisoner. It was a distressing experience and at times writing this book has also been painful.

My business with Japan is unfinished, however, and will remain so until the Japanese government fully accepts its guilt and tells its people what was done in their name.

For as well as being a lucky man I am an angry man. We were a forgotten force in Singapore that vanished overnight into the jungles of Burma and Thailand to become a ghost army of starved slave labourers. During the Cold War those of us who survived became an embarrassment to the British and American governments, which turned a blind eye to Japanese war crimes in their desire to forge alliances against China and Russia.

It was our great misfortune as young soldiers to be swept into the maelstrom of the now largely forgotten Asian holocaust planned and perpetrated by Japan's militarist leaders. We were not just prisoners but slaves in Japan's vast South-East Asian gulag, forced to become a vital part of the Emperor's war effort.

Millions of Asians died at the hands of the Japanese from 1931 to 1945. Like the allied prisoners, the British, Americans, Australians, Dutch and Canadians, they were starved and beaten, tortured and massacred in the most sadistic fashion.

Some time ago I saw a television documentary in which a Japanese railway engineer revisited Hellfire Pass, where we slaved and died on the Death Railway. He claimed that nobody had died and that prisoners had been well cared for. The prisoners and press-ganged natives who worked on the railway died in such vast numbers that to me this was equivalent to Holocaust denial. This book is my answer to those who would doubt the scale and awfulness of Japan's murderous policies during the war.

Germany has atoned for the holocaust its Nazis conducted in Europe. Young Germans know of their nation's dreadful crimes. But young Japanese are taught little of their nation's guilt in the death of millions of Asian people, the enslavement of Korean 'comfort' women, the Rape of Nanking, the Bataan Death March, the extermination of allied prisoners on Sandakan, the revolting human 'experiments' conducted by the Japanese Army on prisoners in Unit 731 and the use of slave labour on the Death Railway.

Japan's reluctance to admit its crimes has now become a major issue in the red-hot crucible of South-East Asian politics, and rightly so. Both China and Korea have objected to Japanese school textbooks that underplay war crimes committed by the Japanese Imperial Army.

In September 2008, at the ripe old age of eighty-nine, I travelled to San Francisco to be reunited with an old friend – the USS *Pampanito*, which torpedoed the hellship *Kachidoki Maru*. I took part in a remembrance ceremony on Sunday 14 September 2008 exactly sixty-four years to the day after we were sunk in the South China Sea en route to Japan from Singapore. I stood in the control room where Lieutenant Commander Paul Summers, captain of the submarine, had tracked the *Kachidoki Maru*, moved in for the kill and given the order to fire. I also stood in the forward torpedo room from where five torpedoes were fired at me on that fateful night when so many poor souls lost their lives. As I watched tourists from across the world take snapshots of the grey instrument of war, I tried to make sense of it all. I could not explain why I had wanted to come to San Francisco and put myself through a lengthy flight but I had felt it needed to be done. I felt I had to lay some demons to rest, sink them to the depths like the hundreds who lost their lives in that faraway sea. It was a therapeutic process, much like writing this memoir.

Of course both mentally and physically I have never fully recovered from my experiences. In the early years after the war the nightmares became so bad that I had to sleep in a chair for fear of harming my wife as I lashed out in my sleep. My nose had been broken so often during beatings that I could not breathe through it and required surgery. The tropical diseases that racked my body gave me pain for many years and have made me a guinea pig still for the Liverpool School of Tropical Medicine. I have never been able to eat properly since those starvation days and the stripping of my stomach lining by amoebic dysentery. All these years later I still crave a bowl of rice. In my seventies I developed an aggressive cancer that doctors believe may have been linked to my exposure to radiation at Nagasaki. The skin cancer I am currently battling is unquestionably the result of slaving virtually naked for months on end in the tropical sun.

My time as a prisoner of the Japanese helped shape and determine my path in life just as much as my childhood did. Like it or not, the horrors did happen to me and to thousands of others. Yet some good has come out of it. My ordeal has made me a much more patient, caring person. Inspired by the devotion of our hard-pressed medics on the Death Railway I was able to care for my young daughter when she was ill and for my late wife, who required twenty-four-hour attention in the last stages of her life. While in Japan, and working with my friend Dr Mathieson, I vowed to spend the rest of my life helping others and I am pleased to say that I have done so. It is where my satisfaction comes from nowadays.

I have tried to use my experiences in a positive fashion and have adopted a motto from them, which I never tire of telling others: 'There is no such word as "can't".'

I have not allowed my life to be blighted by bitterness. At ninety years of age I have lived a long life and continue to live it to the fullest. I enjoyed a long marriage to my wife and I have been fortunate to have a family and to enjoy their success. I have amazed my doctors, my friends, my family and myself by remaining fit and still enjoying my passion for ballroom dancing. I have found companionship too, with Helen, my dancing partner. We run tea dances together and help and support each other. I keep myself alert by painting and teaching my fellow senior citizens how to use the internet. I am grateful for my present way of life, after all the turmoil that life has thrown at me – and thankful to have retained my sense of humour.

Most importantly I now visit schools to tell pupils of what really happened in the Far East during those terrible war years. In my ninety-first year I am fortunate enough, despite the best efforts of the Japanese Imperial Army, to have the vim and vigour required to tell a new generation of how we suffered.

Scandalously our sufferings, which have haunted all of us Far East prisoners of war throughout our lives, were only recognised by the British government in the year 2000, when it offered compensation of £10,000 to the remaining survivors. Unbelievably the British taxpayer had to pay out that paltry sum not the culpable Japanese government.

I hope that this book will stand as an indictment of the criminal regime that ran Japan during the war years and the failure of successive Japanese governments to face up to their crimes.

But I hope too that it will be inspirational and offer hope to those who suffer adversity in their daily lives – especially in these difficult times.

Life is worth living and no matter what it throws at you it is important to keep your eyes on the prize of the happiness that will come. Even when the Death Railway reduced us to little more than animals, humanity in the shape of our saintly medical officers triumphed over barbarism.

Remember, while it always seems darkest before the dawn, perseverance pays off and the good times will return.

May health and happiness be yours.

Alistair Urquhart
Broughty Ferry, Dundee
July 2009

One

Will Ye No Come Back Again?

Everyone remembers how they heard the news. On the
morning of 3 September 1939 I was working at the warehouse. As I scuttled around the empty cavern of a
building, the sound of my footsteps echoed off the high
tin roof. At either end the main doors, which allowed the
trucks and carts to drive straight through for loading,
were closed. I had the place to myself. It was a Sunday
and I wasn't meant to be working but I was an ambitious
young apprentice of nineteen, keen to make my way in the
world and to get on. The older men, workers who had
been with the firm all of their days, said that if you rolled
your sleeves up and kept your mouth shut, you could
have a job for life. It sounded good to me. For a lot of
people the thirties were still 'hungry' and you counted
yourself very lucky to have a job 'with prospects'.

I had been in the warehouse since 8 a.m., making up loads for the lorries, to beat the Monday morning rush. Better to get ahead of the game than to chase your tail later. If a job's worth doing, it's worth doing well and all that. At around a quarter to twelve I was searching for crates high on the mezzanine floor that looped around the draughty walls, when I heard footsteps below on the concrete. I tensed up as a voice shouted, 'Who's up there?'

The stentorian tones of the managing director were unmistakable. The big boss! He had slipped in unnoticed through the side door.

'It's just me, Mr Grassie,' I said nervously, stepping out of the shadows to peer down at my boss and his furrowed brow.

John Grassie looked at me incredulously. I was wearing my usual work attire, including a sleeveless jumper over my company shirt and tie, even though I wasn't supposed to be there – Lawson Turnbull & Co. Ltd paid no overtime.

'What in God's name are you doing here, laddie?' demanded Mr Grassie. 'Get off home. Don't you know war has been declared? Your family will want you home.'

I did not really appreciate the gravity of those words: 'war has been declared'. I certainly had no conception of how they would change my life. But there was a strange urgency in his voice that made me obey Mr Grassie instantly. He locked up behind me as I set off on my old bike to make the seven-mile journey home. As I hurtled along the deserted streets my mind raced with the possibilities. Chief among them: Would I be called up?

I lived with my parents, auntie, sister and two brothers in a newly built granite bungalow on the western fringes of Aberdeen, the 'Silver City of the North' as it was styled by dint of its glinting granite buildings. When I got home Mum and Dad, Auntie Dossie, my older brother Douglas, younger brother Bill and younger sister Rhoda were all in the living room, grimly gathered around the wireless set.

Prime Minister Neville Chamberlain, who only months before had promised 'peace for our time', had just announced that Britain was at war with Germany. I was born in 1919, the year that the First World War, 'the War to End All Wars', had officially been concluded. Now here we were a mere twenty years later taking up arms against the same foe. The irony was not lost on me.

After the disaster of the First World War, my father never imagined the powers that be would be stupid enough to lead us into another one. But it transpired that Chamberlain was no match for Hitler. When the conversation inevitably came around to conscription, Father turned to me and said, quite straight-faced, 'At least your surname begins with the letter "U". You're at the end of the alphabet and the war will be over when they get to you, son.' I thought ruefully of the troops in 1914 who were told they would be 'home by Christmas' and kept my doubts to myself.

Unlike so many in the north-east of Scotland, the Urquharts were not a military family. Indeed the motto of the ancient Urquharts was curiously unwarlike for a Highland clan and its admonition to 'Speak well, mean well, do well' could have been written specially for us.

My father George was an exceptional mathematician and a teacher of English and Latin at the private commercial college he had helped to found in Aberdeen. He was a clever man. Born the son of humble textile mill workers in the Angus county town of Forfar, he had won a scholarship to the local academy and for the times his progress was an unusual example of social mobility. He was the only one of fourteen siblings to make it out of the mill. But he was systematically diddled by a business partner and his ambitions were never fulfilled. Accordingly we lived in what were politely referred to at the time as 'straitened circumstances'.

Dad had started the business school with a fellow teacher called Billy Trail. While Dad headed the general education side of the college, Mr Trail was in charge of the clerical school, which taught typing and office skills. Mr Trail became a very close family friend. It was the third partner, Mr Wishart, the one who looked after the finances – a little too well – who did the diddling. In the early 1930s it became apparent that there was not enough money in the business account to pay the wages. Dad and Mr Trail confronted Mr Wishart. He said he would sort the situation immediately. The books were soon corrected but the thieving had gone on for many years. The police should have been called but neither Father nor Mr Trail was very business-minded and they just got on as best they could.

During the First World War Dad had become the first in our family to enlist in the British Army when he joined Aberdeen's local regiment, the Gordon Highlanders. Like so many others of his generation, he would know the horrors of the Battle of the Somme and was discharged on medical grounds in 1916, having been gassed and suffering from shellshock. In later life whenever there was a clap of thunder in a storm he would begin to tremble and shake. As a youngster I used to wonder why he did that. It was only years after that I realised the sound brought back the terrors of trench life and the big guns booming overhead, day and night. Like many of his generation he never talked of his wartime experiences. Later, after my own hellish war, I would learn why.

On the very rare occasions the adults did speak of it they did so in hushed tones. The trenches of the Western Front were a vast, industrialised slaughterhouse – where youth was squandered in a way that the old Highlanders, for all of their bloodthirsty ways, could never have imagined. Looking back I wonder now what effect the war had on my father's life. Perhaps before it he had been an exuberant, outgoing character, full of small talk and fun.

Certainly the father I knew was remote and distant. He had survived the Great War and the Great Depression. He was content to live out 'a quiet life', and small boys like me should most definitely be seen and not heard. I pressed him on his wartime experiences but he never encouraged my curiosity. The thousand-yard stare that glazed over his eyes whenever the subject came up, or when he heard the wireless's news bulletins of faraway battles, spoke volumes.

*

After the outbreak of the Second World War, I went back to work as usual and waited. It did not take long. On 23 September, just a few days after my twentieth birthday, the dreaded letter from the War Office dropped through the letter box at home.

When I returned from work Mum handed it to me and with nervous fingers I opened one of the few letters that had ever been addressed to me personally. The envelope, stamped ominously 'On His Majesty's Service', was addressed to 'Mr. Alistair Kynoch Urquhart, 9 Seafield Drive West, Aberdeen'. Its contents informed me that four days hence I was to report to the Gordon Highlanders' headquarters at the Bridge of Don barracks near the seafront on the northern outskirts of Aberdeen.

With a sinking feeling I looked at the letter again and again. But there was no mistake and no opting out. Far from being the last to be called up, I was one of the first. Suddenly the realisation hit me: 'I will lose my job!'

Since the age of fourteen I had been working at Lawson Turnbull, plumbers' merchants and electrical wholesalers, which stretched along most of Mealmarket Street in central Aberdeen. Previously I had attended Robert Gordon College, a well-known and prestigious grammar school, along with my brother Douglas, who was eighteen months my senior.

When my father's income fell our parents could not afford to keep us both in study. I had a two-year bursary but when that ran out the family simply could not pay for me to attend school. To help my mother out I had to get a job and quickly. I applied for several positions and within a fortnight, even though I was shy of my fifteenth birthday and still wearing short trousers, Mr Grassie took me on as an office boy. I was so proud. Ignoring all of the usual distractions I raced home in exultation to tell Mum the good news. I was elated to start work at a wage of 5/- (25p) per week. The hours were long, 8 a.m. till 5.30 p.m. Monday to Friday, and included Saturdays till 1 p.m.; on Christmas Days we were allowed to go home at 3 p.m. But I was thrilled. It was a good job with the possibility of advancement. And I would be contributing financially at home.

To begin with I never had any one special role in the company. I just did what was required. One day I would be packing crates bound for Wick in the far north of Scotland and on the next my puny teenage arms would be hoisting cast-iron baths on to the back of flatbed trucks. I really enjoyed it apart from the cold. There was no heating in the wide-open warehouse and you still had to wear a collar and tie. I had to buy my own company coat and I would wear my collar and tie over the top. It looked ridiculous but it was better than freezing to death. I also used to stuff straw in my boots, which worked amazingly well.

The bosses believed that every employee should start at the bottom, in the dust. Those who showed any particular potential or aptitude were given the chance to learn each facet of the business, which was wide and varied. One day, after a couple of years running office errands, I was called into the managing director's office. Full of apprehension and fearful of losing my job (something that was a sin in those days), I gingerly entered the office to be told the amazing news that I was to be offered the job of trainee warehouseman with a wage of fifteen shillings a week. Promoted upstairs to the showroom my first task was wiring and hanging electric light fittings throughout the front room. I worked in the showroom for a year serving customers who came in off the street. I really enjoyed serving the public. I sold them bathroom suites, shower cubicles, light fittings and lamps. We also had a wide selection of Royal Doulton chinaware and were renowned in Aberdeen for being cheaper than the rival shops because of our connections with their bathroom people. After a while they had me making up bathroom suites and partitions myself, so I got to become a joiner as well. After learning the ropes in the showroom I worked in the electrical department for six months. There was so much to learn. Luckily my immediate boss Sandy Anderson knew the trade backwards so I watched and listened, and soaked it all in.

There were no tea breaks and I got an hour for lunch. Most men would bring flasks to work but with no canteen area in which to take lunch communally I preferred to go home. At the lunchtime whistle I would race home on my bike. Mum would have a bowl of steaming-hot soup ready for me to devour, along with an Aberdeen 'rowie', the local savoury bread roll made with so much salt and butter that folk sometimes called them 'butteries'. Then I would pedal back to work, avoiding the speeding trams and not even stopping to watch the hurdy-gurdy man, whose organ and dancing monkey had entertained and mesmerised me for hours as a schoolboy. It was a bit Dickensian but we were just so grateful to have a job.

So it was with some trepidation that I approached conscription. I loved my job and did everything I could to keep it. Around Aberdeen in those days there was not a lot of employment. The shipyards, textile factories and paper mills had all been badly hit by the Depression and we lived in constant fear of becoming 'idle'. Knots of men, desolate and dejected, gathered at the street corners. The men who had beaten the Kaiser were defeated now – by unemployment. And we were all desperate to avoid their fate.

I was under the impression that the government had given some sort of order to the effect that jobs would be kept for men when they returned from war but these assurances all seemed very vague. There had been terrific scandals after the Great War when men, including police officers, returned home to find that promised jobs had gone. Mr Grassie, however, was adamant that his men would have jobs to return home to. He was a veteran of the 1914–18 war and it was important to him that 'his boys' go to war. It was equally important that their jobs were kept for them when they came home and he was very sincere in his determination to do this for us.

I had only four days to prepare myself for basic training. In that period my stomach churned and I shook a bit! I had not left home before and the prospect of joining up was very intimidating. In fact the furthest I had travelled was eighty miles south to Dundee, where my grandparents lived. I did not know it at the time but I would not even be allowed out of the barracks for the first six weeks of basic training.

Finally the day of departure dawned. My work colleagues had already wished me well, with some of the older men, veterans of the First World War, offering the sage advice, 'Remember, Alistair. Keep your heid doon.' On my last day at work Mr Grassie even shook my hand – for the first time in the six years I had worked for him.

At home Rhoda, Bill and Doug stood back, white-faced and cowed by the sudden emotion of my leaving. The adults knew the reality of war. There were lots of tears from Mum, and Auntie Dossie was inconsolable. They had lost their brother Will at the Somme and my departure brought back terrible memories. Mum sobbed quietly but Auntie Dossie cried uncontrollably and clutched at my arm.

'Don't go! Don't go!' she pleaded. 'Oh Alistair, stay a wee while longer.' It was an awful moment and, try as I might, I could not stop the tears rolling down my cheeks.

'I'll be all right, I'll be OK,' I replied. 'Don't worry, I'll be home soon.'

Then Father intervened and shook my hand manfully, making me promise that I would 'look after myself'. As ever he controlled his emotions and overcame whatever dreadful memories he had of earlier partings for the Great War. Doug stepped forward and imitated Dad, shaking my hand firmly. At last I wrenched myself free, swung my rucksack on my back and headed for the tram to the Bridge of Don barracks.

The Gordons had lost nine thousand men in the First World War and suffered a further twenty thousand casualties. Every family in the north-east of Scotland had been affected. Now I was taking the same road my father had taken all those years before. His journey had led him straight to the gates of hell, to the Battle of the Somme, where Britain's 'pals' battalions were decimated and the army suffered sixty thousand casualties on the first day. I could not help wondering what the future held in store for me. But Dad did not offer any advice. He knew by then that I was self-reliant and that I would tackle this challenge in the same head-on manner that I had everything else.

When I got to the main gates of the Bridge of Don barracks I gritted my teeth and strode purposefully through without looking back. I put the tearful departure from home to the back of my mind and reported straight to the guardroom. A sentry volunteered to take me to the looming stone barracks. It was the coldest place imaginable, a stone's throw from the North Sea and further north than Moscow. In the centre of the vast barracks room, which I was to share with twenty-seven other equally nervous young men, sat a dismally unlit iron stove.

As I was to find out, we would be given a weekly fuel allowance of coal and when it ran out that was it. The only warm place was the NAAFI (Navy, Army and Air Force Institute) canteen, which also sold beer, cigarettes, tea and coffee. I would occasionally relax in there to get some heat but I was not a drinker or a smoker. In fact at the age of twenty I still had not even touched a drop of liquor.

I had been one of the first to arrive in the barracks. Men continued to trickle in as we took stock of our new home and put together the iron bed frames. We were a mixed bunch, made up of farm-workers, servants, labourers, fishermen, apprentice engineers and plumbers. There were no university students or graduates. We were rough and ready. Perhaps that was why we had been selected in the first draft, the expendable? The atmosphere between everyone was a little strained to begin with. There was a lot of grumbling at lives suddenly being turned upside down and becoming regimented, and no gung-ho euphoria about fighting for King and Country. We were quiet and subdued, apprehensive and waiting for something to happen.

On that first day we were issued with our kit at the quartermaster's store. Rough blankets, kit bag, toiletries, toothbrush, uniform, fatigues, boots, socks, underwear, cap, overcoat and a gas mask were all shoved into our grasp. Rifles came later. Some of the kit was new but most of it was very much second-hand. The uniforms were ill-fitting and faded, the gear rusted and tired.

After a restless first night we sprang out of bed for roll-call at 6 a.m. and gathered outside on the parade ground for physical training, or PT as it would become known. After energetic exercises on the spot, jumping up and down, and a run around the barracks square, I discovered somewhat to my surprise just how fit I was compared with the others.

*

I had always been very sporting. From an early age I represented my primary school at football, playing other schools on Saturday mornings and for the Cub Scouts in the afternoons. When I went to grammar school I took up swimming, rugby, cricket and athletics. On Saturdays I played rugby for the school colts in the morning, football for the Scouts in the afternoon, before gymnastics with the Scouts in the evening. I could not have fitted much more in if I had tried but I never thought anything of it.

Sunday mornings were spent at Aberdeen swimming pool, a salt-water pool down at the seafront. I was a member of the Bon Accord Swimming Club and no matter what the weather was like I would be there every Sunday at 6 a.m., shivering and keen to get stuck in. An excellent coach put us through our paces, all the swim strokes, except the butterfly, which was not even thought about at that time. I managed to complete my life-saving badge – and later all the swimming lessons really would be a 'lifesaver'.

After a Sunday morning doing lengths in the icy water I would cycle back home and make breakfast for my mother and father, who were still in bed. I would cheerfully serve them ham and eggs with fried bread and tomatoes.

Sport and Boy Scout activities took up most of my weekends. I had joined the Cubs when I was seven and then graduated to Scouts, managing to gain my King's Scout Badge. I took it seriously and was very proud when in 1935 our patrol won the coveted Baden Powell Flag as best troop, in competition with the rest of the Aberdeen Scout groups.

When I left school to start my working career I could not participate with the Scouts as much as I had previously but I still went to meetings on Friday nights and kept up football with them on Saturday afternoons. And I persisted with the summer camping trips, which were always a highlight of the year. We went to spots across Aberdeenshire and quite often down the coast to Montrose in Angus, a favourite for me because the town hall held a dance on Saturday nights. By that time dancing had become a major part of my life.

When I was aged six my parents dragged me off to Highland dancing classes. Reluctant at first, I came to enjoy it and progressed to tap dancing. These classes lasted until I was sixteen, when I thought about getting into ballroom dancing. I hadn't been in a proper dance hall and wanted to know what I was doing before I went and made a fool of myself. Despite the steep cost of 2/6d (12.5p) for ballroom dance classes, which accounted for around a third of my weekly wage, I bit the bullet and went for it. On Saturday afternoons I cycled to a dance studio in Bridge Street, where the classes were led by Mr J. L. McKenzie, a first-rate professional dancer. He taught waltz, Highland and dance hall steps. He was also a very good ballroom teacher. I threw myself into it and quickly became quite proficient.

My best pal, Eric Bissett, who worked alongside me at the plumbers' merchants, was one of the few of us who had a girlfriend. But when we went out on Saturday nights Eric and his gal always struggled with the dances and the various steps. After much pestering I relented and offered them some free tuition, asking my parents if we could use our living room as an impromptu dance studio. Dad did not approve but Mum was in favour and won the battle. She always had the final say over Father in such matters. So Eric, his girlfriend and a few other pals would come round to the house on Thursday nights for lessons. We would clear the living room, pushing the furniture to the walls, and I would teach them all to dance. After that we were always out together dancing.

The first time I went to a dance hall was a magical experience. The place was a fantastic, glittering palace with hundreds of young men and women queuing to get in. Inside, the girls were on one side of the hall and the boys were on the other side. We would all be eyeing each other up, with the boys working up the courage to cross the floor to ask for a dance. Quite often you got beaten to the girl of your choice and there would be a spat. After a while I got the hang of it and started to book dance partners. I would give a girl a dance and then ask her for the next slow dance or quickstep. If she agreed and someone else later asked her for that dance, she would politely decline and say she was already booked. I always went for the ones that I knew could dance.

The Palais de Dance was a very popular venue on Diamond Street in Aberdeen. It was a picturesque granite building purpose-built as a dance hall, with a proper floor, seating all round the edges and a balcony that served tea and coffee. It was the posh place to go, with a higher admission price and a middle-class clientele. It did not sell alcohol but most of us were teenagers or just in our early twenties anyway and we did not care for the stuff. Some of the working men would go to the pub first and then go to the dance but it was frowned upon and girls would often refuse to dance with men if they could smell liquor on their breath. If the men complained, they were thrown out.

The Palais was a happening place to be and had a great house band but my favourite venue was the Beach Ballroom on the promenade. It was a much bigger place than the Palais de Dance and the floor was sprung on chains. You could dance all night and not get tired. It was also more working-class and I felt more at home. Dances would start at seven-thirty or eight in the evening and I would usually meet my friends there. I would always say to the girls that I would see them inside – it was a polite way of saying, 'I'm not paying your admission fee!'

On Friday and Saturday nights there would be a live band at the Ballroom. Since it was such a big venue the operators managed to attract all the big dance bands of the day, including Joe Loss, Oscar Rabin, and Henry Hall and his famous BBC band. If Joe Loss played the Ballroom on a Friday night, he would give a concert on Sunday night. The Ballroom would be filled with rows of chairs and he would play light opera and Gershwin. It was fantastic to see the top acts of the day in my home-town playing music made especially for ballroom dancing. Victor Silvester, a professional dance teacher from London, had his own band and took many tunes of the day and put them to the tempo of the fox-trot and rumba. My favourite dance was the slow fox-trot. Everyone tells me that it is the most difficult but I always found it very easy and girls would line up to dance it with me.

The dances would usually finish at 10.30 p.m. On Fridays they would have late dances, which would last until one in the morning. I had no problem dancing all night and would never sit out a dance. I would dance in my suit and never take off my jacket or tie.

If I had the money, I would sometimes take a girl I had met at the dances to the pictures. Everyone who took girls would try and sit in the back row, in the chummy seats. There was one girl, Hazel Watson, whom I danced with most. I was always trying to pluck up the courage to ask her out. She was a couple of years younger than me. Hazel was a beautiful blonde with sparkling blue eyes and she just loved to dance. She was one of the few that could keep up with me and I got to know her very well. She worked at the paper mill, 'using her fingers', and my group of friends would often meet up with her group on Sundays.

On Sunday afternoons Eric, myself and two other pals, Bob, a shipyard worker, and Alec, a shop clerk, would go to Duthie Park. Sometimes a trio would be playing in the Winter Gardens there and we would meet the girls we had danced with the previous night.

On Sunday nights we would go to Union Street and walk 'The Mat', a promenade route that took us from Holburn Junction down towards the sea to stop at Market Street, and back up again. There would be hundreds of young people doing the same thing, boys walking one way, girls coming back up the other. We would go up and down four or five times an evening, stopping in shop doorways to talk to bunches of girls whom we knew from the dancing.

My main interest in girls was whether they could dance or not. I rarely had any money to take them out anyway, so I stuck to work, dancing, sport and Scouts. Sadly there were no girlfriends for me. Nonetheless it was a happy time.

Far away dark clouds were gathering. Even in remote Aberdeen there were ominous portents, with local men volunteering to fight against Franco in Spain and violent clashes in the streets when Sir Oswald Mosley's black-shirted fascists came to town.

When I got into the Army and basic training at Bridge of Don I was super-fit and without doubt the fittest man in my regiment. On the obstacle course I was always way ahead of the pack. If there was a quicker way of doing things, I always found it.

After the officers had put us through PT, a chillingly cold shower was followed by breakfast. Then the commanding officer would give his usual speech. He paced up and down, reciting the King's regulations and welcoming us into the British Army. When he was done we were ordered back to the parade ground for the regimental sergeant major to have a go at us. He was one of the usual ferocious and special RSM breed to be found within the British Army and had a wonderful command of a spectacular range of foul-mouthed and highly inventive insults to bestow on his hapless new charges.

But he certainly did have grounds for ripping into us. What a right bunch of idiots we must have looked! Some men literally did not know left from right. Some boys on bayonet drill could not even stab the huge straw-filled sack suspended in front of them. Half of them couldn't run, never mind anything else. Nothing but plodders, I thought. The apoplectic RSM would storm around looking about ready to burst a blood vessel, shouting in their faces. 'What a shower,' he would mutter as he shook his head and stomped off. He knew he had his work cut out for him. He was used to dealing with the regular Army. But those soldiers had volunteered for a career in the military – we were all conscripts, not even reluctant volunteers. A big difference.

During bayonet drill the officers were determined we should picture the sack as a real person. 'It's him or you! Give him the cold steel!' they would shout as you charged these men of straw with your rifle jousting out in front of you. Some men would hesitate before the sack and pathetically poke or prod it, much to the fury of the officers. They urged you to 'put your war face on' and scream a bloodcurdling war cry as you ran up and thrust your bayonet right through the sack. I really hoped that it would never come to the real thing, face to face, but I trained as if it were 'do or die'.

In the afternoon we had light-machine-gun drill. We learned to dismantle and put Bren guns together again, and generally get the feel for them and how they worked. The Bren gun was the 'workhorse' of the British infantry. Introduced in the mid-thirties, it fired up to five hundred rounds a minute of the same .303 ammunition used in the Lee Enfield rifles that we would carry. It was designed by the Czechs in Brno and manufactured in Enfield, hence it became known as the 'Bren' gun.

By four in the afternoon we were usually done for the day and were dismissed to our barracks. I spent the time polishing my boots and blanco-ing (whitening) my webbing and polishing the brass buttons on my tunic. Others played cards, read books and generally dodged. I took to Army life better than most. There had been discipline in the Boy Scouts and I had reached the level of patrol leader before becoming a Rover Scout, so I was used to it. Plus I had had to be disciplined for my job. But others really struggled with it. If anyone stepped out of line, the Army had some inventive punishments lined up for them. They might be given seven days of 'jankers', punishment duties such as performing in full kit with their rifle presented in front of them or peeling endless mountains of spuds. The most soul-destroying punishment of all was the mind-bending task of painting coal white.

Eventually we received rifles for .22 shooting practice. Once adept with the small-bore rifles we progressed to .303 training in the nearby sand dunes. I had never fired a gun before and was surprised by the powerful kick that the .303 gave you. But I became a reasonable shot.

As well as the bayonet practice and obstacle courses, we trained in hand-to-hand combat. I was coping well, especially at the fitness tasks. There was a level of competition between the men, which the NCOs would try to play up as much as they could. It was more good banter than anything else but it was a healthy way to train. The NCOs were also quite obviously picking out people for the overseas draft.

Of the original twenty-eight of us, eight failed to make the grade. I was one of the unlucky twenty selected to go to war. After being selected for the draft I was immediately given seven days home leave. I had to wear my uniform in public but it was great to get back home. My own bed had never felt so warm and cosy! While I enjoyed Mum's home cooking and being around loved ones again, I could never fully relax because I knew I would soon be leaving again. I was *really* leaving home this time. We knew we were being sent somewhere but we never had any inkling as to where it might be. The short stay at home gave me time to reflect on the past six weeks and on what lay ahead.

The Gordon Highlanders had a proud military history dating back to 1794, when the regiment was raised by the 4th Duke of Gordon. Many of the original recruits were drawn from the huge Gordon estates to fight Napoleon's armies during the French Revolutionary Wars. The first recruitment campaign was assisted by the Duchess of Gordon, who was said to have offered a kiss as an incentive to join her husband's regiment. Winston Churchill described the Gordons, who helped expand the British Empire with service on the frontiers of India, Afghanistan, Egypt, Sudan and South Africa, as 'the finest regiment that ever was'. The Gordons were famous in and around Aberdeen and were always at the forefront of battle, a fact highlighted by their terrible losses in the First World

War. I would strut around town ramrod-straight and proud to wear the uniform of my local regiment. Both terrified and excited at the prospect of seeing some action, I did my best to keep my emotions in check.

A small clue to our ultimate destination came soon after I returned to the barracks. I was sent straight to the quartermaster's storeroom and issued with tropical fatigues and a topee. I personally had no idea where we were headed. As far as I was concerned it could have been anywhere around the Mediterranean or the African desert.

We were due to leave immediately but as luck would have it Aberdeen was hit by one of the worst snowstorms in its history. Snow piled up and trains halted. Everyone was well and truly snowed in. The pace of recruitment had picked up and, with the barracks filling up, my 'shortened' platoon of twenty marched to Linksfield School hall a few miles away to wait instructions. It was to become our home for a full three weeks as we waited out the snow.

To prevent us going completely stir crazy the bosses allowed us out between 7 p.m. and 10 p.m. We could not go home, even for a visit, but the fresh air did us good. I went to local dances whenever I could, even though I had to dance in my uniform. We had no one in charge of us for most of the day, until a sergeant or corporal would arrive at seven in the evening to check us in and out. I made friends with most of the men in the unit and we all got on pretty well, which helped. Thankfully there was no bullying of weaker members or cliques scheming in corners.

One or two men looked to me for some leadership since I was prepared to take charge of situations. But I never really bonded too close to any of the men. I was civil with them all and I got on with my own affairs. Like so much of Army service it was a boring time.

At the end of November the snow finally lifted. We marched the four or five miles into town, down Main Street, to the railway station. On the train there were no seats for us and we had to sit in the corridors on top of our kit bags. It was freezing cold and as the train rattled south it followed the familiar route that I had sometimes taken to cycle to Dundee to see my father's parents, retired textile workers in the Empire's great 'Juteopolis', where hundreds of smokestacks from the jute mills belched out a thick pall of smoke across the city sarcastically described in postcards of the day as 'Bonnie Dundee'.

We passed through the fishing town of Stonehaven with its picturesque harbour. Near by spectacular Dunottar Castle towered above sheer cliffs, jutting out defiantly into the grey waters of the North Sea. Here 'Braveheart' William Wallace had burned the English garrison alive in the castle chapel and, later, 167 radical protestants had been squeezed into a small dungeon and left to die in Scotland's own 'black hole of Calcutta'. I shuddered to think of it and was glad that we had moved on from the cruelty of the Middle Ages, or so I thought. Next we passed through Arbroath. The lofty ruins of the red sandstone abbey dominated the skyline, rising above the cottages of the fisher-folk in the area known as the 'fit o'

31

the toon', where each house seemed to boast a haddock-smoking shed in the backyard, producing the famous Arbroath 'smokies'.

For a lot of people Arbroath was the spiritual heart of Scotland. In 1320 the Scots had boldly announced their determination to resist English domination. The words of the famous Declaration of Arbroath echo across the ages: 'It is in truth not for glory, nor riches, nor honours that we are fighting, but for freedom – for that alone, which no honest man gives up but with life itself.' Now it was us that were to be fighting for freedom and a more reluctant band of freedom fighters would be hard to imagine. William Wallace and his men may have been warriors. We were most definitely not. A collection of timid, ill-trained clerks and farm boys, we were to be pitched into a conflict that would plumb the depths of medieval barbarism – against a ruthless and blood-drenched foe with a decade of fighting experience.

As we shoogled across the Tay Rail Bridge, the piers of the old bridge poked out of the waters below, serving as an eerie memorial to all those who had drowned in the famous disaster of sixty years before. I was quite literally entering an unknown world. My thoughts turned to home and a happy childhood. Mum, Dad and Auntie Dossie would be hugging the kitchen fire now, and I smiled as I thought of Dad and Auntie Dossie bickering over who should poke the coal fire, the only source of heat in the house.

Dossie was Mum's sister. Her real name was Kathleen but she was known as Dossie. Mum and Dossie were as thick as thieves, always laughing and joking. They would constantly be ganging up on Father. I don't know how he managed to put up with the two of them.

My father was a very serious, regimented man. He lived his life wrapped in the security of a grey suit and a rigid routine. Every night when he returned home from work at the college Mother would have the tea ready to put on the table. Father sat at the head of the table and was always served first. Talk was strictly discouraged, as was reading. To us he was the strictest father in the world.

After dinner he would sit in front of the fire. Ignoring the incessant chatter between Mum and Dossie, he would read a library book for half an hour then put it down and pick up his card tray and play patience for half an hour. Then he would read for half an hour, play patience, and so it went on until it was time for bed. It would be the same story every night except on Saturdays, when at nine in the evening he would catch a tramcar to Castlegate. He would pop into the same pub to stand at the bar and drink a half pint of beer. Then he would go to the market, where he could buy unsold produce cheaply, and come back with some discounted fruit or meat. He did that every week – year in, year out. He was a real creature of habit.

Dad stayed an aloof figure in the household. Born in the reign of Queen Victoria, he was a product of his generation and Victorian in many ways. He maintained a stiff upper lip and whenever he went for a walk in the evenings he selected his favourite walking stick. Mum never went with him but his plain willow stick always did.

He walked to work but he never used the stick in a business situation, only for pleasure. I can recall seeing a photograph of Father with around a dozen of his friends and they are all clutching walking sticks. I still have his stick and it is one of my great treasures.

My fondest memories of Dad are from the time in 1935 when we moved from rented accommodation into our bungalow in Aberdeen. He decided to convert the attic into two bedrooms and selected me as his labourer and assistant. It was a great time and I was as proud as punch. He was a marvel to watch, a real craftsman with his hands. He was about five foot six inches, slim, with light golden hair, thinning across the top, which I noticed when he crouched down to hammer in the nails. He also sported long sideburns, which both of my brothers would later imitate. He taught me how to swing a hammer properly, install joists, hang wallpaper and decorate.

After completing the conversion I shared an attic room with Bill, who was six years my junior. With such a big age difference we pretty much went our own separate ways – although I did ensure that the local bullies never picked on him when we played in the street. Bill was small and skinny and often hid behind Mother's dress. Rhoda shared a room downstairs with Auntie Dossie. Doug, as the eldest, enjoyed the largest attic room all to himself – something that was a source of constant irritation to me.

Doug was clever and like a number of such people was rather lazy. He was very laid-back and liked reading and music, both of which were much too sedate for me. He enjoyed cricket and I teased him endlessly over its being a game for softies. Even though he was older than me, and slightly taller, I used to goad him mercilessly. 'Softie! Softie!' I would taunt until he snapped. He would become so angry that he would launch himself after me with a ridiculous running action, all uncoordinated arms and legs, shouting, 'I'm going to kill you!'

But I was always too quick. I would bolt out of the house and run into our neighbour's house, right through their living room and kitchen and out the back door to safety. The women all knew me and used to scream at me to get out but they were never really too bothered. It was all part of the game; we all got along well in a caring community.

Growing up I was not exactly a bad child but I was in trouble on a regular basis. Discipline at school was very strict. The teachers made liberal use of their 'attitude adjusters'. Some used the cane while others preferred the fearsome Lochgelly tawse, a thick two- or three-tailed leather strap, named after the Fife mining village where it was produced and which stung for hours after it struck your wrists. I got belted frequently for talking in class but made sure I kept quiet about it when I got home to avoid further punishment. Father liked peace and quiet when he came home from work, and I was so full of energy that I used to drive him up the wall. I would run from room to room, mindlessly slamming doors or rushing past him and knocking his book off its perch. He was the disciplinarian whenever I got into trouble. He would never castigate me verbally, he would just methodically fetch his razor strop and track me down to wherever I was cowering. He would bare my backside and strap me, leaving stinging red marks. If it was a particularly dire offence, I would be sent to my room without dinner. He never shouted. I knew that if I did something wrong and he found out about it, he would punish me for it. Happily most of the time Mum and Auntie Dossie shielded my behaviour from him.

While us kids were at school and Dad at work, the house was left to the sisters. Dossie did the housework while Mum did the cooking. She was a great cook and the kitchen was very much her domain. Cooking smells would emanate from it all day and pots would bubble constantly on the stove. I can never actually remember entering the kitchen in the daytime and her not being there.

My mother, Gertrude, was the best mother I could ever have had. Mum was slightly taller than Dad, around five feet eight inches with a slim build and dark brown eyes and hair that she always wore in buns on each side of her head. She had a great sense of humour and was a terrific conversationalist. Mum's parents were quite well-to-do. Her father was a sales representative for a big London firm and she had attended Albyn School, a private establishment in Aberdeen, where they had lived in Hamilton Terrace in the posh west end of town. She was also very musical and was a great pianist, just like my brother Doug. Auntie Dossie was musical too and a marvellous singer. On special occasions we would all gather around the piano in the lounge for a sing-song.

Mum was a real Scottish cook. Nothing went to waste and every penny was a prisoner. The Scots have a reputation for thriftiness but most of them would defer to Aberdonians when it comes to frugality. Hearty soups and broths, mince and tatties, dough balls, stovies, pies, crumbles and steam puddings were conjured up from her tight budget. People used to love visiting our house. Aside from the great food, Mum was a wonderful host. Most of the day she went around the house without her teeth in. But as soon as the doorbell rang there would be a frantic scramble to find her gnashers and pop them in – much to our mirth. She had a bubbly personality and a deeply caring side that made her aware of everyone's existence. She always ensured the conversation flowed and involved everyone. Even when she was serving food or stirring pots she would be engaging with people and making them laugh. She was never flustered. While she had her own opinions – and would fight to make them heard – she never spoke ill of anyone.

Placid and calm, Mum was the polar opposite of her sister. Yet they complemented each other so well. They were always in high spirits when together and kept the house full of warmth and love. Rhoda took after Mother in all respects. She was like a miniature version of Mum and very much a girly girl who loved her dolls and pretty dresses, make-believe and tea parties. She steered well clear of Doug and me, especially when we were up to our rough games.

Auntie Dossie was a very bonnie woman but had never married and always lived with us. She was diminutive, barely touching five feet tall, and walked with a slight stoop. Her extraordinary shock of grey hair was the only hint that she was no ordinary person. There were times when she was more 'dotty' than Dossie. She was splendidly eccentric, great with us children and we all loved her.

She did have one boyfriend but after a while she ended the relationship, explaining to my mother, 'He's got very hairy legs, I couldn't possibly marry him.' Sometimes Dossie did things without first engaging the brain and nothing could encourage her to change gear. She constantly had a cheap Woodbine cigarette hanging from her mouth, even when doing the housework. The thin white fags would stick to her bottom lip and she'd natter and dust without ever removing the cigarette. She lit the next smoke with her last one. But she never smoked in front of the fire. Dad objected to the smell and she respected that.

Dossie also had the habit of rubbing her leg mindlessly while sitting in front of the fire. On one occasion while Mum, Dossie and Dad were sitting at the fire, she was rubbing away at her leg, the action becoming ever more furious. Dossie, who always sat between Mum and Dad, turned to Mother and said, 'Gertie, I've no feeling in my leg.'

Mum replied, 'You idiot. That's my leg you're rubbing!'

They were always laughing hilariously and prattled on for ever. But sometimes Mum was the absent-minded one. On one frosty winter morning, the day that the bin men collected the rubbish, Mum told Dossie that she was going to take the bin from the back door out to the street to be emptied. She went out, bracing herself against the chill, walked down the side path and handed it to the bin man. Back in the house she shivered and said to Dossie, 'It's awfully cold out there today, Doss.'

'No wonder,' Dossie roared with laughter. 'You haven't got your skirt on!' At the realisation that she had shown her bloomers in all their glory to the bin man, Mum rushed to her room, suffering equal measures of embar-rassment and amusement.

All of the kids in our street used to gather on the piece of grass down from our house to play football and cricket. During the 'lichty nichts', the long summer evenings of northern Scotland, we could play for hours after dinner and my parents had a job getting me inside. Auntie Dossie would have to come out and shout us in. By contrast the winters in Aberdeen were long, dark, frosty and bitter – trapping us indoors all evening. I was never one to sit and read a book and always had to have something to do with my feet or hands. I think that is why Mum gave me the job of collecting the messages from the Co-operative.

There was no pre-packaging and everything was made up to order. When you bought butter, for instance, who-ever was working behind the counter would take it out and pat a golden yellow lump into a rectangle and wrap it in brown paper. All of the rice, tea, coffee, barley, lentils and things were taken out of sacks, weighed and put into paper bags. I used to love their bread. It was pan-baked and would have crusts on five of six sides. The sixth side would be white bread. On my walk back home I would pick at the warm bread and scoff it down, hoping Mum wouldn't notice. The shop assistants in their yellow aprons were always nice, especially to us kids. There was great banter but they looked out for us, making sure our change was firmly in our grasp before we left, saying sternly, 'Now go straight home. No dawdling.'

Eighty years later I can still remember our Co-op number – 28915. I would get sent down to buy our food – bread, milk, everything really. We had to quote that number every time we bought something. Every year there was a dividend that was paid out. The payment amounted to two shillings and sixpence in the pound so it accumulated quite well. It arrived just before we broke off for the six-week summer school holidays and Mum would buy us a pair of leather sandals and a pair of khaki shorts, which had to last all summer. We used to slide down rocks at the beach, exploring caves, climbing trees, and when we ripped them or tore holes in them it was a case of tough luck. I spent most of my summers wearing tattered and torn shorts.

I earned my pocket money by going for the groceries. Every Saturday Mum would pay me the princely sum of a penny, which after much deliberation I duly spent at the local sweetie shop, a sparkling Aladdin's cave boasting shelves groaning with row upon row of gleaming glass jars proudly announcing their sugary contents. Granny Sookers, boilings, horehounds, barley sugar, butterscotch, pineapple chunks, eclairs, bull's-eyes, pear drops, humbugs, candy twists, aniseed balls, Edinburgh rock, peanut brittle and Turkish delight were all available by the quarter-pound. They had trays too, for us kids, lined with sweets of all colours, shapes and tastes. I usually plumped for liquorice swirls or sometimes McCowan's Highland Toffee, which I could savour and make last for most of the day.

As we rattled south on the train the thoughts of life in Aberdeen were a useful distraction from the tedium. Our uncomfortable journey through blacked-out England seemed to take for ever, with numerous unexplained stops and detours into sidings where the train shuddered and clanked to a halt. The country was slowly grinding into action, stretching its sinews and mobilising for war.

Eventually, after a day and a half of constant travelling in freezing and cramped conditions, we arrived at Dover early in the evening. The local 'Betties', the wonderful ladies of the Women's Voluntary Service, greeted us with tea to wash down our hard-tack rations. Soon after we were ushered on to an awaiting trawler, which had been commissioned to take us across the English Channel to Cherbourg in the darkness of that very cold winter's night. Herded on to the deck we had only our kit bags to serve as seats. Slowly the trawler edged out of the harbour and into the Channel. It was a rough crossing and my first experience of sea-sickness. Within an hour the relentless heavy swell had me, along with many others, hanging over the rails being violently sick. I decided to move up near the bridge, thinking if I went higher I might not feel as if I were dying. From out of nowhere a hand grasped my shoulder and a voice said, 'Here, laddie, get this down you.' The trawler captain handed me half a mug of brandy and I did my best to gulp down the burning liquid.

It was the first time alcohol had passed my lips and it tasted so awful that I could not imagine how anyone could actually enjoy the taste. The captain waited until I had finished then told me to go and sit at the stern. Thanking him, I did so and felt a bit better.

By November 1939 there was a great fear of German U-boats and aircraft patrolling the English Channel so the captain prolonged our misery by zig-zagging for hours to avoid contact with submarines. Dawn was breaking when we arrived at Cherbourg. I was grateful to set foot on foreign soil for the first time. Terra firma never felt so good. At a large hall we had tea and biscuits and a few hours later were shepherded on to a train for the next part of the journey – to where we did not know. If the train down to Dover was uncomfortable, then the third-class coach of the French train was even worse. But at least we had seats this time, albeit hard wooden affairs.

We seemed to travel for days, the train stopping even more often than we had coming down through England. Everything was so different in France. Even the trains. They were more like box carriages. As we watched the endless French countryside roll past, the men became apprehensive and conversation faded away. Compared with Scotland's majestic mountains, green hills and lochs, this part of France seemed bare and featureless.

Tired and weary, we finally arrived at a large port city that we were told was Marseilles. Billeted overnight in a school hall, we marched the next morning to the harbour and went straight on to a liner that had been converted into a troop ship. It turned out the vessel was the SS

Andes, and once at sea we were told it would be taking us all the way to Singapore. I had never expected to travel in my life and now was setting sail for a distant land, one of those coloured pink on the school map of the world – to indicate that it was 'ours', a part of the British Empire.

Conditions on board the *Andes* were much better than we had experienced earlier on in the journey. There were about ten or twelve hammocks to a cabin. For most of us it was the first time we had ever seen hammocks and they took some getting used to. Getting in and out of them was especially tricky. It made for a few comical efforts, with some of the larger men jumping into their hammocks, spinning around and being spat out on to the floor! But once I got used to it, it was heaven compared with what had gone before. At least the weather was warmer, and as we had set sail from the shores of Europe an Army band on the quayside played the haunting Scottish Jacobite song, 'Will Ye No Come Back Again?' It brought a lump to my throat. Yet we never imagined that so many of us would not be coming back again.

We ploughed on into the Mediterranean accompanied by destroyers and other vessels in convoy – and, just as the trawler had across the English Channel, we kept changing course. Our first stop was to be Port Said at the head of the Suez Canal – a ten-day voyage away.

During the trip full Army training was in force. The day started with PT, followed by arms drill then weapons training. Between noon and 2 p.m. we had to rest. In the afternoons there was more drill and other warfare activities, with a few sessions of boat drill thrown in. This prepared us for abandoning ship. Sirens and whistles would suddenly fill the air and we had to make our way to the lifeboats, ready them and stand by. It was always a complete shambles. People forgot to bring their life-belts and men would be running all over the place, getting in the wrong positions or ending up with the wrong regiment. I just hoped it never came to the real thing or we would be in dire straits.

Movement about the ship was restricted. You couldn't just go up on deck whenever you pleased. Much like prison, you were let out for a daily constitutional and, much like prison, there was some homosexual activity too. At first I was shocked by this. It was illegal at the time and aside from the odd joke I had never encountered it in Aberdeen. Those who were 'that way inclined' were quite open about it. They never bothered the rest of us and people were fairly tolerant. But we were all starting to get on each other's nerves.

My group of twenty were the only Gordon Highlanders on board. There were Argyll and Sutherland Highlanders there too, though in truth they were Lowlanders recruited from Glasgow and around their headquarters at Stirling Castle and we did not really get on. Rivalries between regiments were common, with much name-calling and ridiculous insults relating to the Gordons' alleged fondness for sheep. Sheer boredom led to a lot of bickering on board, even among ourselves. Tempers frayed and insults flew over the most trivial things, especially in our sleeping quarters where the steel walls amplified every sound or movement. There was plenty of petulant kicking of hammocks and cries of, 'Can you not lie still for five minutes!'

Once we arrived at Port Said approximately half of the forces on board got a twelve-hour pass to go ashore. I was not lucky enough to get one so I stayed on board sun-bathing and by now getting a good tan, looking more like a fit and fighting man every day – or so I told myself.

The following day we sailed through the Suez Canal and into the Red Sea. Going through the canal was quite an experience. We had been taught about this amazing feat of engineering at school but it seemed so narrow that you felt you could reach out and touch both sides. By now, though, the temperature had soared and some of us longed for the snow-covered north of Scotland.

Our next port of call was the British colony of Aden (now Yemen), a strategic port and prized British base in the Gulf of Aden. Shore leave was granted to those who'd had no passes at Port Said and we went ashore in groups of a dozen or so.

It was a real eye-opener. A lot of the men had only ever seen other white people before. Growing up in Aberdeen with a busy harbour, I would often see different national-ities down at the docks but I had seen nothing like this. It was an alien world. Hawkers pestered us endlessly, selling watches and other cheap trinkets. The heat was getting to me. Blond hair, pale skin and blue eyes might have been OK growing up in the cool climes of northern Scotland but in this heat I really struggled. To my untravelled eyes the locals appeared shifty and my nose recoiled at the squalid stench of open drains, strange cooking smells and the foreign spices of the place. I was happy to get back to the ship just as soon as I could.

During our leisure time on board we played deck quoits and cards and read and wrote letters back home. But after Aden life became tenser. There was a lot of activity in the Indian Ocean and we had a number of 'musters', fearing that German submarines were operating there. It was the first time that I conceived of any danger and felt under threat. It had all been so unreal up until then. When we arrived safely at Calcutta, the next port of call, I was again granted leave. But I was so repelled by what I saw that I declined to go ashore. It looked a filthy, dirty, poverty-stricken place. Stores were taken on and the next day we sailed out across the Bay of Bengal and down the west coast of Burma and the Malay Peninsula.

Finally on 22 December 1939, three weeks after we had set sail from Marseilles, we arrived at our destination – the colony of Singapore. The diamond-shaped island at the tip of the Malay Peninsula was developed by Sir Stamford Raffles in the early 1820s to become the 'Emporium of the East'. This trading crossroads was Britain's greatest fortress east of Suez – and a terrific prize for the expansionist Japanese Empire. Protected by huge fifteen-inch guns that pointed out to sea to deter naval assault, it had become the 'Gibraltar of the East' and was believed to be impregnable.

As we pulled into harbour I went up on deck and marvelled at the sight. The docks were busy with ships and teeming with wiry, brown-skinned coolies heaving impossibly huge loads on to their backs to unload into the massive warehouses and go-down sheds. Behind the sheds I caught my first glimpse of Singapore's impressive skyline, like nothing I had ever seen before. Squinting into the scorching Singapore sun, I could see rows of white buildings and dominating them all were the sleek art deco lines of the Cathay Building skyscraper, its spire reaching into the cloudless sky. I could not help thinking of the grey granite of old Aberdeen, wreathed in the freezing 'haar' that rolled in off the chilly North Sea. Home was a world away. But this was it, I thought. My new home. It was an exciting and exotic new beginning.

Two

Jealousy

Our knees wobbled down the gangway and, glad to set foot again on solid ground, we staggered bow-legged along the quayside to a row of Army trucks waiting to take us to the barracks. A gruff transport officer instructed us to hoist our kit bags, which contained all our worldly possessions, into the back of the small pick-up trucks.

We clambered up, eight to each green open-top truck, and sat with our feet on our bags. It was only mid-morning but the sun was high, the city already alive and raucous. I was more than glad to get off the ship. It had become so monotonous and tensions were running high. It felt a whole lot safer to be back on land. We still did not know what was in store for us but we were getting accustomed to that by now. The fear of the unknown had started to lose its edge.

Singapore was a sexy posting for British colonials, who enjoyed a privileged, bungalow-dwelling existence. They had servants to prepare their Singapore sling cocktails, grown men, known as 'boys', to run their households, and ayahs, native nannies, to look after their children. During the twenties and thirties the explosive growth in the automotive industry had created a terrific demand for the rubber grown in the vast plantations up-country in Malaya. The material was shipped out to Europe and North America from Singapore's heaving port. The outbreak of war had further boosted demand for rubber and Malaya's other great export, tin. Fortunes were being made and Singapore was a boomtown. The island even boasted its own Ford factory, the only car manufacturing plant in the whole of South-East Asia. Symbolic of Singapore's affluence was the shimmering splendour of the Cathay Building complete with a large air-conditioned cinema. It was an opulent existence for officers and colonials, with no shortage of exotic nightlife at places like Raffles Hotel – all strictly out of bounds to us ORs as the 'other ranks', the non-officers, were known.

The sheer diversity of the population was amazing. To us it was a kaleidoscope of humanity. There were Chinese, Javanese, Indians, Tamils, Malayans, lots of Eurasians and even a sizeable Japanese minority, several of whom had been busy spying for their motherland. It was an ethnic melting pot and a political cauldron. Refugees from the Japanese invasion of China in 1937 had flooded in and set up aid organisations to channel arms back to the Chinese resistance.

While louche British expatriates recreated the Home Counties in the tropics and sipped their gin slings in the country club, Singapore was seething with political intrigue among groups who had very different ideas about the future of the British Empire. Malayan nationalists, Chinese nationalists and Indian nationalists vied with Malayan communists, Chinese communists and Indian communists, not to mention Japanese sympathisers. And then there were the Buddhists, Muslims, Jews, Christians, Taoists, Sikhs and Hindus!

The driver told us to hang on. It would be a bumpy eighteen-mile ride to our barracks, situated at Selarang, east of the city, past Changi village on the Changi peninsula. As we bounced along the dusty, unpaved roads, gripping on for dear life, I saw for the first time how poor the place was for the vast majority of people. As we trundled past rickety open-fronted shops and shacks, a heady mixture of tamarind, cinnamon, nutmeg, wisps of incense, frying fish and rotting fruit invaded my nostrils. Groups of Chinese men were hunched over benches clattering down mah-jong tiles with great flourishes, gambling and shouting.

The sights, sounds and above all the heat hit us like a sledgehammer. I looked at my intrepid fellow conscripts who were also soaking up their new surroundings. We had never seen anything like it. Small, tan-skinned men were standing around fires frying green bananas in their skins while others cracked coconuts with machetes, tossed their heads back and drank deeply. After passing through Singapore City and its bordering villages, we were soon in

the countryside, and countless rice fields and banana plantations.

Finally at the end of the forty-five-minute journey, we
arrived at Selarang, the home of the 2nd Battalion of the
Gordon Highlanders. I noticed immediately that the fenc-
ing did not extend all the way around the barracks and it
seemed a rather sleepy haven. As we approached the
parade ground I saw five blocks of two-storey concrete
barracks, with open verandas overlooking the square.
Little did we realise that this inoffensive-looking complex, designed to house 820 men, would later become the
scene of one of the most infamous episodes in the history
of the British Army. These blocks were to be our new
home and they were certainly modern and a bright change
from the grim greyness of our Bridge of Don base.

Joining a regular battalion of time-served soldiers was a
daunting prospect to us rookies. We unloaded our kit and
were ordered to the dining room for lunch, where Chinese
cooks gave us British food. After we had eaten, the commanding officer Lieutenant Colonel W. J. Graham
welcomed us to Singapore. He was an authoritative
figure, who quite obviously came from a 'good' family.
He certainly spoke better English than we did. He gave us
an informal pep talk right there in the dining room, welcoming us and reading a lot of the King's regulations from
his wee Army book.

He reminded us of our great traditions and the need to
uphold the honour of the regiment. The Gordons seemed
to have been in so many of the key battles fought by the
British Army. The buttons on our white spats were black –

in memory of our commander during the Napoleonic Wars. The details of his interment were taught in verse to generations of British schoolboys as 'The Burial of Sir John Moore after Corunna'. At Waterloo the Gordons had grasped the stirrups of the galloping Scots Greys when they charged into Napoleon's troops with the cry 'Scotland Forever!' – a scene immortalised in Lady Butler's famous painting. It was certainly a hard act to follow and frankly we hoped that we would never be required to do so.

Colonel Graham then went on to speak about Singapore itself and the dark dangers that lurked therein. Pacing up and down before us innocent recruits he suddenly announced to our surprise: 'Venereal Disease! I'm sure you all know what it is. I can tell you now that it is rife among the Chinese, Malays and Eurasians. Any soldier contracting the disease will be charged and severely dealt with.'

Talk about being punished twice for one crime!

He warned us to watch our wallets when in the city and also reminded us that the military police would pick us up and bring us in front of him if we were spotted without wearing proper uniform – including our thick, red-checked, woollen Glengarry caps, despite the intense heat.

He finished up by saying, 'Tomorrow you will rest and draw equipment from the quartermaster's stores and familiarise yourself with your surroundings.'

After the commanding officer's speech we were split into our companies – A, B, C and D. I was assigned to D Company, along with three others from my platoon of new arrivals. We joined the barracks and tried to settle in. But we were the new meat and fresh targets. We got some amount of ribbing, most of it good-natured but some below the belt and bordering on bullying. Like a new football club signing entering the changing rooms for the first time, there was plenty of macho posturing and mock sexual advances towards us 'pretty young things'. I decided to muck right in and do the best I could. I was sure that I could become a good soldier and be better than most of my tormentors anyway.

The following day, after a sleepless night, was spent mostly drawing equipment, clothing and rifle. When the officer in the quartermaster's store handed me my rifle I thought he was kidding me on. I stared at the antique gun and turned it over and over in my hands. With utter disbelief I saw it was dated 1907 – a bashed-up relic from before the First World War. I realised that the rifle and its accompanying bayonet, along with my webbing and buttons, would require much cleaning, polishing and general elbow grease to bring it up to the standard of regular soldiers, whose long experience in Singapore gave them the edge over us.

We paraded for inspection and for extra drill by the RSM. Unsurprisingly not one rifle or bayonet passed. When the drill commenced the regulars hanging over the balconies on all sides of the parade ground took great delight in our pathetic and shambolic performance. They hooted and hollered, subjecting our efforts to merciless and withering comment. For two solid hours in the heat of the afternoon sun we sweated and toiled. With our fatigues soaking we were a bedraggled spectacle when dismissed and we stumbled back to our respective barracks with bleeding toes and red-raw feet.

Christmas Day in 1939 was celebrated in real traditional British style. The officers mucked in for a change and served up generous carvings of turkey with all the trimmings and plum pudding to the men. The dining room had been decorated with festive bunting and there was a cracker for each man. All of us enjoyed the atmosphere and it was probably the most euphoric we had been for weeks. But less than a hundred miles north of the equator the temperature was well into the nineties and it did feel strange to enjoy festivities without being wrapped up in woolly jumpers and scarves. It was my first Christmas away from home and would be my last celebration for six long years.

For the first six weeks at Selarang us new recruits had our own drill and weapons training in the morning, and went our separate ways in the afternoon to complete basic training. This was simply an extension of the Bridge of Don training – the same drill, just done in tropical conditions. Being fair-skinned, I found the heat got to me more than anything. But it never stopped me from giving my all and I was as good as any in the squad. Myself and the three others from the original Bridge of Don platoon pretty much stuck together during those first few weeks. We had yet to be accepted by the regulars so we stayed close and kept each other right.

Once a week we went down to the rifle range on a stretch of virgin hillocky land at the back of the barracks.

We enjoyed letting out our frustrations on the trigger of the Bren gun. Rifle practice was fun too, even though I could hardly hit a barn door with my defective gun. We would usually start target practice from a hundred yards, which seemed the preferred distance to keep your enemy at, but occasionally a bit further.

The officers would also order us on weekly route marches of ten miles or so over uneven ground – sand dunes, semi-jungle – never a proper path, hauling full kit and rifle. They kept us pretty fit – they had to stave off the boredom somehow.

By four in the afternoon we were left to our own devices until dinner at six. Most days we would walk the three or four miles to the neighbouring Roberts barracks, home of the Royal Artillery units. They had a twenty-five-metre outdoor swimming pool that they let us use. After a hard day of training the cool of the pool was fantastically refreshing and reinvigorating. We would eke out as much time as possible before we had to get back to Selarang in time for dinner. If you were late, you went hungry.

The speed at which the sun went down was something that I never really got used to. It was dark by 6 p.m. After dinner I sat on my bed in the barracks, spitting and polishing, and writing letters home. I had never written as often as I did in those early days. I would write to Mother mainly and would include notes to my whole family. Mum would tell me news of home to keep me updated. But she never mentioned Douglas for some reason I never quite understood. I think that maybe she did not want to worry me as I later learned he had gone off to be a glider pilot. I wrote occasionally to my old pal Eric, who had joined up with the RAF, and also to Hazel Watson, the girl I danced with before I left. On days of extreme boredom I would think of Hazel, who seemed to become more attractive and intelligent with every day and every mile that passed between us.

At the end of the six weeks us conscripts were considered passable as soldiers. Without fuss or fanfare we became fully trained members of our respective companies. Aside from the regular training sessions, each company was assigned to guard duties.

Now that I was in the Army proper, spit and polish was the order of the evenings, with drill, manoeuvres, guard duties and PT during the day. Bizarrely each day between 1 p.m. and 3 p.m. the whole camp came to a standstill for a compulsory siesta. Every man *had* to be in his bunk during that period. I disagreed with this from the start. The enemy seemed unlikely to suspend hostilities to allow us time to rest during the hottest part of the day. One's body gets accustomed to the habit of daily routine. It was hardly suitable training for jungle warfare but our superiors thought differently. This ridiculous routine, a hangover from the days of the Raj, was fairly typical of the complacency that served the British so badly in Singapore.

During training with D Company I soon found favour with the commanding officer, Captain W. H. Duke. Noticing my high fitness levels, he was particularly interested in my athletics background. I told him that I ran

220 and 440 yards at grammar school and generally spent my life sprinting here and there. He was impressed by what he saw and I, along with another of the new conscripts, wee Davie, was put through training in athletics for the annual battalion championships between companies. He told us to be ready for training at 6 a.m. the next day.

The following morning I was on the parade ground going through my exercises. Captain Duke, Sandhurst-trained and the best officer I had ever served with, produced a pair of spikes. I was familiar with spikes and had used them many times back home, although wee Davie found them difficult and took some time to get used to them. Captain Duke was himself an excellent runner, particularly over the 220-yard races. Training was held for an hour across from the guardroom on the pedang – not an athletics track, just a patch of coarse grass that served its purpose for us very well.

Captain Duke watched us intently as we sprinted laps, timing with the stopwatch that hung permanently from his neck. He was very softly spoken but knew how to get the most out of us. After a few laps he would come up and give some technical tips, like how to run the bend or how to maximise your stride – things that the sports master at school never taught. I improved a lot under his tuition.

We wanted to shine as individuals and trained hard. But we also wanted the Company to perform well. I was allotted to run the 440- and 880-yard races while the other chap was given the mile race. Captain Duke did the long jump and high jump duties were shared by myself and wee Davie.

Finally the day dawned for the battalion sports day. I was extremely nervous throughout the day before the event kicked off at 4 p.m. on the pedang where we had trained. I wasn't too sure why, as I had competed in various events back home without any such nerves. I guess after all the stick we had taken from the regulars I wanted to prove myself in my own way. I was certainly out to win. All of the officers, their wives and children were there, along with the company support, cheering us on from the sidelines. Stakes had been hammered into the ground to mark out the makeshift track. It was covered in bumps and rises that could put you off your stride but since I had practised on it I knew all the bad bits and dips.

After a shaky start I managed to hit my strides and win the 440-yard race, while wee Davie won the mile event. I didn't fare as well in the 880 yards but still finished a credible third. I also won the high jump and the officer won all of his events as anticipated. Our 220-yard relay team was augmented by a fairly good runner, and with Captain Duke as anchor man we came in a solid second. On that showing we lifted the cup for 1940. There was no hugging and kissing, no grand party, just back to the barracks to spit and polish and get ready for the next day. But the grin on my face remained for a good while.

Athletics helped get me out of the cocoon that is military life. And after the battalion championships I decided to travel into Singapore as often as possible to break the tedium. However, as a conscripted private paid just a shilling a day, less deductions for my keep, and when converted to Singapore dollars, it was nigh on impossible to leave the barracks more than once a month.

But the more I did get out, the more I encountered the local colonial population. And the more I saw of them, the less I liked what I saw. Most of the white people, rubber planters, mining company managers or those working for the government, conducted themselves with swaggering arrogance and had nothing but contempt for the armed forces who had been sent out to protect them. On one day off I thought I would venture into Singapore. I had heard that the air-conditioned Cathay cinema was showing *Gone with the Wind*. I caught the 'piggy bus' and got dropped off downtown. Walking along the pavement, or 'sidewalk' as they called it, I had my first experience with the local colonials. Two chaps dressed in sandals, khaki shorts and immaculate open-collar cotton shirts were striding towards me. As they approached one of them said to me in a pukka upper-class English accent, 'Hey, soldier. You have to get off the sidewalk to let us past.'

I stopped in my tracks, stunned. 'Excuse me,' I said. 'Who are you talking to?'

'You. Who else?' one of them sneered.

Bristling with rage I replied, 'Why do you think I'm here? I didn't want to come to Singapore but we're here to defend you and there's no way I'm getting off the pavement for you or anyone else.'

Greatly affronted they threatened to report me to my commanding officer and stormed off pompously. I stood there shaking my fist at them. 'You do that! But I'm not moving off this sidewalk!'

I was still cursing them as they disappeared from view. If this was how they treated us, goodness knows what they meted out to the native rubber-tappers. It was a miracle that there was not more trouble, I thought, as I marched to the cinema. I had never been treated like that before and it was disgusting to witness these English and Scottish colonials and their diabolically superior attitude to all and sundry. I swore never to become like them and arrived at the cinema only to discover that the screening had been cancelled – which did nothing for my mood.

A few weeks later I received an unexpected invitation to lunch from a chap called Ian, who was engaged to my cousin Cathie Kynoch. He was a fellow Aberdonian – a very large proportion of the colonials were Scottish – and managed a rubber plantation in the Singapore area. I was pleased to have been remembered and excited at the prospect of meeting people outside the stultifying confines of the military. Naturally I dressed immaculately in Army 'whites', my formal attire, and made my way to the exclusive club in the middle of Singapore City. I clutched my invitation to a club usually out of bounds to the likes of me and as I approached suddenly felt extremely poor. The club was housed in a huge white building that had been converted from a former mansion house. I walked up the palm-lined pavement and, finally plucking up the courage, entered the teak-panelled drinking club popular with expat traders, rubber planters and their guests. As I went in I felt the welcoming cool of the air-conditioning and the swish-swish of the ceiling fans. The louvred blinds kept out the heat of the sun and white-jacketed bar tenders were shaking cocktails. It was another, well-heeled world. I could sense all the men in the room sizing me up, the only non-civilian there, and felt extremely uncomfortable under their disdainful stares. I walked up to the long bar beside the vacant snooker table and under the swooping of the fans took my bearings. The all-male clientele were standing, drinking brandy and gin slings in equally copious measures and smoking cigars and expensive filtered cigarettes. Shouting at the Chinese waiters and making derogatory comments, they were much the same arrogant characters I had seen abusing the rickshaw drivers in the streets of Singapore.

I was wondering whether to turn around and leave when a large man with a bloated face and stomach came forward and introduced himself as Ian, my cousin Cathie's fiancé.

To my horror the man was one of the two planters who had tried to chuck me off the sidewalk. If he recognised me, he concealed it well and offered a sweaty palm. I shook his hand automatically. In a loud and artificially acquired pukka accent, he asked, 'What'll you be having to drink, good fellow?'

'Iced lemonade,' I replied, noticing the smell of alcohol on his breath and the red lines that webbed his eyes.

'What? Iced lemonade?' he roared, as if I had just asked for Hitler's barber.

'Yes, just iced lemonade, thank you.'

He tossed his head back laughing, shouted to a waiter to fix my drink, and went back to his pals, who were in stitches. A few of his drinking buddies came over and attempted some forced small talk. Ian came back over and said, 'So you're *just* a private, then?' in a voice loud enough for everyone to hear.

My lemonade arrived and despite not being particularly sour, it certainly went over that way. I downed it rather quickly, made my excuses and left. On the bus journey back to barracks I kicked myself for not having asked Ian if he had yet volunteered for the Malay Volunteer Force. He would be roped in eventually and I doubted that he would fare very well.

When I got back to the barracks I immediately sat down and wrote a letter to my cousin: 'Dearest Cathie, I had never met your fiancé before I came to Singapore, but now that I have, I urge you in the strongest manner possible not to marry him. He is no good for you. He will ruin your life.'

I will never know whether it was my letter that changed her mind but I was delighted when she called off the engagement soon after.

During this period the news coming from home was worrying. Dunkirk, especially among the Highland regiments, was viewed as an unmitigated disaster. Churchill had ordered the 51st Highland Division to undertake a rearguard action to allow the beaches to be cleared of allied soldiers. Three hundred thousand men got off the beaches but forty-one thousand, including virtually the entire Scottish army in Europe, had been killed or captured at St Valery. The Black Watch, the Seaforth Highlanders, the Cameronians, the Argyll and Sutherland Highlanders and two battalions of our own Gordon

Highlanders were all either wiped out or marched into Germany as captives. It was a terrible thought. But in Singapore it was business as usual – still very much a 'phoney war'. We never even had a blackout.

Somehow even the good news that came from home in late summer, when the RAF and our allies got the upper hand in the Battle of Britain, had a downside for us. The home islands were under attack and planes were needed to defend Britain. But where did that leave Singapore? There were mutterings in the barracks that we could be the 'next Dunkirk', a sitting duck without adequate air cover. Singapore was known as the 'Naked Isle' and that is exactly how it felt without a sizeable RAF contingent.

When I wasn't taking part in athletics or exploring Singapore on the cheap, I threw myself into the training. The various companies of 112 men alternated guard duties at the barracks with stints at the governor's house across the causeway on the Malaya Peninsula in Johore, and Blakang Mati – the small island at the foot of Singapore where the mighty British guns pointed out to sea. Each guard posting was for one week. The most sought-after duty was guarding the governor's house and only the best men got selected. I did more than one stint at his house and I welcomed it like a vacation. It was a great number. The governor had a beautiful, lush nine-hole golf course as smooth as a billiard table, which we were allowed to play in the evenings, and the pace of life was even slower and more relaxed. At night, like something out of a Hollywood movie, huge chrome-plated limousines would pull up at the house and glamorous diamond-clad ladies in long, flowing dresses would step out and set our hearts aflutter, their escorts resplendent in white bow-tied evening wear and full regimental dress. In this idyllic existence, as the strains of the latest dance numbers drifted across the impeccable lawns, it seemed unthinkable to the governor, Sir Shenton Thomas, and his entourage that it might all come to a sudden and dramatic end.

Once in a while the battalion was ordered up-country to Port Dickson for jungle warfare training. On my first manoeuvre I walked straight into a tree that was home to a colony of red ants. Hordes of inch-long stingers swarmed all over me and were completely crazed at my sudden interference with their natural habitat. They were biting like mad all over my body, especially around my head and face. I cried out in pain and danced around like a mad man. I was in such a state that other men rushed to get the ants off me. I was in pretty bad shape and was taken off to hospital at Port Dickson where I was given antihistamine and took days to recover.

Aside from the armies of angry ants I enjoyed jungle manoeuvres. It was a welcome change from the humdrum existence of camp life. It was good too to put your training into action, even if I found the premise and the practice somewhat childish. We were supposed to attack a certain target and the officers would send us on the most ridicu-lous routes. Their tactics seemed antiquated and obvious, and would have us weaving through the jungle – the enemy would have seen us coming from miles away. The officers were completely out of their depth and just playing at soldiers. They had no jungle warfare expert on hand to assist them. They would have us setting off on manoeuvres and tell us to report back to a certain point by 3 p.m. – but you would never do that if you were fighting an enemy, you wouldn't stop until you reached your objective. We were short of supplies and fuel, which meant that exercises sometimes had to be curtailed. There were times when it was quite farcical, a cross between *Dad's Army* and *It Ain't Half Hot Mum*. I kept my mouth shut of course.

Mail from home was slow and heavily censored but the local newspaper, the *Singapore Times*, kept us up to date with how the war in Europe was progressing. Almost daily it featured a headline announcing, 'Singapore Impregnable', and ran lengthy articles on 'Fortress Singapore'. But the more our impregnability was trumpeted, the more I began to doubt it.

The regular soldiers never dreamed that there would be a war in the East. I used to shudder when I thought about it because I knew it would be a calamity. Our officers were in a situation beyond their understanding and our training lacked both skill and urgency. We had no tanks because in its wisdom High Command believed that they were not suited to the terrain. This was all too laboured, too tired, with too much hanging about wondering what was to be happening next. You cannot afford to do that when you are fighting someone.

After fifteen months at Selarang I was taking part in weapons training when I was summoned to the orderly room. Scratching my head I could not begin to imagine what I had done wrong. I arrived at the office and the lieutenant in charge quickly put me out of my misery. He said that I had ten minutes to pack up all my gear and report to the guardroom. I was being given a compulsory transfer to the Royal Army Service Corp, specifically the garrison adjutant's office at Fort Canning, overlooking the city of Singapore. Fort Canning was the headquarters of the general staff and the Royal Corps of Signals. I was to take over from Lance Corporal Mackie, who was being returned to the regiment. Someone at the company must have looked at my CV and seen that I had office experience from civvy street.

A platoon truck was ready and waiting when I reached the guardroom and I was soon on the way to my new home at Fort Canning. I had only vaguely heard of it before and I didn't know where it was. As the truck rumbled back in the direction of Singapore City, I was filled with excitement as well as apprehension and not too sad to leave Selarang. I saw the move as something of a promotion, even if there had been no mention of my gaining a corporal's stripe or more money.

After crossing the island and heading up the hill that led to the headquarters we arrived at Fort Canning, occupying a commanding position on what was the original site of Sir Stamford Raffles's first mansion. A complex warren of tunnels and underground bunkers, the so-called 'Battlebox' of Britain's South-East Asia command, was largely situated underneath the reservoir that provided Singapore City with much of its water supply. It had all been constructed during the 1920s when Singapore was transformed into a fortress complex to counter growing Japanese ambitions that even then were perceived as a threat.

We reported to the guardroom where the garrison sergeant major came down and met me. He was a remarkable sight and did not instil a great deal of confidence to say the least. He reeked of drink and, bent over like a hunchback, suffered from some kind of degenerative deterioration of the spine. To cap it all he wore rimless glasses and sported a huge white ten-gallon cowboy hat. This bizarre spectacle left me speechless. I certainly would never have guessed he was a sergeant major, if it were not for his insignia. He grumbled a welcome and sent for someone else to take me to my sleeping quarters, a hut by the reservoir. A ramshackle affair standing away on its own, the cabin was incredibly cramped, having barely enough room for me to stand with my kit bag, but it was my own space with its own key. After living alongside other men for so long it was such a welcome change.

I dumped my stuff and was taken to the office, where the garrison sergeant major tried to explain what my role would be but was incredibly vague. I wasn't completely sure he knew what I was to do either. He mentioned something about dealing with 'general correspondence' and typing up Part 1 and Part 2 orders that came from HQ.

My official title was Garrison Adjutant's Clerk and apart from Garrison Adjutant Fowler in the office the only other worker there was a Tamil. I could not understand why the Army would employ a Tamil to do the payroll of the garrison when there were people like myself able to do the job. He had access to our strength and manning levels. He spoke very good English but we never got on. He had worked in the office for several years and

I was extremely suspicious of him. As concern over Japanese agents and their fifth column activity grew, I made my suspicions known but was told to forget about it. Typically I was told he was 'OK' and 'had been with us for years'.

I had a heavy workload and things were made more difficult by the garrison adjutant and the garrison sergeant major, who were both unreliable and often completely absent from their posts. Frankly they were a couple of imperious boozers. Adjutant Fowler would disappear around lunchtime and I would be lucky if I saw him back again. If he did come back in, he was usually drunk and incapable. He would shut himself in his office, lock the door and fall asleep. This became an embarrassment on many occasions when HQ telephoned for one or the other to go across to the underground headquarters – the labyrinth of corridors and offices, operations rooms and corps of signals under the reservoir.

On my first day I sat down to type at my desk below the only window in the office. The first piece of paper I had to deal with stopped me in my tracks. By a strange coincidence I saw my own name written at the top. I had to type up the official papers of my own promotion: to acting unpaid lance corporal. The next day I dealt with another item of personal interest: my company transfer and promotion to paid corporal, which took effect from that date. It was a significant pay rise and my monetary woes were suddenly resolved.

But the inefficiency of the place shocked me. It was totally slap-dash. Whatever mail came into the office got glanced at cursorily and set aside. No one would want to deal with it and things just piled up. While the garrison adjutant was off living the life of Riley, I knuckled down. I worked very long hours, starting at eight in the morning instead of the nine o'clock required starting time and working through till 10 p.m. most nights. Despite the mountain of work that lay ahead of me, and my reservations over my Tamil co-worker, I enjoyed the job. They left me alone to get on with things and I think I did a better job than the previous fellow. There were no drills or parades and the accommodation was a lot better. I played tennis at courts in the grounds of the fort with some of the signal and medical corps officers. I quickly made friends, more so than at Selarang.

I became very friendly with a signals man from Blackpool called Tommy Barker. A lot older than me, about thirty-five, he had been in Singapore with the Territorial Army for a few months before war was declared. We got talking one night in the mess room and discovered a mutual passion for ballroom dancing. Tommy, who had a wife and kids back home in the north of England, talked about the Tower Ballroom and the great times he had had there. He had seen all the major ballroom championships and was well versed in who was at the top then.

As the passes were issued by our office, most weekends I could easily obtain a ticket to leave the fort. So Tommy and I agreed that we would visit the dance halls of Singapore at the earliest opportunity.

We did not have long to wait. One night in the mess

room tombola was being played. Tommy and I put in a dollar each and were lucky enough to win the 'full house', amounting to the small fortune of a hundred Singapore dollars. The following night, having obtained passes, we paid a pittance to catch the piggy bus from outside the barracks, travelling with the locals, Chinese and Malays into Singapore. Getting off downtown we began wandering the streets, looking for a place to blow our new-found riches.

My ears perked up as some distinctive sounds came floating down the evening street. We followed the sound and arrived at a dance hall, tucked away just off a busy Singapore street. It was called the Happy World and seemed to be jumping. Hardly able to contain my joy we rushed inside and I was delighted to see that its floor was quite large and of good quality, and that a live band responsible for those mesmeric sounds we had heard was in the corner and well into a set.

Sitting around the perimeter of the floor were some very beautiful Chinese, Malay and Eurasian girls. I wanted to start dancing as soon as possible and collared a soldier walking past to ask him what the local etiquette was. He suggested we order a drink and sit down while he explained how it worked. He told us that the girls were known as 'taxi dancers'. To dance with them you had to buy books of tickets and for each dance the girl must receive one ticket. As I had never experienced anything like this before, I was bemused to say the least. I could not imagine anyone in Aberdeen charging for a dance!

We sat sipping our drinks and watched the performance of the mainly service personnel with the taxi dancers.

There were, of course, Chinese men and other nationalities there but they seemed to drink and not dance. It did not occur to me at the time that they were probably minders or pimps. Most of the girls were prostitutes. They would let you know that dancing was only a prelude to later goings-on and would go off with men at the end of the night, having negotiated a price.

I was particularly interested in seeing Tommy dance and was not to be disappointed. He had a style all of his own and seemed to float across the floor. I loved watching him. But he was a big man, tall and bulky, and after each dance he would be breathless and sweating, needing to have a seat, puffing and mopping his brow with a hankie.

After finishing my drink, and having weighed up the girls, I decided to go for it. I bought some tickets and ventured on to the dancefloor. I nervously proffered a ticket to a Chinese girl and asked her to join me in a modern waltz, hoping she might just be able to dance. Thankfully she was a reasonable dancer and able to follow my leads. It was difficult to tell if she enjoyed dancing with me or not but on subsequent dances she seemed happy just to dance and made no untoward advances.

I was soon out of tickets and went back and bought some more for one dollar. The band played a popular tango, 'Jealousy'. I never could resist that music and sought out the Chinese girl again and took her back to the dancefloor. She gave a very creditable performance and it was thoroughly enjoyable. It was rather difficult to dance with a strange partner but it all went very well. We danced late into the night.

Tommy and I soon had the bug and, carefully managing our winnings, we vowed to return to Singapore City the following weekend. The New World dance hall was open on Sunday afternoon and worked on the same principles as the Happy World. We managed to get passes to go and got there as soon as we could. Some of the girls from the Happy World club were there, including the girl I had danced with the previous week. This was a spot of luck for me and the smile I got when I asked her for a dance was most gratifying.

Tommy and I never went out alone and we arranged our outings to suit his shifts. One night at the Happy World we saw a notice that advertised an amateur ballroom championship to be held the following Friday night.

'Why don't you have a go, Alistair?' Tommy said.

'Why don't you?' I replied.

We talked about it all evening. Tommy was very persistent, to such an extent that he approached my Chinese partner, the lovely Nita, to ask if she would enter the championship with me. But since she could not speak English he was unable to make her understand. I was relieved and hoped that would be the end of the matter. But Tommy had the bit between his teeth and went up to four Chinese men sitting at another table to ask if any spoke or understood English. Apparently one did so Tommy persuaded him to approach Nita and explain what was wanted. After much excitable conversing in

Chinese the chap came over and said that she had agreed, despite being extremely nervous.

It was arranged that we would be there on Friday, and as Tommy and I returned to the fort I tried to persuade him to enter too but he was adamant that he would simply be the cheerleader.

Friday night duly arrived with the two of us, dressed in whites, with highly polished brass buttons, looking as good as one can in Army uniform. For once the dance hall was full when we arrived. Lo and behold, Nita was dressed in a beautiful long white evening gown and had a very special hair-do. This was very pleasing and in my own bashful way I managed to convey to her that she looked stunning. We had a few dances together before the competition started.

Tommy was fussing and telling me just to go out and enjoy it. He helped put a number six on my back as we sussed out the competition. The Chinese were dressed in tails, while the Navy, Army and Air Force all had representatives. The dances were waltz, slow fox-trot, quickstep, tango and Viennese waltz.

I said to Tommy, 'It's a foregone conclusion. A Chinese couple will win it.'

'Nonsense,' he said. He handed me a whisky on the rocks to tame my nerves, which were beginning to spiral out of control. I couldn't get on the floor quick enough when the first dance was called. Nita and I took the floor with another twenty couples.

Once the music started we danced well and Tommy, who had a very loud voice, started shouting, 'C'mon number six! Go number six!' Out of the corner of my eye I saw Tommy recruiting more cheerleaders and he soon had a whole gang of people chanting for 'number six'.

Things were going well, especially in the slow fox-trot and the tango. Between dances Tommy kept saying, 'You've only got the Navy chap to worry about but I think you're well on top.'

'Do you think so?'

'Absolutely. Keep your head. Nita is doing great, you two haven't made a single mistake.'

After a final faultless dance Nita and I, number six, were adjudged the winners. For our efforts we were presented with a small cup and a 'Big Ben' Westminster Chime metal clock.

We were popular winners and I think my pal's cheerleading experience learned in Blackpool got the judges thinking 'number six', whether consciously or subconsciously.

The manager of the Happy World came to our table with a bottle of bubbly and brought Nita to join us for the rest of the evening. Lots of people came over to congratulate us and I felt quite the celebrity. When things quietened down a very well-dressed Chinese gentleman approached our table and asked if he could join us as he had a proposition for me.

'Pull up a seat, sir,' said Tommy quickly.

The Chinese gent asked if I would go along to his studio to give some lessons on how to dance smoothly. Tommy thought it was a great idea and practically decided on my behalf. So it was all arranged for Sunday afternoon and I launched into a new and all too brief career teaching the 'dancing girls' of Singapore how to fox-trot. They came and collected me at the fort gates and took me back after the classes. It was perfect.

Teaching dance without a grasp of Chinese was every bit as difficult as it sounds. I suggested that I demonstrate with one of the girls so that the permanent teacher could understand what I was trying to impart. So it was back to basics for the class. They learned steps from the teacher, who was using a Victor Silvester book on dancing but had not grasped the basics of ballroom dancing himself. Each class was based on balance, posture and walking through the steps. Initially I spent time working with the men because they are to be the leaders and I explained that all dances came from the hips. Then with the ladies I explained how to avoid getting their toes trodden on.

A few weeks later they were progressing well enough to introduce some variations to the basic steps. The Chinese were very good at learning and had supple bodies. Suffice to say that a few really good, smooth dancers emerged from the class and most of them went on after the class to the New World dance hall, where I met up with Tommy who benefited from all this by getting free dances for the afternoon, as the teacher paid for the girls' tickets.

As I approached my second Christmas in the tropics, the band was playing on in Singapore but the new Japanese government, headed by the war-mongering Prime Minister Tojo, was keen to call a different tune. By now Britain was fighting for its survival in Europe and the Japanese could act to seize Malaya and half of the world's rubber and most of its tin in one fell swoop. Tommy, a corporal in the signals department, kept me in the picture about the latest developments and Japanese movements. It had been obvious for some time that things were hotting up. Reinforcements were arriving from Britain and in February 1941 the *Queen Mary* would sail in with six thousand Australian troops to bolster the Singapore garrison and strengthen the lines up-country in Malaya. The pace of evacuation of women, children and civilians was also increasing ominously.

Singapore began to resemble less of a boomtown and more of a frontier town. As reinforcements continued to pour in tensions between the Australians and the Argylls sprang up and regularly spilled over into massive punch-ups and wild drunken brawls. The Argylls were even known to take their bugler with them to summon reinforcements when the inevitable boozed-up battles broke out.

On 2 December HMS *Prince of Wales*, the brand-new battleship that was the pride of the British Navy and which a few months earlier had hosted Churchill and Roosevelt's North Atlantic talks, steamed into Singapore accompanied by the mighty HMS *Repulse*, a First World War-vintage cruiser. These two naval giants and a handful of destroyers were intended to act as a deterrent against Japanese aggression, in what seemed like a throwback to the era of gunboat diplomacy.

But the Army also had a plan, Tommy revealed. 'Matador', he said, swearing me to secrecy, was the code-word that would signal an imminent Japanese invasion.

The British, Australians, Indians, Gurkhas and Malayans would launch a pre-emptive strike and turn our beaches into killing fields, forcing the Japanese back into the seas.

At Fort Canning we waited for the inevitable. We waited for Matador, and we waited and waited . . .

Three

Land of Hope and Glory!

One evening Tommy sat down next to me in the mess with a worried look on his face. 'I think the Japs are coming. Keep it to yourself – the bosses are talking about launching Matador.'

The news was hardly unexpected but having your worst fears confirmed was still pretty grim.

'I thought they would be coming,' I said, reading the seriousness etched on Tommy's face. He was greying at the temples now, the distance between him and his family ageing him more than any number of late-night nappy changes or trips to the park with his young children.

He said, 'Hopefully we'll be prepared for them but I doubt it as much as you do. We are going to be in for a rough ride.'

'Let's just hope the Nips are as disorganised as we are.'

'Invaders are always organised,' he observed glumly, slumping back in his chair.

'Are you scared, Tommy?'

'You betcha. You?'

'You can say that again.'

Britain was on the horns of a dilemma. It wanted to defend Malaya and Singapore but did not want to provoke the Japanese into a war, especially with Britain standing alone against Germany. It was an unenviable position and led to constant dithering and indecision at the top.

Our commander, General Arthur Percival, had an unfortunate appearance and looked like a typical upper-class 'chinless wonder'. He was nicknamed 'The Rabbit' but in fact was a tough and brave soldier who had been heavily decorated in the First World War and had fought in Ireland, where in 1920 the IRA put a price of £1000 on his head. He had also fought in Russia against the Bolsheviks. Percival was fully aware of the Japanese threat and of their likely tactics. Yet Singapore, despite its immense prestige and strategic value, was critically lacking in heavy armour and air power.

I also felt that everything was far too laid-back in Singapore. In one sense it was understandable. Britannia had ruled the waves since the Battle of Trafalgar in 1805. And we had defeated the Germans in the 1914–18 conflict. Undoubtedly, though, there was an undercurrent of complacency and racial supremacy too. It was inconceivable that the greatest Empire the world had known could be defeated by little yellow men who had poor eyesight and could not see in the dark. All kinds of mumbo-jumbo was repeated in relation to the Japanese and their alleged weaknesses. We were told that they were inferior soldiers and had only ever fought other 'inadequates' like the Chinese. We were even told that their pilots were hopeless because they had a poor sense of balance, owing to their being carried on their mothers' backs as babies! We would soon learn the hard way.

The eighth of December 1941 in Singapore was a balmy summers' day just like any other. The only unusual thing was the failure of our 'trusty' Tamil to show up for work as normal. The tempo of work at the base had really increased and late in the evening I was still dealing with papers in the office when, at around 10 p.m., a tremendous explosion just fifty yards from my small office sent me diving under the desk for cover. Japanese bombs had started raining down on Fort Canning.

The first bomb had exploded on the nearby tennis court, leaving a ten-foot-wide crater on the baseline and rocking my office. Huddled under the desk, scared to death and waiting for the next bomb to drop, I realised this was it. War. I would finally learn why my father's hands shook during thunderstorms.

I should have known that 8 December was to be the day. The mystery of the Tamil's non-appearance was now solved. He was never seen again, confirming in my mind my earlier suspicion that he was a spy for the Japanese and had been ciphering secret information and documents out of our office, from beneath our noses.

While the Japanese were targeting Fort Canning and the naval base at Singapore from the air, their army was landing up-country on the eastern coast of Malaysia – on the undefended beaches originally identified in Matador as landing points. Imperial shock troops blooded against Chiang Kai-shek's Chinese nationalist army, Mao Tse-tung's Communist guerrillas and Marshal Zhukov's mechanised Red Army in Mongolia strolled ashore in neutral Thailand and walked into Malaya virtually unopposed.

Thousands of miles away on the other side of the Pacific, in a separate time zone, it was still 7 December, a sleepy Sunday morning in Hawaii. The bulk of the United States' Pacific Fleet was moored at Pearl Harbor when Admiral Yamamoto's dive-bombers struck without warning on a day that President Roosevelt predicted would 'live in infamy'.

For the next two days the bombs kept falling. Oddly Fort Canning suffered very little. Whether it was because the fort was situated on a hill or because the Japanese calculated that they could not get to the underground complex, I never knew. But we escaped most of the bombs. They always seemed to fall short and the main buildings bore little actual damage.

Singapore was not so lucky. The city was ill-prepared for this oriental blitz. On that first night no order was issued to black out the lights in the city and from Fort Canning I looked down to witness the incredible sight of Singapore ablaze with street lights, their glow acting as a magnet for Japanese bombers and their fighter escorts, which buzzed around the city like wasps around a jam pot. There was insufficient British air support either.

Hopelessly outnumbered our pilots took to the air on suicide missions. Tragically some of our planes were also shot down by our own anti-aircraft batteries. Soon the Japanese had mastery of the skies and a great black pall of smoke hung over the city. Singapore was burning.

At the same time reports came flooding in from upcountry in Malaya and most were utterly depressing. Japanese troops under General Yamashita, who would later become known as 'The Tiger of Malaya', were storming south at an unbelievable speed, relying on bicycles and the ingenuity of their engineers, who quickly restored sabotaged bridges and roads. Critically the Japanese infantry was supported by three hundred tanks. The war machines that the British Army had decided were unsuitable for conditions in Malaya cut swathes through our lightly armed troops.

On 10 December General Percival issued a special order of the day. He announced, 'The eyes of the Empire are upon us. Our whole position in the Far East is at stake. The struggle may be long and grim but let us all resolve to stand fast come what may and to prove ourselves worthy of the great trust which has been placed in us.'

On the very same day we received the shocking news that HMS *Prince of Wales* and HMS *Repulse* had been sunk by Japanese bombers with heavy loss of life. A vital component in our defence had gone and the loss of these mighty ships had a devastating impact on our morale.

Incredibly, with the enemy bearing down on us, the bungling continued. Colonial civil servants refused the Army use of civilian telephone lines or transport for the wounded from up-country. Railway officials were adamant that civilian passenger trains run as normal while Red Cross and troop trains were shunted into sidings. It was yet another example of the complacent colonials and their snooty attitude towards the Army, Navy and Air Force. Did they think we were out there for a picnic? Their lack of cooperation played right into the hands of the Japanese whose active fifth column was wreaking havoc with our lines of communication and had been working on intelligence for many years prior to the invasion.

The paperwork was dropping on my desk even more frequently than the bombs that fell around us. I had moved a camp bed into the office so I could be there twenty-four hours a day to handle urgent papers. Besides, sleeping in my small wooden hut all on its own, exposed on the banks of the reservoir, was an unattractive option.

On the day the *Prince of Wales* went down a lance corporal marched into the office and handed me a piece of paper signed by Colonel Graham himself. The Gordon Highlanders were sending three boy soldiers to Fort Canning and I was to be put in charge of them. It ordered me to look after these three boys, two of whom were brothers, for 'the duration of hostilities'. They had joined the Army as bandsmen and Colonel Graham had given them the option of trading their uniforms for civvies and going with the civilians. To their credit they decided that they had joined the Army as Gordon Highlanders and it was their duty to stay on and fight.

And so fourteen-year-old Freddie Brind, his elder brother James, fifteen, along with sixteen-year-old John Scott were sent to me that very day. It was a bit scary. I had never had the responsibility of looking after anyone other than myself. It would have been bad enough if there hadn't been a war on! I had no idea why I was chosen to look after them. There must have been some discussion at Selarang as to what they should do with the boys and perhaps they thought they would be safer at Fort Canning than anywhere else. They could hardly have sent them out with the troops.

When the boys arrived they looked as if they had just walked in from the Bridge of Don barracks. Shiny as new pins they were in full Gordon Highlander uniform with kit bags at their sides. They were petrified, like startled rabbits caught in headlights, and twitched nervously at the constant air raids. I had not had a chance to think what to do with them but felt the safest thing was to accommodate them in the basement below the office. It was not very habitable but it was safer than being above ground, especially in my isolated hut just begging to be bombed. At least here I could keep an eye on them. Acquiring three iron bedsteads and an old wooden cabinet, I took the boys down and set them up a makeshift home. I commandeered as many magazines from the mess room as I could and took those to the boys as well – anything to keep their minds busy.

They were pretty relieved to be ensconced in the basement and were so glad to be out of harm's way, relatively speaking. When the siren sounded to signal a momentary all-clear I let them up into the office and kept them occupied with some work. They were fairly obedient, through sheer terror more than anything else. Freddie, despite being the youngest, was most definitely the ringleader. A little under five feet tall, with hollow cheeks, he was dark-skinned with a mop of curly brown hair and brown eyes. He was the dominant personality by far and always getting his older pals to follow him. He was very cheeky and ribbed me endlessly but in quite a likeable way. I could never be mad with Freddie. He had a way of flashing a smile, with big wide eyes that glinted in good humour, or turning a phrase, which made you think butter wouldn't melt in his mouth. Even with people telling him to go to hell he would break into a grin and shrug. He was the most charming of rogues and a real artful dodger.

If Freddie was the extrovert, his brother Jim was the exact opposite. He was about the same height but slightly sturdier and had very little to say, to the point where I thought he had a speech difficulty. He did not stutter or stammer yet he was a slow speaker and found the right words hard to come by. Maybe because Freddie spoke so fast and so frequently Jim had allowed himself just to fade into the background.

The Brinds lived in Singapore. Their father had completed a twenty-three-year stint with the Gordon Highlanders and his last posting was in India, where both boys were born. On leaving the Army he moved the family to Singapore where he took over warden duties at Changi jail, the purpose-built prison constructed by the British. He stayed on at his post in Singapore and was subsequently captured by the Japanese. The boys' mother and sisters successfully escaped from the besieged island on one of the last ships out and returned to the family's original home in Brentwood, Essex.

Like Jim young John never said a word either. He was an Aberdeenshire farmer's son, tall and gangling, but dour and rather simple. He followed Freddie around like a lamb and I could not get through to him.

Christmas Day 1941 was a day like any other. Bombs were falling and in Singapore City innocent men, women and children were dying. Up-country in Malaya the fighting was intense. Reports cascaded into the office and the boys were as scared as hell. It was the first time in my life that I had not celebrated Christmas and I smiled to myself as I thought of what it would be like back in snowy Aberdeen. How I longed to be there with my loved ones. It was always my job to polish the silver and set the table, a task over which I took infinite care. After gorging ourselves we would gather round the piano and Mum and Doug would take turns to play our favourite tunes. The festivities always ended the same way, with Auntie Dossie singing her party piece, 'When You Come to the End of a Perfect Day'. I had a good singing voice too and would join in. I thought of them all that Christmas and wondered when if ever we would meet again. And then I vowed that we *would* meet again and that I would join in singing with Dossie, at the end of a perfect day.

Across the South China Sea in Hong Kong it was anything but a perfect day. After a seventeen-day siege the British surrendered to the Japanese. Hours earlier

Japanese troops had entered the city and celebrated Christmas in their own special way – by torturing and massacring sixty wounded patients and doctors in St Stephen's College Hospital.

Watching the progress of the war through the correspondence that passed over my desk only heightened my anxiety. It was like a tide that could not be stemmed and the Army was in full retreat, fighting valiant but ultimately doomed rearguard actions. Civilians were fleeing down the Malay Peninsula and heading for Singapore, desperate to escape.

During this time, when boredom had well and truly set in for the boys, they either got hold of my hut key or opened its door by force. Whatever their method of entry they managed to get in and rummage through what few personal possessions I had. They found my gramophone and records and went through all of my photographs. When I found them ransacking the hut I chased them out and ordered them into the basement, where I gave them a hell of a rollicking. I lectured them about respecting other people's property and privacy. Jim and John were very apologetic while Freddie was typically all milk and honey.

They were lucky lads. Just two days later the hut received a direct hit during an air raid. It was blown to smithereens. Nearly everything I owned, including all of my personal belongings, was lost. Luckily I still had some clothes and personal photographs, including snaps of my family and Hazel, in the office and counted myself lucky not to have lost them.

My happy childhood helped me to survive. Summer holidays at my grandparents' home in Newtonhill. In ascending order: Bill, Rhoda, myself and Douglas. (Urquhart Family)

My maternal grandfather William Kynoch. My mother's family were quite well-to-do unlike the parents of my father who were humble weavers. (Urquhart Family)

My father as a young man (standing second from the left), rambling on Royal Deeside. Many of his friends would not survive the First World War and Father was never the same after being gassed and shell-shocked at the Somme. (Urquhart Family)

Calm before the storm. Cricketing with my colleagues from Lawson Turnbull & Co. Ltd in the summer before the war. I am pictured second from the left in the middle row.
(Urquhart Family)

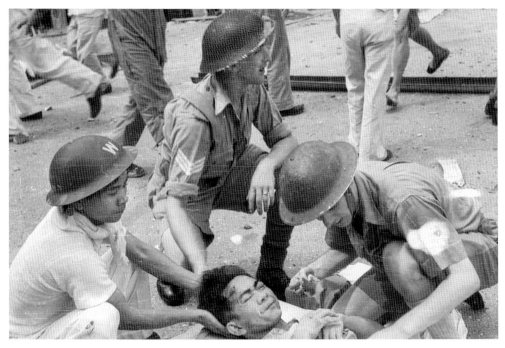

Singapore was hopelessly prepared for the Oriental blitz launched by the Japanese in their surprise attack of 8 December 1941. (Australian War Memorial 011529/10)

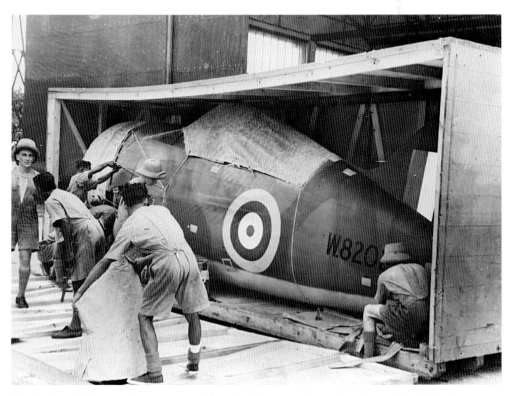

Too little, too late. RAF personnel frantically unpack an American-built Buffalo Brewster. The Japanese dominated the skies over Singapore. (Australian War Memorial 012129)

Banzai! Japanese troops take a break from the murderous Sook Ching massacre to celebrate their conquest of Singapore. This propaganda picture was taken at the Singapore waterfront the day after our surrender. (Australian War Memorial 127905)

The square fills up at Selarang Barracks as 17,000 men are squeezed in. I feared that we would be slaughtered at any moment. Young Australian George Aspinall risked his life to take this photograph of the infamous Selarang Incident and kept the film hidden in his water bottle for the duration of the war. (Australian War Memorial 106531)

Australian prisoner Murray Griffin graphically captured the chaos as men flooded in to Selarang Barracks. (Note the officers avoiding hard labour.) (Murray Griffin, Australian War Memorial ART25084)

These rice trucks became stifling steel coffins when more than thirty men were herded into each for our six-day, 900-mile trip north to the Death Railway. (Rod Beattie/Burma–Thailand Railway Memorial Association)

Murray Griffin's depiction of the march from Ban Pong. The death march was a true nightmare, ill and starved, we covered 150 kilometres through dense jungle, much of it at night. (Murray Griffin, Australian War Memorial ART25077)

We worked for up to eighteen hours a day on the cutting at Hellfire Pass. Eventually the sick were drafted in to break stones in the searing sun while lying on stretchers. (Murray Griffin, Australian War Memorial ART25081)

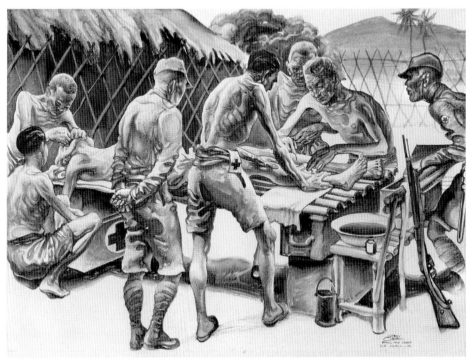

Everybody suffered from tropical ulcers. We scooped out the rotting flesh with sharpened dessert spoons. I cured mine with maggots but others lost limbs. Chungkai was full of limbless survivors. (Murray Griffin, Australian War Memorial ART25052)

This photo was taken early as the prisoners still have trousers and are yet to be reduced to skeletons. (Australian War Memorial)

An example of a typical bridge, built in the most unlikely places in the most challenging of conditions. (Australian War Memorial)

Up-country, meanwhile, Malaya was the scene of bitter hand-to-hand fighting. Australian, Indian, Gurkha and British units distinguished themselves with heroic but increasingly ineffective resistance. The Japanese were 'distinguishing' themselves too, and there were alarming reports of barbaric massacres of civilians and allied prisoners. In Penang the occupying Japanese promptly massacred seven hundred local Chinese, beheading and bayoneting them.

The fighting was getting closer to Singapore all the time. So were the atrocities. On 22 January 1942, after fierce fighting at the village of Parit Sulong in Johore, retreating Australians were forced to leave behind their wounded. What followed became the first of many atrocities against allied prisoners. The Japanese General Takuma Nishimura ordered them killed and his subordinates gleefully obliged, bayoneting, drowning and burning alive the wounded men. Over 160 Australians and Indians died. In a separate incident at Bukit Timah twelve captured Argylls were tied up with barbed wire and bayoneted. One survivor played dead and was helped to safety by friendly Chinese.

At midnight on 31 January 1942 the Australians and Gordons withdrew from the mainland and the ninety remaining survivors of the Argyll and Sutherland Highlanders were ordered by General Percival to retreat across the causeway that linked Malaya to Singapore. Bagpipes defiantly skirled the Argyll tune 'Hielan Laddie' as the last men out of Malaya crossed on to the island. Some high-ranking officers used Red Cross ambulances for their retreat over the causeway before it was blown up by the Royal Engineers.

Now Singapore was on its own. The only force that could have helped us was lying at the bottom of Pearl Harbor. A mish-mash of eighty thousand men from at least half a dozen nationalities and from both regular and volunteer regiments, some with little or no training, were defending the island with rapidly diminishing air support.

Morale plummeted and when our engineers blew up the huge British naval base to deny its use to the Japanese it plunged even further. The whole point of 'Fortress Singapore' had been to protect the giant Keppel naval base that we had just blown up on Churchill's orders. It was obvious that the game was up and troops began to desert in large numbers. Singapore, which had very few air raid shelters for the civilian population, stood in chaos and an epidemic of lawlessness and looting broke out. There were thousands of deserters, particularly among the Australians, who were more 'bolshie' than us and who could see that it was impossible to fight without air cover. Many of these men fought to get on to the ships sent to rescue women and children and the military police were forced to fire over their heads to stop them storming the gangways on to the ships. Dozens swarmed aboard by shimmying up the mooring ropes so desperate were they to get out and escape. Yet incredibly troop ships were still arriving, disgorging into this abyss more young Australians, many of them poorly trained. Some had literally never fired a shot. They were lambs to the slaughter. It was an awful waste.

Fort Canning soon became the prime Japanese target. For the first two weeks of February the Japanese kept up a barrage of bombing and shelling aimed at the underground Battlebox and its surroundings. To us huddled on the hill, ridiculously poorly armed and basically defenceless, the shelling was much worse than the bombing and more accurate too. The shells whistled in all the time and we could only pray that our names were not on them. We were just so vulnerable. The boys were especially scared and stayed below in the basement. Even the normally effervescent Freddie remained uncharacteristically quiet and subdued. It was a terrifying time for all of us.

On 8 February, just two months after the first bombs fell, the Japanese landed on the island and intense fighting ensued. From our hilltop position we could see much of the action. A few days later they entered Singapore City and then on 14 February came the terrible news that Japanese soldiers had committed a massacre at the Alexandra military hospital. Three hundred and twenty-three patients, doctors and nurses were systematically murdered in the shadow of the Red Cross that was meant to protect them. The invaders actually bayoneted some of the patients on the operating table.

When I read the signal about the massacre I could not believe my eyes; it sent my stomach into knots and my mind reeling. But I resolved to keep quiet about it. There was no point in spreading fear and alarm.

Churchill had urged a fight to the end and General Archibald Wavell, our supreme commander, told troops that it would be 'disgraceful' if the much hyped fortress of

Singapore were lost. But to me it was inevitable that we would fall. All of my previous experiences in Singapore, the arrogance, frivolity and sheer ineptitude suggested we were no match for anyone, let alone a well-organised and determined aggressor.

On 15 February, shortly after the news of the Alexandra massacre arrived, the shelling stopped and a ceasefire was proclaimed. With good reason Percival feared another 'Rape of Nanking', the 1937 massacre which had seen the Japanese slaughter three hundred thousand Chinese over a six-week period. With water cut off and no air cover the situation was deemed impossible. During humiliating negotiations in the Ford factory, Percival was bluffed into surrendering to an overstretched and much smaller Japanese force.

Amazingly, for reasons unknown, no order was given to us to destroy the files at Fort Canning and when the Japanese came marching in twenty-four hours later they helped themselves to all of our military secrets.

The end of the shelling came as a relief but we lived in terror of the Japanese arriving and the fear of the unknown gnawed away at us. The boys kept on asking what would happen to us. Naturally I kept the news of the Alexandra Hospital events to myself. I did not want to panic the young lads, who were fearful enough already. After two weeks of shelling and now surrender, we were a bag of nerves. I think that feeling sorry and concerned for the boys prevented me from feeling sorry for myself.

On 16 February the Japanese entered Fort Canning. Sometime during mid-morning I was stood in the office with the boys, when looking out the window I saw Japanese soldiers for the first time. The privates came ahead of the column and rushed buildings, bundling everyone outside. The boys went extremely quiet and retreated into the corner of the office. Barely able to keep my voice from breaking I whispered, 'Be very quiet and do what they say.'

Then suddenly two Japanese soldiers burst into the office. They were quite young and very volatile – excited and angry, their eyes looked filled with fury and hate. Yammering and screaming in Japanese, they began jabbing their bayonets at our chests. It was so petrifying, I felt as if the bayonet had pierced my heart and I was staring death in the face. The boys behind me looked on in abject, open-mouthed terror. I had no idea what these soldiers in their mud-coloured, oversize uniforms were saying but in a daze I handed over my old rifle and put my hands over my head. Thoughts of Alexandra Hospital raced through my mind.

They punched, slapped and kicked us outside, where an astonishing sight met our eyes: hundreds of men filing out of the underground bunker, their hands above their heads, fear writ large across their ashen faces. They lined up alongside us. Then everyone was rounded up at bayonet point into rows and left standing. As we waited for a long time in the burning midday sun, some of the Japanese privates went down the rows of fearful soldiers snatching watches off wrists, cigarette lighters, packets of cigarettes, pens, money, stealing anything of value. No one had the temerity to object to the thievery. Many officers had their faces slapped indiscriminately and their epaulettes ripped off, their caps thrown to the ground.

A Scouser corporal whom I knew from around the base was standing beside me and the boys. He whispered in my ear, 'Can't one of the officers do something? This is looking serious, Alistair.'

'Just keep your mouth shut. There's nothing to be done. We're at their mercy now.'

As we stood there in the blazing sun without food, water or shelter, the horrible reality broke over me in sickening, depressing waves. I was part of Britain's greatest-ever military disaster, a captive – just like some 120,000 others captured in the Battle of Malaya. I was a prisoner. It was a gut-wrenching realisation to think that my liberty was gone and no telling for how long it would be so. I kept a brave face on for the boys, whose eyes were on stalks but who stayed mute. This was the worst moment of my life.

Hours later the Japanese commander arrived, strutting in front of his car. He looked us over disdainfully, scowling with a mixture of disgust and contempt before barking orders to his officers and promptly leaving. They put us into columns and told us to march. We didn't know where to; we were little more than cattle to our captors. But it transpired that we were to cover the eighteen miles to Changi. The Changi peninsula housed the famous prison, the Selarang barracks and a sprawling ramshackle complex that would become a vast permanent POW camp for twenty thousand prisoners. I dreaded to think how different Selarang would look and what awaited us.

We were in a very poor state on the march from Fort Canning to Changi. Utterly dejected and deep in despair we trudged along, prodded on by bayonets and with stragglers subjected to vicious treatment by the Japanese. There was no defiant singing and little display of pride. We felt defeated and downtrodden. The sheer uncertainty was the worst thing. What was going to happen to us? The thought kept on returning. In the back of my mind the Alexandra Hospital massacre loomed and I really thought that the same fate awaited us. The boys were as anxious as I was but to begin with they did not really show it. They were still in shock.

Then, as we marched along the dusty road, without warning a horrific sight confronted us. We came face to face with a thicket of severed Chinese heads, speared on poles on both sides of the road. The mutilated bodies of these poor souls lay nearby and the heads, with their eyes rolled back, presented a truly shocking spectacle. The sickly sweet smell of rotting, putrefying flesh smothered us. Retching and fighting the instinct to be sick, I shouted to the boys to keep their eyes to the ground. For the rest of our march spiked heads, mainly Chinese, appeared at intervals in this way. The Japanese had been busy with their samurai swords and had created a hellish avenue to terrify and intimidate. The tactic certainly succeeded.

Unknown to us we had just walked into the middle of the 'Sook Ching' massacre, a well-planned Japanese purge of Chinese opponents, both real and potential. More than fifty thousand Chinese were murdered with the sickening sadism that seemed endemic in the Japanese

Army. The worst of thoughts now flashed through our minds.

Next I saw a column of at least a hundred Chinese civilians being marched across a pedang in the same direction as us. They wore white shorts and white T-shirts but were blindfolded. It struck me then as strange that we had not also been blindfolded. The future of these hapless Chinese, I thought, looked especially gloomy. It was obvious that they were about to be killed. Paradoxically it made me feel a little better about our own immediate future – after all we were not blindfolded.

About a week later I heard that the Chinese we had seen had indeed been massacred – machine-gunned along with hundreds of others on the beach at Changi. British POWs on a work party had to dig a mass grave for hundreds of bodies. When I heard that news my already diminishing spirits sank even lower. I felt that we were sitting on a time bomb and it would not be long until it went off.

During the march we saw plenty of other frightening and dismal sights. Bloated and shattered bodies of all nationalities, both civilian and military, lay strewn everywhere covered in great blankets of flies. Some of the local population lined the streets, waving Japanese flags, welcoming the invaders with open arms. They sneered and spat and snarled at us. Only the Chinese seemed restrained – they knew only too well what Japan's offer of 'Asia for the Asians' really meant, but many of the Tamils, Malays and Sikhs fell for it. It was heartbreaking to see, yet after what I had witnessed I could understand their predicament. A few days earlier the Union Jack had fluttered proudly over the Cathay Building; now the Japanese 'Rising Sun' flew in its place. The sun had well and truly set on Imperial Britain's Far East hopes. Many locals were left with little choice but to support the latest batch of colonisers. A very brave, mainly Communist, minority fought on.

By the time we got to Changi it was dark and we were in bad shape – exhausted, dehydrated and traumatised. The army buildings on the Changi peninsula were designed to accommodate four thousand men and in those first days of captivity we were over fifty thousand. The camp was already crammed full with thousands of prisoners and the barracks were also beyond capacity – the only space left was standing room in the barracks square. I kept the boys with me and had to be pretty firm with Freddie because he wanted to go off on his own and search for some spare space for us.

The mood was one of complete devastation and total desolation. It was degrading beyond words and humiliation hung over us like a heavy black cloud. There were no toilets, you just had to go where you stood. The Japanese had surrounded the perimeter and had machine guns trained on us. It was hopeless. To try to escape or organise a mass rush would have resulted in a massacre.

More and more POWs kept flooding into the camp. The arrival of each fresh group added to our dejection and bewilderment. We eventually found a space to lie down and get some fitful sleep.

The next morning prisoners came around with pails of food, ladling out servings into the mess tins we had brought with us. It was a kind of stew with green vegetables in it. We had not eaten in twenty-four hours and it tasted delicious. It was the last 'proper' meal we would get for some time. There would be only rice from here on in.

Food and the lack of it would swiftly become an obsession for all of us prisoners. The rice we got was sub-standard, quite literally the sweepings off the warehouse floor normally considered inedible, contaminated with vermin droppings, maggots and all sorts. We were grateful for every grain of it. The food was always served outdoors on the parade ground, for breakfast, lunch and tea, from four huge cast-iron pots. The Gordons had their own line and allowed no pushing to the front. We all knew what we were getting and how much of it. It was tough to stomach the plain rice after a while and you really had to force it down.

It was particularly difficult for the boys. But Colonel Graham took an enlightened view and decided that they should get more food than the rest of the POWs. They received a cup and a half of rice to our single cup, which the cooks factored into the total. Had other prisoners known I am sure that there would have been objections to their extra half-cup. But the boys knew they had to keep it to themselves so as not to cause resentment. Had there been any trouble over it, though, I would have stood up for them. They needed the extra sustenance more than we did. They were going through puberty and needed what little extra boost a half-cup of rice could provide.

Once most of the prisoners had moved out to occupy other buildings on the peninsula, we had some more space and moved into our old barracks. It was total chaos. Fights sparked like wildfire over perceived prime positions. Fists flew at the smallest infringement of space. Thankfully the officer in charge of assigning places put the boys and me into a small wooden outhouse building. It had been used for storage previously but it suited us fine, with just enough room for four camp beds and little else. Not that we had any possessions anyway. All I had were the clothes on my back, a cheap wristwatch, a few pencils, my mess tin and my cache of photographs. I was pleased to have our own space and the boys were happy too.

The shower facilities were based in the main part of the concrete building complex and the cold water was on only briefly – usually for an hour in the morning. You could not drink it because it was not boiled and the risk of getting ill was too great. But it did help to try to wash some of the dirt and grime off and it made us feel better for a short time. I tried to get the boys to wash every day. While the other two took some persuading to shower, Freddie required no prompting. He was always fussy about his appearance. I had one piece of soap, which we shared. We had to make it last, which was very difficult with cold water because it was so difficult to work into a lather. When it came to brushing your teeth there was no toothbrush, just some water and your finger. As for shaving there were of course no razors so most of the POWs were fully bearded.

At first we simply felt relieved that the killing and the shelling had stopped. We had survived and over nine thousand of our comrades had died. But there was a lot of anger in the camp too. Many men had been captured without having the chance to engage the enemy or even fire a shot. Some argued endlessly over who was to blame for our downfall. 'If only we had been sent tanks. If only we had enough aeroplanes. If only we had launched Matador. If only we had sunk the Japanese Navy before it got too close. If only . . .'

Churchill wanted to keep Singapore British but it was well down the list of priorities when it came to resources – behind the defence of Britain, the campaign in North Africa and the need to send arms to the Russian front. In my view the 'pukka sahib' officers, who incredibly still insisted on having their batmen in the prison camp, were partly to blame. The government was more culpable and Churchill even more so. It was a view that I never missed an opportunity to express. Gradually, though, the recriminations subsided and we found another great topic of conversation.

Food. It haunted our dreams and thoughts. Hunger was turning into starvation. We were beginning to waste away, the sensation of taste becoming a distant memory. Some of the men already suffered from debilitating vitamin deficiencies and the quest for food became a matter of life or death. It was at this point that the indomitable Freddie and his fantastic foraging skills came to the rescue. One day after weeks of little more than rice, he rushed in to the hut clutching his Glengarry cap to his stomach: 'Alistair! Alistair! Look what I've got! Look what I've got!'

We all hunched over as he carefully opened the Glengarry to reveal his treasure trove – a clutch of gleaming white eggs! Our eyes widened in disbelief and our taste buds went into overdrive. Freddie, our magnanimous provider, was triumphant. We drooled as we fried up the eggs and stared in amazement at them bubbling in the pan, the sizzling sound a symphony to our ears. The familiar smell had us dancing around with excitement. Never, ever did a fried egg taste so good and every succulent mouthful was made to last.

Soon Freddie was so well liked in the camp that he became the unofficial Changi mascot. Darting about the place he refined his scavenging skills and brought smiles to the faces of men who had little to smile about. I had a special, almost paternal relationship with him but others felt protective of Freddie as well. There was something about his nature that you could not help but warm to. Some of the older prisoners, men with families who had sons in their early teens, saw them reincarnated in Freddie. He was a reminder too of our lost youth. I hated to think what Freddie was up to when he was out of my sight. He was such a curious person and never afraid of bursting into a group or conversation. I was always afraid he would fall in with a bad crowd and I would lecture him constantly on the perils of life.

But Freddie was irrepressible and became well known around the camp and well liked by all the men. He had such vitality and could bring energy to any situation. Nobody had a bad word to say about him; he reminded them of life before the camp, of a better world that existed beyond the wire in a different time and place.

Most nights the boys and I went up the grassy hill that dominated Changi to chew the fat. Boredom was a huge problem, not just for the boys but for me too. Invariably it led to depression and we did all we could to fight it. I managed to snaffle a deck of playing cards, which helped pass the time. We played endless games of whist and rummy, while snap seemed to be the boys' favourite. We chatted about the possibilities of what could happen to us. I would say to them, 'Look, you're just young boys. The Nips won't do anything to you.' I think the older boys believed me but Freddie would look at me sceptically and keep his concerns to himself.

After enjoying the spectacular sunset we would talk for hours under the moonlight. The Brinds had never been to Scotland and I would tell them all about life in Britain. Freddie would sidle up and grill me about my life. He wanted to know everything, personal, professional and otherwise. He was eager to learn about life and was especially nosy about girls, and Hazel Watson in particular.

One evening hundreds of men milled about our normal spot up the hill. There was to be a concert, a break from the grinding monotony of camp life. As a music lover I was thrilled. The boys were excited too. Somehow, goodness knows how, a piano had been dragged all the way up the hill. It was a brilliant moonlit night and as the musicians arranged themselves total and respectful silence descended on the huge crowd. Had it not been for the sound of the crickets and the tropical breeze, we could have been in the Albert Hall. Then a solo violinist, a professional with the London Philharmonic called Denis East, stepped forward and the plaintive notes of Mendelssohn's Violin Concerto reverberated around the hillside. It was the first music we had heard for months. I sat entranced, and the boys, strangers to classical music, were agog – spellbound by Mendelssohn's magic. For a few minutes the beauty of the music lifted us out of the camp and reminded us of the greatness of the European civilisation that the Japanese militarists despised. Some men wept. When East finished several stunned seconds passed before rapturous applause and cheering broke out. It was so beautiful.

Eventually the Japanese guards present got bored and left. When they had gone an altar was set up and an interdenominational church service held. It proved a welcome morale booster. Even people like me, not especially religious, found it comforting. It was to be my one and only church service during three and a half years of captivity but it struck a real chord and made me think seriously about Christianity for the first time. When the padre finished his sermon on our mount in Changi prison, thousands of miles from home, hundreds of voices joined in a moving rendition of 'The Old Rugged Cross'.

The first verse seemed so appropriate to all of us caught up in the fall of Singapore:

On a hill far away stood an old rugged cross,
The emblem of suffering and shame;
And I love that old cross where the dearest and best
For a world of lost sinners was slain.

The Brinds were both devout Roman Catholics. Freddie never talked about his beliefs but the brothers were always missing on Sunday mornings and were friendly with the Roman Catholic padre. The Japanese did not allow church activities yet there were obviously secret masses going on – at considerable risk to all involved. I never enquired because I did not want the boys to think I was spying on them. Freddie always wore a crucifix on a silver chain, which he kept tucked under his shirt. If the guards had discovered it, they would have taken it from him and given him a beating.

During this bleak period when the days dragged on for ever, Freddie scored his greatest triumph. On one of his regular snooping missions around the sprawling camp complex he stumbled upon a clandestine cooking operation run by a Swiss gentleman – the former head chef of Raffles Hotel no less! Along with two or three of his friends the master chef had set up a concealed cooking stove in a basement of one of the buildings. Needless to say, Freddie quickly befriended the chef, who took the boy under his wing, and one evening we were invited for some food.

The endless diet of rice had long lost its appeal and the invitation prompted frenzied speculation as to what would be on the menu. The vegetable stews served in our early days had ceased and the rice rations had already been cut. So we were just incredulous after we nervously entered the basement and the exotic and glorious aromas overwhelmed us. The chef showed us how to make an omelette and then carefully cut it up and served us each with an equal portion. It was a mouth-wateringly magical moment, the omelette delectable in the extreme.

Thanks to Freddie, who spent his days scavenging food to give to the chef to cook, we were invited back regularly. We used to joke about how as Other Ranks we had been banned from Raffles Hotel before the surrender but now had our own personal chef. It was brilliant. We got our ration of rice and eagerly took it to him. He was quite a character, short and stout, not much taller than Freddie. A typical chef, he had a fiery temper but good humour in equal measure. He idolised Freddie, who never failed to cheer him up.

This culinary conjuror would transform our weevil-ridden rice into mouth-watering kedgeree, delicious risotto and savoury rice balls – it did not mean more food but more variation and taste. One of my favourites was a risotto of plain rice that the chef would add all sorts of spices to – God knows what – and it tasted superb. As prisoners fixated with food your stomach never let you forget that you were hungry. You became obsessed with when the next meal would be and when that time arrived, with the portion sizes. All eyes stared beadily at the pail of rice and the server to ensure that you were not being cheated.

Lack of food and the dire conditions were beginning to take a serious toll on everyone. Myself and the boys all came down with dysentery, which tore at your stomach lining and had you running to the squalid latrines dozens of times a day. Then in May 1942 I suffered my first bout of malaria. With no sprays or mosquito nets the place was alive with insects. I was lucky. At this stage the medical officer still had a little quinine. The boys looked after me and I stayed in the hut, wrestling with the shakes, sweats and fever, while they were delighted to be rewarded for their efforts with the rice ration that I was too ill to eat. As I suffered they grinned and wolfed down the extra spoonfuls of rice.

During this period of camp life Changi was still quite a disciplined and organised place. British and Australian officers were basically in charge of running the camp and the Japanese left us pretty much alone. The only time we saw much of them was when they searched for radios. On these frantic occasions the Japanese turned everything upside down, taking anything that was a benefit or bonus to us. Books, bibles, pens and paper were all taken away.

Our regular guards and sentries were Sikhs, who had served with the British Indian Army. Around thirty thousand of the forty thousand Sikhs serving in Malaya went over to the Japanese, who promised India independence. The Sikhs who refused to switch sides were treated appallingly as prisoners and some were executed.

The Sikh guards dressed in turbans and obviously despised us. You could see the hatred in their eyes. But they were rarely violent towards us. I had heard stories of the brutal treatment they dealt out to other POWs but I never saw it. We had once been their colonial masters, now the boot was on the other foot. I hated the fact that they had sided with the Japanese but that is human nature, I suppose.

One day a few weeks after our arrival at Changi Captain Faulder, the education officer, approached me.

He enquired, 'Are you the one in charge of these lads?'

'Yes, sir.'

'I've heard a lot about them. Turned down the chance to go with the civilians, eh? Remarkable.'

'Indeed, sir,' I said, wondering where this conversation was heading.

Captain Faulder then decreed, 'Very well. Urquhart, I would like you to take classes so that these lads can get their British Army General Certificate of Education while they're here. Might as well spend this time wisely.'

'But I'm not a teacher, sir. I've never taught in my life.'

'Nonsense,' he said. 'You're sufficiently educated to teach them the basics. We've got a room for you to start immediately. Come along, I'll show you.'

I trotted after him to another outhouse building near by. It might once have been used as a type of lecture room because it had a blackboard easel and a tiny stump of chalk, a long trestle table and three chairs.

'This should do you,' Captain Faulder said, standing with his hands on his hips, admiring the choice of classroom.

He said, 'I'll get you some exercise books and some pencils. You can start straight away.'

I thanked him and he marched off, leaving me scratching my head, wondering how the heck I was going to teach these rascals anything. After the shock had subsided I recognised that it could be a positive thing. At least it would keep my mind busy and away from depressing thoughts.

The following day class started at 9 a.m. With my only previous teaching experience being dance classes for Eric and co. in the living room back home, I decided to concentrate on English and maths, and also Latin, since my father had ensured I was a fairly accomplished scholar. There are so many Latin words that tell you what the English meaning is, I thought the boys would benefit from my personalised syllabus. There were no books or manuals to call on so my own ideas had to suffice. We worked for two hours on the basics and I tried to keep them interested by asking questions relating to the outside world. While Freddie was by far the most intelligent, he was also the most restless. He was forever day-dreaming out of the window or distracting the others, who were slower and inarticulate. Jim was rather backward in his work and his ponderous handwriting was almost unintelligible – like a hen's scrawl, as I used to tell him. They hated the lessons more than I did but it kept us all occupied.

After two hours we stopped for lunch and a break. We continued in the afternoon for a further two hours but the schedule was flexible. If I got fed up, which occurred frequently, the day would be called off short, much to the boys' delight.

After three months they were ready to sit their exam. I had high hopes for Freddie but was unsure as to how the other two would fare. Much to my surprise and general delight they all passed and received handwritten certificates, signed by me, that confirmed completion of their British Army General Certificate of Education. Hastily typed up certificates were later presented to the boys and

Freddie was extremely proud of his, especially when he learned that his Army pay would now be increased! Not that it did any good in the camp.

Meanwhile most of the men went on work parties during the day. I was very lucky, exempted since I had a duty of care towards the boys. The others went to the very docks where I had landed less than two years earlier or to the aerodrome to clear trees. In the first few months the men could work hard in the tropical heat because they were in relatively good health. But as their health deteriorated and their body weight dropped due to the poor diet, fewer and fewer of them came back from the work parties. Many were visibly withering away and, suffering from dysentery or malaria, dropping like flies. The officers had even to designate a new work party whose sole function was burying bodies.

The work parties taken to Singapore harbour to work on the docks, unloading shipments of rice, sugar, meat and vegetables, plundered as much as they could. For starving men the temptation to help themselves was just too great. The Japanese deemed stealing food the most heinous of crimes. Some paid with their lives for a handful of rice. Guards administered savage beatings with iron bars, staves and pick-axe handles that left men paralysed and blinded and others dead. The dreadful dangers, however, did not stop starving prisoners from taking their chances.

There was constant paranoia in the camp that some men were acting as spies for the Japanese. Anyone seen being called to their offices regularly and who returned unscathed was singled out as suspicious. Of course some men might have been chiropodists or something, called in to work on the officers' feet or whatever. But it did not stop fevered speculation and tongues wagging among bored men. If there was a particularly strong suspicion that someone was in the pockets of the Japanese, or 'Jap happy' as it was known, they would be confronted. I heard rumours that some men were even murdered; their bodies disposed of head first into the latrines. Surprisingly, though, the men who secured jobs working in the Japanese cookhouse or helping in the storerooms were never castigated by the rest of the men. They were obviously better fed but there was no jealousy. It was more a case of 'fair play to them'.

As the weeks turned into months in 1942, there were plenty of rumours circulating in the camp about the progress of the war. We heard of a huge armada sailing from England with the RAF to save us, of major sea battles, of Japan running rampant through the Pacific and taking island after island. The Russians had reached Greece. The British were winning in North Africa. And so it went on. Through his interpreter the Japanese commander would take great glee in announcing, 'The mighty Japanese empire is taking over India and Australia.' It got into your mind and you did not know what to believe. We would ask our officers for any information but they were just as in the dark as we were.

The lack of contact from our families also got us down. Men wondered how their families were surviving the bombing of British cities, if sons and brothers had been conscripted. The lack of letters from home made us feel like a forgotten army and we were anxious that our families knew we were OK. In June the Japanese had allowed us to send a message home. I had filled in my little card with the message: 'My Dearest Mother, I am in good health and spirits and being well treated. Hope you are well. Much love to all at home. Please do not worry too much. Please let Hazel know and give her my love. With all my love, Alistair.' But we never knew whether the cards had been sent or not. (In fact I was to send a total of six of these cards during captivity and all of them arrived in Aberdeen after my return home.) By now every prisoner was suffering from depression, and coping with 'black dog' was the hardest thing a prisoner ever encountered.

That was why the concert parties were so important. I had been mesmerised by the concert on the hill above the barracks; then one day it was announced that there was to be a stage show on the parade ground of Selarang barracks. We all trooped along on the night to be treated to a burlesque show entitled 'Tulips From Amsterdam'. It was hilarious and with Japanese guards in the audience, pretty near the knuckle. The concert party had devised all kinds of skits sending our captors up, with great music too and we all sang along to the hits of the day. The indisputable star of the show was a drag artist called Bobby Spong. Dressed up to the nines and positively glamorous, when he came on stage the audience went wild, the boys besides themselves laughing, hooting, yelling and cheering – and no shortage of indecent suggestions. We laughed until our sides nearly split.

It was to be our last laugh at Selarang. A couple of weeks later at the beginning of September, things turned nasty, very nasty. The Japanese had decided to tighten the screw and increase control over the camp. Unbeknown to the prisoners they had plans about what to do with us and blind, terrorised obedience was central to those plans. The strange limbo we inhabited, in which we lived as prisoners but under British authority, was drawing to an end and the Japanese wanted to impose their authority.

A new regime headed by Major General Shimpei Fukuye wanted to transform Changi into a proper prison camp. A few weeks earlier four prisoners, two Australians and two British, had tried to escape from up-country in Malaya and Fukuye demanded that all the allied prisoners should sign an undertaking not to do this. Escape attempts were futile and doomed in my view. But our officers refused to sign as a matter of principle. The first we knew about this row was on being told to report to the Selarang barracks. As we made our way there, thousands of men were doing the same, streaming in to the barracks from all directions. The Japanese had decreed that all prisoners must be inside the barracks by 6 p.m. – anybody outside after that time would be shot. It was the beginning of a terrifying stand-off that became known as the Selarang Incident.

Seventeen and a half thousand men crammed into the Gordon Highlanders' barracks designed to accommodate fewer than a thousand men. It was appalling. We had no space and what little water we had was for cooking only. Latrines had to be dug in the middle of the barracks square but we could never get near them, the place was so heaving with men. Somebody worked out that the population density was one million men per square mile. Outside of the crammed barracks in the parade ground there was very little cover for the men and we baked in the sun. Our officers warned us that we would face a court martial if we signed and that the Japanese were breaching the Geneva Convention that allows prisoners the right to attempt to escape without facing punishment.

The Japanese could not have cared less about the Geneva Convention and had no intention of observing it. To rack up the pressure they ordered the execution of the escapees and the British and Australian commanding officers were instructed to attend. It was a brutal, botched affair during which the Sikh firing party had to shoot the men several times. They shot some of the prisoners in the groin and the poor chaps had to plead to be finished off. Refusing blindfolds the condemned men displayed fantastic bravery and the British and Australians still refused to give in.

We were playing a dangerous game. The Japanese could not stand to lose face and we knew that they were capable of anything. Crammed into the parade square we were so vulnerable, deprived of all items of war. There was no possibility of an uprising. Personally I was riddled with fear that the situation could escalate into a massacre.

At various points during the stand-off the Japanese would drive in a dozen lorries covered in tarpaulins.

These would reverse into strategic positions in front of us covering all points. Then at a signal the tarpaulins would be torn off in unison to reveal machine guns mounted on the trucks, four soldiers at the ready on each. Their guns pointed at us, the Japanese would start screaming. It was all part of the terror tactics they so enjoyed. We responded by singing 'Land of Hope and Glory'. The national anthem was banned and this became our theme song, our only weapon and I doubt if it was ever sung with more fervour. The Aussies would pipe up with 'Waltzing Matilda', and sometimes a chorus of 'There Will Always Be an England' would ring out. As conditions deteriorated and more men went down with dysentery and diphtheria, singing was a way of keeping our spirits up. But I always believed that we were all going to be massacred.

On the third day of the stand-off conditions had become really desperate and men began to die of dysentery. I tried to keep a brave face on things for the sake of the boys but it was an awful ordeal. We were down to half rations, constantly thirsty and had hardly room to lie down – sleeping was a problem.

Still we stuck it out and then the Japanese played their trump card. They threatened to transfer in two and a half thousand sick and wounded men from the hospital in the nearby Roberts barracks. It would have been mass murder and reluctantly our officers agreed to sign but insisted that it be recorded we did so 'under duress'. At last it was over. We were ordered to sign a piece of paper that read, 'I the undersigned, hereby solemnly swear on my honour that I will not, under any circumstances, attempt to escape.'

We all lined up to sign and it seemed to take ages. Some men signed as 'Mickey Mouse' or 'Robin Hood', while 'Ned Kelly' was a popular choice with the Australians. After standing in line for hours it finally came to my turn. I signed as 'AK Urquhart' but deliberately made it an illegible scrawl so I could deny it if need be.

Once you signed you were moved to your new barracks, or camps as they now were. As Gordon Highlanders we stayed put at our barracks in Selarang, along with some members of the Malay Volunteer Force. The Japanese used Selarang as a propaganda victory. They could tell their population how cowardly we were, how easily they took Singapore and that we were a feeble enemy.

The Selarang Incident was mentally and physically draining. We had been on an emotional roller-coaster, playing for the highest stakes. It also marked a dark new phase in our relationship with our captors.

We were surviving each day at a time. Every day seemed longer and tougher than the previous day. Freddie was the only one who did not seem to be suffering. One steamy October day in 1942 a British officer's runner found me at my hut and snapped, 'You're to report to Lieutenant Emslie's office straight away!'

'What for?' I asked, annoyed at his abrupt manner, which seemed uncalled for.

The runner looked at me and said with a wry smile, 'You're down to go to a holiday camp.'

I reported to Lieutenant Emslie's office. He said,

'You've been selected to go on a draft up-country. Get organised and be ready for parade at 8 a.m. tomorrow.'

He refused to tell me any more but I suspected that even he did not have more information. I trudged back to my hut, trying to compute the information, wondering what he meant by 'up-country' and working out how to tell the boys. They would be devastated.

Back at the hut I sat the boys down and relayed the news, emphasising the part about its being a 'holiday camp'. They were understandably upset.

Jim said, 'But who will look after us?'

'An officer will make sure you are looked after,' I said, reigning in rampant emotions.

While I was only a few years older than the boys, I had become a father figure to them over the last few months. We had formed a strong bond and it was being ripped apart. They felt abandoned and I felt as if I had failed them.

Four

Death March

I did not sleep a wink that night. I scrunched my eyes tight to block out the horrible visions but all I could see were images of us being taken away to be executed. I imagined us being led into a field and shot in the back, machine-gunned on a beach, bayoneted or beheaded on the deck of some Japanese warship.

The next morning I said my goodbyes to the boys. It felt like leaving my family all over again. None of them tried to stop me going, they knew that would have been fruitless, yet their eyes betrayed their fear and concern. As I went to leave, Freddie grasped my arm and with tears welling up in his eyes said, 'See you later, mucker.'

I reported to the parade ground, trying as best I could to compose myself. Despite my anxiety I had to focus on what lay ahead. I was joined by twenty or thirty other

Gordon Highlanders out of the five or six hundred stationed at Changi at that time. Cleverly the Japanese did not send a whole bunch of men from one battalion together. They always took care to split us up. None of the Malay Volunteers billeted at Selarang had been selected for this mysterious task, whatever it was.

The Japanese officer in charge began shouting in staccato and through his interpreter broke the 'good' news. He told us, 'You have been selected as the best men for this duty. You will go to a holiday camp, where you will work for three days, have four days rest, have good food, good conditions and everyone will be happy if you work hard.'

Our officers had been told that we were moving to special 'rest camps' in which food would be more plentiful than in Singapore. In these hill camps we would be supplied with blankets, clothing, mosquito nets. Even gramophones would be issued at the new camp, along with medical supplies to equip a new hospital. There would be no marching except for short distances from the trains to nearby camps, transport being available for the sick and unfit, as well as our baggage. The ill men would have better prospects for recovery in a 'pleasant hilly place with facilities for recreation'.

Thousands of miles away Japan's European ally Nazi Germany was issuing similar rosy promises of 'resettlement' in the East to Jewish families.

But some of the men, desperate to believe that their luck was changing, actually believed it all and were excited at the prospect of filling their bellies and escaping slavery in the docks. There were cheers and shouts of 'Let's go!' and 'Sounds great!'

Firmly believing that we were about to be massacred I kept silent, my jaws locked with tension. I had seen with my own eyes the Japanese capacity for cruelty and I could not believe this cock and bull story about 'holiday camps'. It was astonishing that so many did.

We were taken into Singapore on the back of lorries, the first time that I had been in the outside world since our capture seven months before. Notwithstanding the burned and bombed-out buildings, Singapore seemed back to normal. The Chinese seemed back to their usual activities, cooking, bartering loudly, playing mah-jong, gambling and dextrously pedalling rickety bicycles while balancing chickens in wire cages on the handlebars. Yet it passed in a blur of colour and noise. I was more interested in where we were being taken. Our officers knew but we did not that we were to travel by train.

By the time we arrived at the station, already hordes of British prisoners were standing about. I recognised the uniforms of men from the Argyll and Sutherland Highlanders and the Royal Artillery. Seeing such a large number gave me comfort. Surely they would never massacre *all* of us. Hundreds of men milled around, slow in their movements, mindful of the Japanese machine guns. Some prisoners were being herded into tiny steel goods wagons in randomly selected groups of thirty-five to forty. The Japanese mixed everyone up, separating them from the herd-like safety and companionship of their regiments. You could see close friends drifting apart in the mêlée and all the while trying desperately to stick together.

The trucks had previously been used for transporting goods like rice, sugar and rubber. They looked like shipping containers but were smaller with large sliding doors. Those squashed inside the wagons were pleading with the Japanese not to force any more men in. Some trying to clamber aboard with kit bags had them chucked off by those already inside, who shouted, 'No room for that. We can hardly stand!'

A young private, a Gordon Highlander alongside me in the truck from Changi, turned and said, 'I hope we get a carriage with some seats.'

'I doubt it,' I mumbled.

Another Gordon piped up sarcastically, 'Aye. One with a window. And maybe a drinks trolley. It must be ninety degrees already. God knows how hot it's gonna be inside those wagons.'

We were taken from the back of the lorry to join the swarm of prisoners embarking on the trains. I felt sick with trepidation. There was an air of sheer terror. Men were almost dancing on the spot, hopping from foot to foot, unsure what to do with themselves. The Gordons who had earlier cheered that we were off to a holiday camp looked horrified.

'They told us it would be like Butlins. This doesn't look like a holiday to me. We're going to die.'

As we neared the train I could hear banging and frantic cries from inside locked carriages: 'Open the doors! Open the doors! We can't breathe! Open Up! Open Up!'

A Japanese grabbed me, separating me from most of the other Gordons, and hauled me towards a carriage, slapping me around the head. I told him to bugger off. I got wedged into a container of around eighteen feet by ten feet with about thirty other men, near the door as I could get no further in. It was incredibly cramped with no room to sit down. The Japanese screamed and lunged at us with bayonets. We practically had to breathe in collectively to make enough space for the doors to close. When they clanged the doors shut I listened ruefully to the jangling of the chain and padlock being snapped into place across the handles, a sickening sound that became familiar to millions of ordinary men and women during the Second World War. What would have been a depressing sound in any circumstances felt like a death sentence in that stifling steel box.

Animals would not be transported like this, I thought. To make matters worse the sides of the steel carriage were searingly hot. They burned any bare skin that touched them, making life even more difficult because there was so little room as it was. I did not know anyone else in the carriage and it was so dark that you couldn't make out faces, just shapes and general outlines. I felt completely isolated. All I had was the ragged uniform I was wearing, my Glengarry, mess tin and my beloved photographs from home tucked deep inside my back pocket.

We stood there for hours before the train started moving. The heat was appalling. Dehydration set in quickly and coupled with the malaria I was already suffering from I began to feel extremely ill. None of us knew how long we were going to be like this but I felt I couldn't take another minute. My despair and depression added to the claustrophobia. It was like being buried alive.

Out of the blue the train lurched forward. It started clacking and clattering and soon picked up some speed. As soon as we were moving some men tried to prise open the doors. They heaved at them, wrenching them every which way, cursing the workmanship and sadistic efficiency of our captors. Where the steel doors met there was an inch gap from ceiling to floor and on either side a half-inch gap, which let in some light, and now that we were moving an ever so slight, life-saving breeze. Realising that being by the door was the prime position, we devised a plan of moving around a place every half an hour. Since the Japanese had stolen our watches we had no way of telling the time, especially in the darkness, but we did the best we could. The gaps in the doors provided a little welcome relief from the torment of the truck.

The smell inside the carriage became unbearably foul. Without toilets the men had to relieve themselves where they stood. Several were very ill with malaria, dysentery and diarrhoea. People vomited and fainted. Dust swirled around the wagon stinging our eyes and adding to our unbearable thirst.

At last after hours of shuffling around like a zombie, trying not to go mad, it was my turn for the gap. I stuck my nose outside the steel tomb in which we were slowly being cooked and breathed in deeply. It was heavenly, the air warm and scented with the pungent dampness of the jungle. It was fresh, and anxious to make the most of it I breathed in great lungfuls. Sadly the pleasure was short-lived and once my time was allegedly up I got shouldered away from the gap, back into the darkness and nauseating stink of a torture chamber on wheels.

We had no idea where we were headed but since Singapore island was at the southern tip of the Malay Peninsula, surrounded by water, I knew we were going north. That much I knew.

Men became weaker all the time. The lack of fluids especially afflicted those with malaria and dysentery. Prisoners who collapsed were given some precious space, while the rest of us had to bunch up even more. The train was forever stopping in sidings and without any breeze from the movement the temperature soared ever higher. No one spoke. We had nothing to say. Besides, I wanted to save my energy. Who knew what was ahead of us?

When night came the carriage slowly cooled to a more bearable temperature. But as we went on the temperature began to fall relentlessly and I spent most of the night shivering. It was at least thirty-six hours before we were allowed out of the wagon. Suddenly the train's brakes screeched on the rails and we were all pushed forward in a mass. The men by the doors peered through the tiny gaps but could report seeing only jungle. When the doors opened the men closest to the exit tried to jump the three or four feet to the ground and collapsed in a heap at the bottom. I tried to walk forward towards the door but could hardly get my feet to follow my brain's instructions. We had been standing so long that we had no control of our legs. When I jumped down I saw some men had suffered head cuts from the fall and were trying to stem the blood with their hands.

The Japanese were dishing out a cup of water and a serving of rice to each man. I joined the queue and looked around. Thick jungle surrounded us on all sides. The stopping point had been carefully selected. There was no escape. The guards did not bother with head counts and would never have noticed if I had dashed into the bush, but from my jungle training at Port Dickson I knew I would not have lasted long. The jungle was such an uninhabitable place, even for the locals, and you could not have trusted them to help you. For the most part they were terrified of the Japanese, who meted out draconian punishments for anyone caught helping us. They also offered substantial rewards to turn in escapees. A sandy-headed white boy like me stood no chance. I was safer staying put; better the devil you know.

When I got my water I gulped it down not knowing whether it had been boiled or not. By that stage I was past caring. If the water and rice, swimming in a noxious green liquid, had a positive impact on my health, it was short-lived. Many of us, me included, had already developed the 'rice bellies' characteristic of starvation and vitamin deficiency.

I sat down in the shade and tried to rest my legs. It felt like I had been still for only a minute, the ache from my feet and legs reverberating up my spine and neck, when the Japanese started shouting, '*Hakko, hakko!* Speedo, speedo!' We had been there for less than an hour.

There was a terrible scrum trying to get the men back on the trucks. Men climbed into different carriages, hoping that conditions would be better, while others who had left kit bags in the wagons returned to find them gone. Accusations flew around and rows were settled only at the blunt end of a Japanese rifle or a kick from a hobnailed boot. Without much thought I returned to the same carriage, having earlier taken a mental note of its Malayan markings.

I clambered inside and recognised some of the faces from the earlier stint. Some of the sicker men required a leg-up to get back in. The doors thundered shut with an awful finality. We were just so helpless. I wondered how long it would be this time, unsure if I could survive another thirty-six hours confined in this oppressive oven.

There was an interminable wait before the train got underway. It was soon night, plunging us into complete darkness, but at least it was cooler and we could lean against the sides of the wagons for extra space and support.

We travelled all night, stopping in sidings frequently – every halt raising our hopes that the hellish journey might be coming to an end. We would stand still and silent for what seemed like ages but was probably less than ten minutes, hoping the doors would open. Then to our despair the train would trundle on again. It went on all night. By the next day I was getting very weak. We all tried to help each other, holding on to men who swayed uncontrollably. More of us couldn't take any further standing up and collapsed to the floor. Eventually I became completely disorientated and had to sit down too.

After another thirty-six hours or so we came to a stop and could hear much activity outside. It sounded like we were getting off. Someone in the carriage said we were at Kuala Lumpur. How he knew that I didn't know. Perhaps he had spotted a landmark through the slit in the doors. When the doors opened we could have been anywhere. It was a built-up area but the buildings were all warehouses and train sheds, with no sign of life other than the ring of Japanese guards, their machine guns trained on us. I jumped down on to the rocky ground, almost going over on my ankle. That would be the last thing I needed, I thought.

It was stupefyingly hot. It seemed that the further north we travelled, the hotter it became. I was permanently drenched in sweat and had a prickly rash covering my back. It itched madly but the pain was worse. It was akin to shingles, brought on by the heat, and simply added to my general woes. I began to question how much more I could take. Every time a man retched or spewed where he stood, covering his shirt and feet, I felt like doing the same. Often the gagging sound was enough to send bile leaping up from my own bloated belly. I never imagined life could get so bad or that I could feel so low.

Again we stopped for rice and water. While waiting for my portion I overheard some Englishmen chatting in hushed tones.

'Thank Christ that's over.'

'Yes. This doesn't look too bad. At least we're not in the jungle. I hate that place, with its creepy crawlies and all.'

'And snakes. Can't be doing with that. No, this will be

fine. Might even get some time off to go downtown and see some dancing girlies.'

I did not share their optimism and was proven correct. Within an hour the bawling started again and the Japanese beat and harassed us back into the steel ovens.

We waited for a long time again before departing. As we stood in the relative darkness I could hear a solitary mosquito buzzing around the carriage. Its endless whirring faded in and out, dive-bombing me but never landing. I stood with my arm raised, ready to wallop it when it came within range. On and on it went slicing through the stifling heat and cutting the silence like a machine gun. No one else seemed to mind its presence. I wondered why it was the only insect invader. It would almost have been better that the carriage be full of flies rather than this perverse sole purveyor of annoyance.

After a while I could take it no longer. I snapped, 'Would someone kill that bloody mozzie!'

No one replied. I even wondered if I had said it out loud. Either the fly bugged only me or everyone else had lost the will to fight a battle in the dark.

Finally the train started moving again. I vaguely heard an ironic cheer go up in the next carriage. It brought a wry smile to my face. By the time we were back up to full pace I could no longer hear the buzzing of the mosquito and a while later I was surprised to find myself missing its presence. It had given me something to concentrate on, a target for what was left of my anger. It was back to the endless clackety-clack of the wheels on the track, the moaning and coughing of the sick men, the itching of my back and the humiliation of urinating in your trousers. On and on we went. Day became night. I leaned against the wagon sides once they had cooled down sufficiently and tried to sleep. It was hopeless. It sounds bizarre but I think I was too tired to sleep. Still no one spoke. It was just too much effort. I felt doomed and resigned myself to death. It would have been a blessing. I considered suicide and began to fantasise that the train would jump its tracks and that I would be killed swiftly without any more suffering. I was so delirious and out of my head that I willed the RAF to drop bombs on us and end our misery that way.

Again and again we stopped at sidings and would pray for the doors to open only to have our hopes crushed as the train picked up steam and rumbled on once more. On the fourth day of this living hell we stopped again in the middle of the jungle. It could have been the same place as our first stop for all we knew. The jungle looked the same to me. We took more water and rice, just a minuscule and mightily inadequate cup of each, and rested for an hour before being rushed back on to the train.

We travelled on through the night and into a fifth day. By now nobody stood. We lay slumped all over each other on the floor, trying to keep off the sizzling sides. I was at my absolute breaking point. Looking back now more than sixty years later I wonder how we possibly got through it. We were all out of our minds. Great hulking men keened and wept like mourning mothers. Others whispered private prayers over and over. I lay, my head resting on a stranger's boot, ready to die.

Just before dusk on the fifth day we ground to a halt, the doors rolled back and the Japanese ordered us off. We had arrived at a village, which we were told was Ban Pong. We were in Thailand. Our nine-hundred-mile train journey was over.

Helping some of the sicker men off the train I noticed a young man in his teens, lying at the rear of the carriage. I remembered that earlier in the day he had had respiratory problems, wheezing uncontrollably. There had been nothing we could do to help him. One of the lads jumped back up and tapped the man's foot.

'Come on, son, we're here – at the holiday camp. Let the games begin.'

The youngster remained still.

'You lazy lout, get up,' said the helper, a note of desperation in his voice. He crouched down over the stricken youth's face. The teenager's lifeless eyes stared back sending his helper recoiling, gasping in horror.

The dead man was lugged off the train. He had probably died of diphtheria, coupled with malaria, dengue fever or dysentery. Some of the prisoners kicked his body into the jungle to decompose alongside the fallen leaves – food for the rats and bugs. I turned my back and walked away. I did not want to see his face and carry that with me; anything that sapped the will to live had to be avoided.

The Japanese officer's translator told us the train journey was finished. Before we could rejoice too much the interpreter quickly added that we had yet to reach our final destination.

We had a fifty-kilometre march ahead of us. Starting immediately. To be completed that night.

I swayed with shock at the announcement, as if I had been punched in the face.

I had no idea how far a kilometre was but supposed it was further than a mile. In my state I struggled to see how I could possibly make it through dense jungle. I was surprised that I had made it this far. It was a miracle it was not *me* decomposing in the jungle beside the train tracks.

The Japanese served up the usual meagre helping of rice and water, and gave us a further serving of unsalted, sugarless rice to take with us. I looked at the rice that barely covered the bottom of my mess tin, wondering how long it would be before I had the chance to eat it. It had already begun to ferment in the heat. All I wanted to do was to eat it, lie down and let death take me. The thought of a march through thick jungle, in darkness, was overwhelming and I sobbed quietly to myself as guards struck us with bamboo sticks and, shouting 'Marchee, marchee!', assembled us into a long column. During the six days that followed it would shorten considerably.

About six hundred prisoners – diseased, vermin-infested and at our lowest ebb – began that march. A handful of Japanese guards and officers organised the line and led us into the jungle. Those prisoners who had brought with them all of their kit and clung to it so tenaciously during the train journey, now ditched all non-essentials. We hastily fashioned stretchers from

bamboo poles and blankets or rice sacks, and loaded on
them those unable to walk. We were entrusted with carrying the sick. It was a Herculean task. All of us were
walking wounded really and in such a decrepit state that
we decided to take turns carrying the invalids.

Trudging north from the railway, leaving behind our
last glimpse of civilisation, we started our death march.
In the bright moonlight we traipsed into the virgin jungle
along a crudely cut path that swarmed thickly with mosquitoes. The Japanese must have prepared the trail for us
beforehand but it was only about five feet in width and
for the most part the soldiers in front had to hack away
with machetes at the encroaching growth. Other guards
carried sputtering bamboo flares that illuminated our
path and threw up weird shadows against the jungle
canopy. We walked three abreast with guards at the
front and between us in intervals. Guards also walked
alongside at points, encouraging us on with thwacks
from bamboo canes and prods with bayonets. If we fell
by the wayside, or stumbled and fell, they beat us. The
blows landed swiftly and randomly, impossible to defend
against.

We were a miserable lot. It was not a march, more of a
stagger. I had to concentrate intently just to put one foot
in front of the other, the undulating ground covered with
treacherous tree roots that you had to be on the lookout
for.

Depending on their mood, every two hours or so the
Japanese would shout, 'Yasume!', and we would stop to
rest for five minutes, collapsing on the side of the track,

flopping where we were. If you were lucky you might fall asleep. The next thing you knew a Japanese boot would be on your neck, its owner screaming at you to rise.

At that first stop I ate the last of my rice. Just as I closed my eyes we were told to get a move on. Silently we rose, again forming into soulless columns, and began walking. It was better to be in the middle of the trio. Bamboo, while remarkable for its diverse qualities, adaptability and usefulness, cuts like razor wire. On the outside of the column you had little chance of dodging blows from the guards or avoiding scraping your arms against the over-hanging vegetation. When the cuts went bad, 90 per cent of the time tropical ulcers formed.

It got to the point where I did not trust any plant. I treated them all as poisonous or dangerous, as many were. A lot of the things that we suffered from, including ringworm, scabies, rashes and itches, came as a direct result of plant contact. The only one I knew to be safe was the hibiscus, identifiable by its lovely silky green leaves. Whenever I saw one I would pick some leaves and stuff them in my pocket. They were packed with vitamins and could be added to rice or boiled to make a stew.

Tree snakes that hung above us from the tropical rain-forest like lianas were another hazard. Roaming the Aberdeenshire countryside I occasionally saw adders and while I never exactly wanted to bring one home as a pet, I knew that they could not kill a man. I did not know just how venomous these slim green slitherers were and had no wish to find out. Yet they were so well camouflaged among the dense foliage that by the time I spotted them they were already hissing above my head, sending icy shivers down my sweaty back.

I also tried to ensure that I was near the front of the column. The stragglers faded to the rear, which ignited the idiotic wrath of the guards, who ruthlessly beat these poor souls and all of the men in their immediate vicinity. Another benefit of being near the front was that you saw fewer men surrendering to fatigue, illness and death. The less you saw the better. Death chipped away at your spirits like a jackhammer.

Nonetheless I did witness the pathetic and desperate sight of two men, both younger than me, being left behind. Anyone who collapsed, passed out or refused to go on was left to die. You would walk past and offer assistance, a hand up or a supporting arm under the armpits. Those too weak to be encouraged to come along were left, slipping down the onward column, which stretched for hundreds of yards. Theirs was either a slow, lingering and lonely death or the swift and brutal thrust of a Japanese bayonet.

Some men had noticeably 'paired up', latching on to friends from the same regiment. They helped each other over fallen logs, egged each other on, shared food and stories. They worked on the basis that two men were better than one, and the companionship must have given them strength. I knew no one and was wholly alone. Never had I felt so alone.

After two days of solid marching we came to a village. I heard that the clearing in the midst of the jungle, surrounded by trees on all sides and dotted with five or six bamboo huts, was called Kam Pong. The villagers were instructed to feed us and ran around at the behest of the Japanese, bowing to the guards' every need, clearly petrified. Some of our chaps tried to quiz the natives for information – where were we, what was near us, could they hide us – but the villagers quickly turned away. Others tried to barter for food or water but met similar silence. I did not blame the locals for pandering to the Japanese; they had no choice.

The villagers served up rice, some boiled water and an extremely spicy vegetable stew. It was delicious but it played havoc with my bowels, instantly sending me running for the jungle. Luckily I managed to do my business without getting a beating and returned to my spot. Around me the POWs were scattered like the aftermath of a mass failed parachute jump. Men lay at all angles, some of them moaning softly, others already asleep. We were told that we would spend the night here so should conserve energy and sleep. I wondered how many 'kilometres' we had travelled and how far we had ahead of us. Those terrible thoughts somehow sent me gratefully into a deep sleep there in the dirt – not giving a second thought to the cobras, kraits and vipers we had been warned about in training.

Through the night I kept waking up with a start. The jungle had come alive. A whole new populace claimed the darkness. Around us echoed strange and terrible sounds – wolf-like howls and a clack-clack-clack that I took for a type of woodpecker. The din produced by crickets, bullfrogs, monkeys and all manner of creatures rose to such a crescendo that it was impossible to sleep soundly. I half expected a man-eating tiger to come and take me.

When I woke in the morning my body ached all over. I stood and almost yelped with pain and stiffness. I was covered in the rich jungle soil. It caked us all from head to toe. The Japanese had awoken with renewed vigour and demanded an even quicker pace today, screaming in our faces, 'Speedo, speedo!' and beating us on. I put my head down and trudged on, fixing my eyes on the back of the sad chap in front of me, not really taking anything in. My mind was switched firmly on to autopilot. I was so out of it that my brain had shut down and was reduced to survival mode. I wondered if it were possible to sleep with your eyes open.

We followed a river for most of the march. I would later learn it was the Mae Klong, which joined the river Kwai – a vast river that rises in the north-west of Thailand near the Burmese border and flows south for hundreds of miles to drain into the Gulf of Thailand. We kept to the right of its muddy brown expanse, shadowing its winding path. It was as wide as the mighty river Tay in my native Scotland. Even when the Mae Klong was out of sight I could hear its low rumbling. Much as we yearned to we never ventured near enough to sneak a drink from it. But the guards often waded in and bathed, taunting us by splashing each other, laughing and loudly enjoying the relief that the cool waters brought.

As the sun dropped below the horizon like a sinking stone the river left our view. Its distant sound disappeared with the emergence of the myriad of jungle noises. After marching in the dark for some distance the guards ordered us to a halt. We would camp on the path overnight. I ate what was left of the rice in my mess tin and fell asleep. It was to be a long, broken night. I felt sick with dread, wondering what was to come next. The question of a holiday camp was now well and truly ruled out. Even the most optimistic POW realised that we had been conned.

Vivid and disturbing nightmares of the surrender at Fort Canning disrupted what sleep I did manage to get. The raging face of the Japanese soldier who took me prisoner at bayonet point haunted my subconscious. I still have those nightmares to this day and the image of the man's face is as clear as if it happened yesterday.

I never dared to take my boots and socks off overnight. They would almost certainly have gone missing. Lying there in my boots I remembered a scene from a Western I had seen at the Capital Theatre in Aberdeen, in which the cowboys were all sleeping on the ground, around a campfire. One chap, drunk on moonshine, was without a pair of boots and proceeded to steal a pair from the guy beside him. It was the way he did it that tickled me. He took an age to slip them off and was very careful not to wake the sleeper. The image stuck with me for some reason and I thought, I'm not going to let that happen to me.

On the fourth day we trooped on again. More and more men were dropping back and being left behind to die. It was noticeable now that the column was shrinking. No one tried to boost morale by song, banter or otherwise. Our spirits were broken. We just kept plodding along, praying it would end soon and that we would get better conditions. We all stank to high heaven. There was no escaping it but after a while we became used to it, like families who live beside fish markets. The Japanese probably did not smell as badly as us since they often bathed in the river. We tried not to get close enough to them to check. Our collective stench most likely increased their already ample disgust for us.

Allowing oneself to be relegated to the status of prisoner, to fall into the arms of the enemy, was highly dishonourable in the Japanese soldiers' minds. In their distorted view of the world death was a more admirable option. The simple peasants who formed the backbone of the Japanese Army had been thoroughly indoctrinated by their fascist leaders. Like their German allies they were a chosen race, a superior people. They were 'the sons of heaven' and we were decadent and effeminate weaklings. Lacking the Wagnerian and Teutonic mythology that cloaked Nazi ideology, the Japanese militarists wrapped their aggressive bid for racial domination in the ancient code of bushido to legitimise it with the Japanese people. Under this samurai code Japanese soldiers committed hara-kiri when captured, undertook suicidal banzai charges and, as kamikaze pilots, crashed into enemy ships.

For us prisoners bushido, the so-called 'Way of the Warrior', gave the guards a licence to murder, maim and torture. The only thing more despicable to them than a prisoner was a sick prisoner, as we first discovered on our death march.

In the months to come many thousands of prisoners would follow in our footsteps and this jungle trail would claim hundreds more lives.

That night we stopped again at a village. We were fed rice, spicy stew and water, before sleeping where we sat. I slept much better, either becoming accustomed to the jungle sounds or just too dog-tired to care.

We went on our way again in the morning. We hauled our sick men along by their arms, their toes dragging in the dirt. My fears of being massacred had long subsided. If they were going to do it, they would have done so by now. I believed that we were being taken to work as slaves on something.

By now covered in scabies and lice, I had been struck down again by the dreaded malaria. As the protozoan parasites raged through my bloodstream, my spleen became tender and enlarged. Walking became ever more difficult and I stumbled more often than not. Some men, whom I had helped earlier on in the journey, gave me blankets to break the fever and to stop the rigors that shook my body like a man possessed.

We walked all day and through the next night, stopping only for brief respites beside the track. It was a final push by the Japanese to get us to our destination, whatever it was, inside six days. Whether there was a date we had to arrive by, I was unsure. It appeared that the soldiers wanted us moving at double-time, rush or not. In the late afternoon, after we had been trudging for around thirty-two hours, we arrived at our final destination – we had completed a 160-kilometre trek.

It took some time for us to comprehend that we had made it, that this small, sparse clearing in the middle of the jungle was 'it', the ultimate objective of our eleven-day journey. There was nothing here, not a single hut. On one side of the clearing lay an array of tools. Pickaxes, shovels, two-handed saws and scythe-like instruments. Seeing them made me wonder again what our purpose here was. An aerodrome perhaps? Were we at a strategic point for the Japanese to launch an air assault on India? The men were gathered, chattering about our future possibilities, when the guard in charge got our attention.

Through his interpreter he told us: 'This is your camp. You make home here. Build own huts. All men work on railway.'

A *railway*! A railway, here in the middle of nowhere. It seemed mad and it certainly never occurred to me that this would be our task. How would they get the sleepers into the jungle? Not to mention the steel railway lines. The British had considered the construction of a railway to link Burma with Siam many years before but concluded it could not be done. Not without massive loss of life anyway.

Finally we had been told of our purpose but I do not think that it sank in properly. All we cared about was that the march was over. Surely things would start looking up. We could not envisage the enormity, misery or savagery of the challenges ahead. I just felt glad to stop walking.

The soldiers had arranged arc lamps in one corner of the clearing, which they led us to now and instructed us to start construction of our sleeping quarters. We all stared at each other blankly. One of the guards, noticing our bewilderment, pointed to the scattered tools and made an A-frame with his arms, yammering away in a language we did not comprehend.

'What are we supposed to do? Build the ruddy Ritz?'

The plucky Londoner who had stepped forth to offer his cockney wit quickly retreated when a guard went for him with a pickaxe handle. It was our signal to get on with it. We snatched a tool each and tried to look busy. They wanted us to clear more trees but we were so knackered that it was totally fruitless. I took a scythe and started hacking at some trees. It was pretty hopeless. The blade bounced off the hard bamboo but at least I appeared industrious in the eyes of our masters.

The Japanese wanted us to build five huts for the POWs, forty men to each. They would build their own huts, while the first thing we were required to build was an awning for the cooks to operate under.

They stopped us after about two or three hours, perhaps realising that we were too shattered to make any progress. Allowed to stop I sat down on the spot and curled up. After thirty-six hours of constant activity I could finally rest. The tropical forest sounds didn't interrupt my sleep that night and I wasn't visited in my dreams. Tomorrow would be a new dawn.

Five

Hellfire Pass

On that first morning they split us into two groups. Half of the POWs had to finish building our sleeping quarters, while the rest of us cleared trees at the camp. As a guard thrust a pickaxe into my soft hands, I could not remember the last time I had endured any hard labour. And this was going to be a far cry from hoisting cast-iron bathtubs on to lorries bound for Highland mansions.

I positioned myself near the trees, away from the guards, and took a moment to watch the other men in action. Some of them were already getting stuck in, swinging their chunkels, heavy Thai hoes, with apparent ease. They were flailing into the earth, digging up roots and rocks. It looked easy enough and after a few awkward swings, some of which grazed my bare shins, I quickly got the hang of it. It was rhythmic toil and I became almost mechanical in my movements. But within an hour bubbling blisters started to appear on my palms. By lunch my thumbs felt painfully disconnected from their sockets and my back ached at its base from all the unnatural movement. There was no respite. The Japanese had no consideration for our poor health or hunger and beat men across their backs with bamboo or rifles regularly enough to make us keep our heads down. It was a long first day and if I had realised then that it was just the first of 750 days I would spend as a slave in the jungle, I would have broken down and cried like a baby.

After another night sleeping in the open with restless centipedes and soldier ants, we went back to work. Through some ingenuity I managed to get selected to help construct the huts. The work was no less frantic but it was less physical and gave the balloon-like blisters on my hands a chance to subside. The only dangers lay in the fact that nobody knew what they were doing. I felt that my Boy Scout knowledge of knots and the outdoors would be useful. Instructing us through an interpreter the Nippon Army engineers spelled out what they required. The huts were to be very basic A-frame structures, using lengths of bamboo for the frame and support struts, and the point of the roof raised to about twenty feet high. We would use slivers of tree bark, or rattan, carefully cut with parangs, Burmese knives about eighteen inches long, to lash the bamboo together. You dampened the rattan before tying it around the bamboo and as it dried it would shrink, providing an amazingly tight fastening. The floor, made with bamboo split in long half-lengths, would have a corrugated effect and be raised about three feet off the ground. We were to sleep on either side of a gangway that ran the length of the hut, which was open at both ends but at least closed at the sides with walls of bark. I volunteered to make the roof, which involved thatching it with atap leaves. It was a good job, not least because I was out of reach of the guards and their vicious tempers.

When I had finished it looked great. But it provided little more than shade; these huts really only created shelter for mosquitoes and disease-carrying flies. During the monsoon season, when the rain pelted down in stair-rods, the water cascaded in and we may as well have not bothered with our roofing efforts. We were permanently damp, working, eating and sleeping in the rain. As result we lost a lot of men on the railway to pneumonia. For many the disease known at home as the 'old people's friend' would become the 'prisoner's friend', offering a relatively peaceful and unconscious end.

This camp would become known as 'Kanyu'. I thought of it as 'Can-You', which I often found cruelly ironic. As the line progressed it would become Kanyu I, when Kanyu II and Kanyu III were built further up the railway that snaked its way through the dense jungle of Thailand towards Burma.

After three days the Japanese considered our huts to be completed. They told us we could add finishing touches in 'our own time'.

On day four we were to begin construction on the infamous Death Railway, the 415-kilometre Burma–Siam Railway through some of the most inhospitable terrain on the planet. The British engineers who had scoped out the possibility of a railway in 1885 were quite right to warn of the massive loss of life it would entail. The construction of the Death Railway was one of the greatest war crimes of the twentieth century. It was said that one man died for every sleeper laid. Certainly over sixteen thousand of us British, Australian, Dutch, American and Canadian prisoners died on the railway – murdered by the ambitions of the Japanese Imperial Army to complete the lifeline to their forces in Burma by December 1943. Up to a hundred thousand native slaves, Thais, Indians, Malayans and Tamils also died in atrocious circumstances.

Even Japanese engineers estimated that the railway would take five years to complete. The Japanese Imperial Army would prove them wrong, however. It had a secret weapon: slave labour. In just sixteen months a railway linking Bangkok with the Burmese rice bowl and its vital oil fields would be completed at a terrible human cost. The single-track narrow-gauge line, just over a metre wide, allowed rice and raw materials to be looted from Burma and Japanese reinforcements to be sent from Thailand for the planned invasion of India.

At first only prisoners of war were put to work at both the Burmese and Thai ends of the railway, with the object of meeting in the middle at Three Pagodas Pass, where the ancient Burmese and Thai civilisations had clashed three hundred years earlier. Then following the United States' success at the Battle of Midway in June 1942, the seas around Burma and Malaysia became a vast hunting ground for American submarines and the pace of work was quickened by working us prisoners to death and drafting in two hundred thousand coolie labourers.

Over sixteen months we would hack our way through hundreds of kilometres of dense jungle, gouge passes through rocky hills, span ravines and cross rivers, building bridges and viaducts with rudimentary tools. It was a huge civil engineering project that would be lubricated with our blood, sweat and tears. But most of all blood.

On starvation rations and with no access to medicines of any kind, we lived in camps buried deep in the remote jungle where Red Cross inspectors or representatives of neutral foreign powers could never find us. A whole army of sixty thousand men had vanished into the jungle at the mercy of our Japanese masters.

On that first morning the guards woke us by rattling canes across the bamboo walls at dawn. It was a sound that would become all too recognisable to us.

'All men worko! Speedo! Speedo!'

A chorus of 'Aye, aye,' rang around the awakening hut. One brave lad replied, 'Keep your head on you Jap bastard, it'll be knocked off soon.' This sort of bravado would fizzle out later when we discovered that many of our guards could understand English.

There was no time, facilities or desire for a wash and shave; it was straight out to form the line for breakfast.

'Cheer up lads, it's ham and eggs this morning,' one prisoner offered from the front.

'Naw it's no. It's porridge the morning,' said another.

Some of the men in the queue cursed the early-morning jokers for mentioning such fantastic delicacies. Thinking and talking about food had become a form of torture – it just drove you mad. We all knew it would be plain rice, just rice. Just like every other stinking day.

The cooks had already been up for a couple of hours – about the only downside of being a camp cook – to heat two 12-gallon cast-iron saucer-shaped pots of rice, 'kualies', and boil drinking water in cauldrons over an open fire. The cooks were fed last, and best. But sometimes when the cooks had had enough, I would manage to get the burned skin of the rice scraped from the kualies. It may have been burned but it tasted so much better.

After breakfast we were paraded in the half-light outside our huts for the count. It was a full squad, a *kumi*, on the railway today. *Tenko*, roll-call, was conducted by guards and overseen by the Japanese version of a drill sergeant, a *gunso*, who made the RSM from the Bridge of Don barracks seem like a playful puppy. It all took time and was done in Japanese. The camps all operated on Tokyo time. Not that it made any difference to us; the bayonet and the boot were our timekeepers.

The count, or *bango*, was conducted in Japanese with numbers one to ten being *ichi, ni, san, shi, go, roku, shichi, hachi, ku, ju*. Number eleven was *ju-ichi*, which took the tenth number and the first, while number twelve was *ju-ni*, and so on. It took some longer than others to get their head around. But you learned seemingly impossible tasks very quickly under the threat of a rifle smashing into your face. The Japanese had especial trouble understanding some of the Scottish and English accents and when inadvertently we offended them they would go berserk. If someone stumbled and forgot what number they were, someone would shout it out for them but it didn't always work and the guards would give the man a beating. Sometimes several beatings would be administered and the count could take up to an hour, which would result in further blanket punishments or reduced rations. I quickly learned that it was best to avoid being in the front rank at tenko, where most beatings were handed out.

In the vast sprawling camp at Changi it had been easy for me to keep out of the way of our troublesome and irritable captors but on the railway they stalked our every move and it was necessary to fully learn the humiliating kow-towing protocol that they insisted upon. If we failed to bow, salute or stand to attention at the approach of a guard, a beating would be administered.

Once the count was complete we formed a line for our tools. Picks, shovels and twin baskets on bamboo yo-ho poles that you carried across your shoulders were all laid out. The saws, chisels and anything else that was sharp and could have been used as a weapon were always kept down at the railway. I could not understand how the Japanese never saw a pickaxe as a potential weapon but I never came across it being used as one, so maybe they were right after all.

As I was handed my pick and shovel a Japanese guard whacked me across the legs with a strop, urging me to follow the men into the jungle. We followed a rough path, weaving through the trees. The only men left behind at camp were a handful of officers, two Royal Army

Medical Corps (RAMC) officers and their assistants and four cooks. There were only six officers and they all shared one hut with the NCOs. Since the Japanese had removed anything that signified rank it was difficult to tell who was an officer and who was not. They had to convince others that they were who they said they were. But I could usually tell after hearing them speak. Most of the officers spoke a different language from the rest of us. And it was not just their posh accents; it was their vocabulary too. Farm labourers and factory workers did not call each other 'old boy' and describe things as being 'quaint'.

It took about an hour to reach our destination, nothing more than a rare and slight gap in the jungle with a rocky cliff just visible ahead in the distance. Later the Australians would dub it Hellfire Pass and I could not have thought of a better name for it myself. The Japanese engineers told us that we had to clear everything between the white markers already pegged into the ground. The pattern was set. Trees would be chopped down by hand, huge tree roots ripped up, boulders shouldered out of our path and great thickets of towering, spiky bamboo cleared.

They divided us into squads. I was on pick and shovel, clearing all the vegetation and boulders in a thirty-foot width. In the middle of the space, where the railway sleepers and eventually the tracks would go, we had to dig down to a depth of about three feet. There we dug up the earth in a twelve-foot-wide strip, which others with baskets on yo-ho poles hauled to one side. After digging down a foot or so we invariably struck clay, which made for even tougher going.

Another squad were tasked with removing the rocks, trees and debris, another separated the roots to dry them out and later burn them. Meanwhile on the pickaxe party some men were going hammer and tong. I said to one chap near me who was slugging his pick as if in a race, 'Slow down mate, you'll burn yourself out.'

'If we get finished early,' he said, puffing, 'maybe we'll get back to camp early.'

But the soldiers would only find something else for us to do. And then the next day Japanese expectations would be higher. Personally I tried to work as slowly as possible. The others would learn eventually but I soon discovered ways to conserve energy. If I swung the pick quickly, allowing it to drop alongside an area I had just cleared, the earth came away easier. It also meant that while it looked as if I were swinging the pick like the Emperor's favourite son, the effort was minimal. Nevertheless under the scorching Thai sun and without a shirt or hat for protection, or shade from the nearby jungle canopy, the work soon became exhausting. Minute after minute, hour after hour, I wondered when the sun would drop and we could go back to camp.

Around midday the Japanese called for yasume. We downed tools and sat and ate rice, which we had taken with us from camp in the morning. When I opened my rice tin I found the contents had begun to ferment. It was almost rice wine and tasted horrible. But I ate it anyway. Lunch usually lasted for around thirty minutes at the railway, depending on the officer in charge. If he were sleepy or tired, it might be longer. We used to love it when he fell asleep!

After lunch we carried on. Our progress became bogged down by a huge boulder semi-submerged in the soil and right in our way. We had to pickaxe around it and try and lever it out with pick handles. It took five men to prise it from its hole and once it was out we rolled it down the hill towards the river. It was the river Kwai that flowed south to join with the Mae Klong, which we had followed during the death march. It remained to our left for the duration of my time on the railway and I never once went in it.

By mid-afternoon we had finally completed the first section. Despite enormous toil and effort over the previous ten hours, our progress had been incredibly slow. We had managed to clear the required thirty-foot width for only about twenty feet. It was the beginning for us of what would become the most notorious railway construction that the world had ever seen. The Japanese engineer came over to inspect our work. He studied the clearing from several angles, using various surveying instruments, before declaring, 'No gooda! Do again! Deeper!'

Utterly demoralised we had to go back to the beginning and manually dredge another foot of soil. We were all in various stages of beriberi, pellagra, malaria, dengue fever and dysentery. A new illness had also started to ravage some unfortunate prisoners. Called tinea, it was nicknamed 'rice balls' because the hideous swelling had the tormenting tendency to attack, crack and inflame the scrotum.

There was never any warning when the dysentery might come on. You could be on a pick when the urge would hit you, sending you scuttling into the jungle to do your business. You might get away with it or you might just get a beating to add to your woes.

A Japanese officer sat on a rock in the shade, overlooking proceedings. If he saw something that he didn't like, he would shout to guards who would come running into the area. You might be working away, completely innocent, and get an indiscriminate beating because of someone else's minor misdemeanour. I came to know which POWs were the ones always getting into trouble and I steered clear of them as much as possible. I thought it took a strange man to always be at the receiving end of beatings and never learn to avoid them. Those men were usually the ones trying to hide in the shade or those who would see a native walking through the jungle and try to barter with them. Always looking for an angle. I did not need those kind of people around me.

By the end of the day we still had managed only a distance of twenty feet. But we had finally dug to the depth the engineers wanted, and just before dusk we wound our weary bodies back through the jungle to camp. I got my rice and water and went straight to the hut and collapsed, my whole body aching with pain. Hands, feet, back, arms, legs were all so sore, especially my back and legs. Eventually out of sheer exhaustion I fell asleep. But when I woke it didn't feel like I had slept at all. I was incredibly lethargic and the pain had increased overnight. I was expecting a long sleep to rejuvenate me, to help me through the next day, which I had envisaged as bringing just the same amount of torture, if not worse. But I felt horrific and that is when I realised I was at rock bottom. I felt lower than the rats that had scuttled through our hut during the night. The whole camp was completely demoralised and dejected; you could see it in the empty darkness of men's eyes. I was glad there were no mirrors – I really did not want to witness the state of my face and read the story of my own eyes.

Nevertheless I heaved my ravaged body out of the hut and got my food. I half-ran to the queue for tools, desperate to be given a pickaxe and shovel once again. I had seen the poor devils struggling on the baskets the previous day and while I was in agony from a day on pick duties, at least my muscles would become accustomed to it. Better the devil you know.

On the hike back to the railway the enormity of our task suddenly dawned on me. During the first day I remembered seeing a great expanse of solid rock in front of us. Only now did I realise that we were going to have to make our way *through* that slab of rock.

The Japanese never allowed us to speak while working. You had to speak with your head down, in hushed tones, to someone, 'Hey, slow down mate. You're making it worse for all of us.'

While I could successfully fake the amount of effort I was putting in on pick and shovel duty, I couldn't escape the toil of carrying rocks in the baskets. It was the most difficult task. You had to be on the move all day, knees buckling under the weight, often down steep inclines. It was especially difficult during the monsoon season and caused more injuries than anything else.

Each day the Japanese increased our task. We had managed twenty feet the day before so today they wanted twenty-five feet. I whispered to the guys in my work party, 'Let's not do it. Let's go slow.'

They all agreed. We went on a go-slow all day, chuckling to ourselves as the shadows lengthened. By the time it got dark we were a little over halfway through what they wanted us to do. But the plan backfired. Instead of returning to camp at 6 p.m., the soldiers set up arc and carbide lamps, bamboo fires, containers filled with diesel fuel, oil and hessian wicks, anything they could lay their hands on, to keep us there well after nine in the evening, until we had finished the task.

No matter what time of the year, summer or winter, it was always dark by the time we got back to camp. Most evenings men would gather outside the huts and chat before they hit the hay. I would occasionally join them but I would stand on the fringes and not say anything. There was not much to chat about, although a lot of men were married and would talk about their families back home. These slightly older men in their thirties and forties seemed to survive in much greater numbers. Surprisingly it was the young men who died first on the railway. Perhaps the older ones were stronger emotionally. Perhaps with families they had more to live for. I sometimes wondered if I would die without having a family and without having had the chance to live a life, and then quickly try to banish these thoughts before getting my head down.

The huts teemed with bloodsucking bed bugs that would emerge just before dawn to torment us. We could never eliminate them; we had no chemicals or anything like that. When you caught them and crushed them they smelled absolutely disgusting. After a few weeks of being eaten alive by bugs while sleeping on the floor of the hut, I decided to try a night sleeping outside. I did not know what would happen to me if I did but I judged it was worth the chance of being bashed by the guards. I always slept near the front of the hut, third man in on the right, and sneaked out during the night, careful not to make a noise, around the side of the hut. I lay down in the dirt. It was undulating but soft and cool. The stars were out and the high sky seemed to muffle the constant malaria-induced moaning of men and the tormented cries brought on by nightmares. The jungle noises by now had lost their edge for me and I fell asleep quickly. When I awoke I joined the breakfast queue, feeling much more sprightly and relaxed than I had after sleeping in the packed and restless hut. The unbroken rest would pay dividends during a day on the railway. I slept outside most nights from then on. Strangely nobody commented on it and no one copied me.

There were some, however, who got up in the night to stretch their restless feet. It was quite normal for men to walk outside and find a cool spot, some wet leaves or damp soil, to cool their 'happy feet' – the name we gave to the very painful burning sensation caused by beriberi, which was brought on by acute vitamin deficiency.

*

A full-time burial party of six men now worked in the camp. It was comprised of the same six souls, who never went out to work on the railway. While digging graves in the jungle was by no means easy work, it was easier, physically at least, than being on the railway. But seeing those poor dead men must have taken a lot of strength and will from the gravediggers.

Just to face the next day required a huge effort for all of us. You did not have the energy to do what our captors demanded. On around a thousand calories a day it was completely beyond our physical being. But it did not matter to them. There were thousands of POWs, not to mention the tens and hundreds of thousands of natives, waiting to replace us. We were slaves to the slaughter and utterly expendable to them.

But even the Japanese eventually realised that some tasks were becoming beyond our physical capabilities. For the previous few months we had been manually dragging huge teak logs to be used as railway sleepers. When we first arrived it would take eight to twelve men to move these hardwood trunks but as we became weaker it took twenty or thirty men to edge them into place. After a while the soldiers introduced two elephants to take over that task, to increase productivity. I had seen elephants when the circus came to Aberdeen and up close these beasts were equally impressive and intimidating. It was pleasing to see them in action, knowing our backs were being saved for another day, but their presence only added to the overall danger of railway life. The logs hung on steel chains around the elephants' necks. The animals

moved them easily but they would swing around dangerously, causing a lot of accidents and broken bones and
taking out plenty of men.

My army-issue clothes, shorts and shirt had long since
rotted from my frame. In a bid to retain my remaining dignity, I resorted to wearing a 'Jap-happy', a simple loincloth
that had become popular among the men. It consisted of a
long piece of white linen approximately six inches wide.
Two pieces of tape or string attached to the ends meant
you could tie it around your waist, while the rest of the
material was drawn from behind under your groin to
cover your bits. The loose end just flapped down in front
of you. It would win no fashion awards but it did the job
and was surprisingly comfortable. Otherwise I was naked.
The more naked I was, the cleaner I felt. But the filth, dirt,
crawling lice, the itch, smell and loss of all freedom and
dignity were hard for any proud man to bear.

The wall of rock that had started off four hundred
yards in front of us was getting closer every day. The
thought of using pickaxes, hammers and chisels on this
great slab of limestone gave me the horrors. I knew people
were dying around me on the railway but I didn't really
want to know. It was too dispiriting. It was difficult to
judge the full toll of casualties and by this stage I had
become so self-obsessed, in a true mental battle just to get
through each day. I had very few friends at Hellfire Pass
and most of us were the same. We all worked so hard
that, just trying to survive, each person became more and
more insular as it became more difficult. It required a
superhuman effort to make it to the end of each day.

Strangely the less we talked to each other, the more we talked to ourselves. Nearly all of the prisoners talked to themselves and I was no exception. Every morning I would tell myself over and over, 'Survive this day. Survive this day. Survive this day.'

Occasionally, often with bizarre timing, I would have flashbacks to funny incidents from my childhood. Several men reported the same thing. Suddenly, quite out of the blue, we would be transported back in time, an astonishing and vivid experience. It must have been the mind's way of coping with the extreme stress. In my case Auntie Dossie would often appear. Images of Dossie doing crazy things would prompt me to great outbursts of hilarity to the point where I would be laughing out loud, tears tumbling down my cheeks. Even though most prisoners talked to themselves, men stared at me in alarm.

'What the hell are you laughing at?'

'Nothing,' I would reply, trying to regain my composure.

'There's nothing funny about this place.'

By this time mental health had become a major issue on the railway. We all suffered from depression. Men were taking their own lives. All along the railway men cut their own throats, put their heads on the railway line and simply walked into the jungle to die. Many developed the 'atap stare' and just looked intently at the thatched roof of the hut – death soon followed. Others went mad because of medical conditions caused by vitamin deficiencies and some just gave up, losing their minds and their self-control. They would fight with anyone over nothing at all, throwing punches, biting and kicking. They needed to be controlled physically but just could not be calmed down. It came to the point where something drastic had to be done to prevent innocent men being killed by deranged fellow prisoners, some of whom had reverted to animal instincts. The decision was made to build our own lunatic asylum to cage these poor souls.

With the agreement of the Japanese, the burial party built two six-foot-square bamboo cages. The 'madmen' could stand or lie down in these, just ten feet from my hut, and they had a bench to sit on. They received food and water but sadly were largely ignored. At night it was awful to hear them in the darkness jabbering and screaming, throwing themselves at the cage sides. The men who went in there never came out alive. Death would have been welcome for them. It was a dreadful thing to see our fellow beings caged like animals but what else could we do?

By now the lack of food at Kanyu I had become a major issue. Only those on work parties received rations. The sick were not given any food so ours had to be divided up so they could have some. The more sick men there were, the less food I got as a worker. It was a terrible situation.

The Japanese decided how many bags of rice we required but the way in which it was distributed was up to our officer. I didn't know how he came to his decisions; we just hoped he was fair.

When the Japanese felt we had been especially disrespectful or dishonest, we would be punished collectively with further reductions to our meagre rations. This happened only on rare occasions, not through any good grace on their behalf, but because the human body simply cannot operate on anything less than the rice we received.

I was really beginning to struggle. While my muscles had become used to the rhythm of work, I had become very ill and weak. Due to the lack of vitamin B in our plain rice diets, all of us had fallen victim to beriberi. In the long term it could be worse than dysentery or malaria. In the short term it gave me a swollen tummy and a tremendous pain in my joints, like a very bad toothache. My eyes too were beginning to give me trouble, stinging from the constant glare of the sun on the dirt and clay. The lack of vitamins entering my system worsened their state and I was lucky not to go blind, as others did. We called the blindness that sometimes came with beriberi, 'camp eyes', and lived in terror of going blind. At first men noticed their range of vision reduce to around ten metres and that everything was blurred. Then they would go blind altogether. The medics assured us it was temporary but I did not want to discover for myself. I also had very little chance of getting a proper sleep and the nightmares of surrender at Fort Canning continued as terrifyingly real as ever.

As if all this was not bad enough I started to suffer from kidney stones, brought on by constant dehydration. I had first had an attack of those devilishly painful daggerballs during my early days in Singapore while still with the Gordons. Downtown when they struck, the pain doubled me over and caused me to actually shout out in public. I didn't know what was happening so I paid a visit to the Alexandra Hospital. They told me to drink lime juice once a day and as much water as I could. Now with mere droplets dribbling past my cracked lips, the kidney stones struck often and with excruciating regularity. With no pethidine or morphine it was sheer hell. A worse pain I have never experienced.

Kidney stones tortured me for the next few years as a POW. The pain was so bad that I started to pray, the first time I had ever lent on God's ear in earnest. Even though I had to attend Bible class with the Boy Scouts, I never believed in a divine entity and was especially sceptical since I was *forced* to go to the classes. Gradually the more I suffered and the more evils I witnessed, the more I began to believe. I turned to God several times. Often I felt my prayers went unanswered. But I somehow lived through this madness and I think that someone must have been listening.

Faith in God could not prevent the beatings on the railway, which were totally routine. The threat of a rifle butt across your head or bamboo cane across your body forever loomed large. For no reason at all wire whips would lash into our backs and draw blood. Some guards would creep up on you and strike the open tropical ulcers on your legs with a bamboo stick, causing intense agony. Often they delivered these beatings with such brutality and swiftness that you did not see them coming or even know what they were for. Sometimes you just happened to be in the wrong place at the wrong time. The Korean guards took a certain pleasure in the beatings. They had express permission to kill prisoners without any reference to higher authority. But most of them would be satisfied to stop at the sight of trickling blood. The beatings, no matter how frequent, never got any easier to take. In fact they got tougher. Each time I took a beating it chipped away, not just at my bones and waning muscles, but at my will to endure them. The dilemma was whether to swallow your pride by going down at the first blow or to retain some of your dignity by taking several blows and standing up to them. If you refused to show that their blows were hurting you, they would fly into rages and the beating could be severe, even fatal.

From an early period the Japanese camp commandant, whom I called the 'Black Prince', became ever more inventive with his punishments. I could not imagine a more sadistic and evil person on the planet. The more heinous the so-called 'crime', the sicker the sentence. Under his instructions the guards had free rein. If they felt you deserved something more than a beating, it meant taking you aside and making you pick up a large boulder. For the rest of the day you had to hold the rock over your head in the blazing heat. Within minutes your already weak and malnourished arm muscles would start to twitch and fail you. Before long you would have to drop the rock, usually the size of a rugby ball or football, mindful you did so without letting it fall on your own skull. When you let go the guards would pounce – fists, rifle butts and boots flailing into your body until you picked the rock up again. It would go on all day. And if the Japanese officer did not think you had learned your lesson sufficiently, the punishment would be repeated back at camp.

The Black Prince was a true bastard. Others called him the 'Kanyu Kid' but I thought my name suited Lieutenant Usuki really well. He was darker than the other Japanese soldiers and strutted around like royalty, his beefy gut protruding from beneath a shabby uniform. He despised us totally. We were scum to him. His absolute power over us and capacity for pitiless brutality made him so terrifying to me.

Long before our decision to incarcerate crazy men, the Japanese had built their own cages. The 'black holes', as they were known, were a higher form of punishment. Those unfortunate enough to be locked inside the semi-subterranean cages, proportioned so you could not stand, lie down or even kneel fully, would be kept in for a month typically. Corrugated iron and metal covered the bamboo to intensify the heat and deprive victims of air and any cooling breeze. Few who went in came out alive.

The Black Prince's right-hand man was Sergeant Seiichi Okada, known to us Brits simply as 'Dr Death'. Short and squat he took the roll-calls and carried out all of the camp commandant's orders. Presumably he was more educated than the other Japanese or Koreans but he was evil to the marrow. Ruthless in the extreme he loved tormenting us. He especially revelled in a sickening brand of water torture. He had guards pin down his hapless victim, before pouring gallons of water down the prisoner's throat using a bucket and hose. The man's stomach would swell up from the huge volumes of water. Okada would

then jump up and down gleefully on the prisoner's stomach. Sometimes guards tied barbed wire around the poor
soul's stomach. Some men died and a few survived. I witnessed this disgusting display only once but it was once
too often. Dr Death also took great delight in hurling
stones and rocks down on prisoners from a lofty vantage
point.

When a prisoner was caught stealing from the Japanese
officers' storeroom, or if a man turned on a guard, they
received the next grade on the sliding scale of Japanese
torture. I called it the 'Indian rope trick', one favoured by
Indians in the old cowboy films. The helpless prisoner
would be tethered spread-eagled to the ground. They
wrapped wet rattan – the same string-like bark used to
lash our bamboo huts together – around his ankles and
wrists, and tied him to stakes in the ground. As the rattan
dried, the ties would slowly gash into the skin, drawing
blood and tearing into sinew and cartilage as it pulled
limbs from their sockets. It reduced even the toughest
men to agonised screaming, and they would be there all
day. I would be almost glad to get out of camp in the
mornings just to avoid hearing their cries of unbridled
pain. It was a way of torturing all of us. Often when we
returned from a day on the railway the men would no
longer be there. Nobody asked where they had vanished
to. I certainly did not want to know. After such a horrific
ordeal death at the end of a Japanese bayonet would have
been welcomed.

The worst of the Korean guards was the 'Mad
Mongrel'. He was slightly more Western-looking than the

rest, with a hard, angular face. A lot of prisoners struggled to tell the difference between the guards, who no doubt thought we all looked the same too. But I could tell and the more time you spent with them, the better you knew which ones to try and avoid. The Mad Mongrel patrolled the railway with a bamboo cane, striking out indiscriminately and often. He had been chosen by Dr Death and the Black Prince for his exceptional cruelty and sadism. On the railway their favourite punishment was getting us to kneel on gravel with ramrod-straight backs. If we sagged, blows to the kidneys straightened up our failing frames.

One day on the railway the Mad Mongrel saw something in my work party that riled him. Before I knew anything was wrong he charged up to me and slammed his rifle butt into my forehead. It knocked me clean off my feet. I was seeing stars but despite being dazed and shaken I got up quickly, to avoid being kicked to a pulp on the ground. I still bear the horseshoe scar, a lifelong gift from the Mad Mongrel.

Within those first few months my trusty army boots that had done me so proud since being issued back at the Bridge of Don barracks finally succumbed to the rigours of the railway. As I negotiated a slope with two baskets filled with rocks on my shoulders, the sole came away from the upper, sending me head over heels down the hill, rocks bouncing out of the baskets and crashing on top of me. I shielded my head with my arms and when I dusted myself off saw that both of my boots had split in two. Many of the men were already going barefoot and it was something I had long feared. I tried to repair the boots by lashing them together with a piece of rattan but it did not last.

My socks had disintegrated long before in the tropical sweat. Now in bare feet I had a new challenge. My feet were extremely soft from living in constantly wet boots and the ground was particularly unforgiving, the jagged volcanic rocks often hiding just below the surface of the topsoil. I knew that the soles would harden up but until then I would have to walk like a cripple. When using the spade I wouldn't be able to use my foot to dig deeper into the soil and would require more upper-body strength. Having no boots also made the ever-frequent trips to the *benjos*, the latrines, even more unsavoury. They were revolting, vast open pits, later covered in after weakened prisoners began to collapse into them and drown. As you approached the benjos you had to wade through the mud layered with the excrement of those dysentery sufferers who had never quite made it. Flies and maggots swarmed and wriggled over this foul mush. It got so bad that we had a bucket of water at the entrance to our hut to wash our feet in. It all added to the misery.

In moments of adversity I would often think back to my childhood and I remembered going barefoot during the long hot summers we spent down at the Aberdeenshire fishing village of Newtonhill, where I was born. My mother's parents had retired there and lived in a house called 'Fairseat', which we nicknamed 'Sair feet'. My elder brother Douglas and I used to go to the beach in the morning. We stayed there all day until teatime, having great adventures that fortunately our parents never knew about. We explored caves, went cliff-climbing and dived off a breakwater that was probably fifteen to twenty feet high. One of the local families, the Cobblers as we called them, had two boys about our age. They would come down to the beach and do much the same stuff as us. But for some reason Douglas and I never really cared for those two lads. One day I remember we had fisticuffs over a burn – standing on either side of it slugging away at each other.

I remembered the magical summer at the age of seven or eight, when my mother's brother, our Uncle Alfie, and Aunt Alice returned home from India, where he worked as a tea planter. They came to visit us at Newtonhill. We got home one day and were surprised to see our auntie and uncle. They took us through to the front room and I saw a white sheet propped against the sideboard. Uncle Alfie said, 'Now boys, we have a surprise for you but you're not going on the main road with these.' He pulled off the sheet to reveal two sparkling, brand-new bikes. It was just amazing and beyond our wildest dreams. We went outside and tried to ride our new bicycles. Once we got the hang of it and mastered them, we went down to the village. The first thing we did was to ride past the Cobblers' house and shout out. We were the only ones in the village with bicycles so you can imagine the reaction!

Reflecting on my happy childhood, my job and my family was a useful tool that I used to get me through some very hard times.

Just after losing my boots I noticed that some of the

men were wearing 'jungle slippers' made of bark and leaves. I heard that one chap in my hut had discovered a particularly inventive way of making sandals from a jungle plant. After hobbling back from the railway I tried to find him. For a change I entered through the back entrance of the hut and noticed a chap from my work party lying alone in his bed-space.

'Hello Bill,' I said to him as I crouched down. He was from Northampton and had left his newly wed wife back in England after joining the Bedfordshire and Hertford-shire regiment. I normally spoke very little on the railway but Bill had a friendly face and we always exchanged quiet words while working.

'Hey Bill, it's me, Alistair.' He looked at me and tried to speak but nothing came out. I could tell that he was suf-fering from an acute strain of malaria. Through the fear in his eyes I could see that he was dying. I sat down beside him and took his hand. It was sticky but cool. His breath was laboured, life fading from him.

I stayed with Bill all night. I nursed him the best I could, giving him some rice and most of my water. As the night wore on he began losing consciousness. He was away with the fairies and by 2 a.m. or 3 a.m. he was gone. Holding his hand I felt it go limp. He twitched for some time after he passed away. When it stopped I fetched the medical orderly and left. When I returned he was gone.

I never went back to ask about the 'jungle slippers', even though I saw some men wearing them around the camp. They did not look particularly comfortable and were already falling apart so I left it. And besides, my experience with Bill in that hut had left me hollow. I even castigated myself for getting involved with another prisoner's problems. Once you got started with sentimentality and grief you were a goner. It was a selfish tactic but I was desperate to survive. I was refusing to let the Japanese win this.

Like on the death march some men found the going easier by teaming up and making a close bond with another prisoner. They would fight railway life together, sharing whatever food or water they had, helping each other wherever they could and always having their back. They even took beatings together to share the blows and the pain. It was not the way for me. I watched the heartache of men losing their best pals and suddenly being left alone. They never usually lasted very long and soon followed their mates to the grave.

By now the cuts on my feet and legs had turned into painful – and dangerous – tropical ulcers. When I suffered scrapes on the railway, or had a rash, I could not tend to it until yasume-time or until I was back at camp. Then I wrapped leaves around the cuts at night to keep the flies off but it was useless, and the ulcers usually spread. They rotted your flesh, muscle and tendons; people were left with gaping holes as the flesh simply fell away. An ulcer would eat deep into your flesh, so deep you could sometimes see the white of bone. Even worse, if you were not careful they could become gangrenous, and many men lost legs that way – by improvised amputation, without anaesthetic or drugs.

I went to the medical hut for advice. In common with most of the men, tropical ulcers had engulfed my feet, ankles and lower calves. I had avoided the medical hut until that point. It was set aside from the sleeping huts and about the same size as ours. The RAMC officer in charge was Dr Mathieson, a likeable character from Paisley, just outside Glasgow, where he had studied medicine. He had come to Singapore about the same time as me and would later, in much different circumstances, save my life. On this my first encounter with him he would at least save my legs.

Sneaking under the cloud of black flies that circled outside the hut like a swarm of miniature vultures, I entered nervously. The overpowering stench immediately had me gasping. Stepping across the cadaverous forms of five or six men who appeared to be rapping on death's door, Dr Mathieson introduced himself.

I had not spoken for so many days that when I went to reply my parched throat failed me.

'Here,' he said, handing me a half-coconut cup of water, 'get this down you.'

I sipped the cool water down and thanked him, asking how his patients were.

Dr Mathieson, in his mid-thirties at that point, appeared weary beyond his years. He was probably on self-imposed half-rations just to keep some spare for his patients. The men had spoken highly of him and many of our doctors were revered as saintly figures.

The doctor took me by the arm and led me down to the far end of the hut away from the men. In a soft west-coast accent, he said, 'Half of these men will die within days. The other half? Who knows? If I had access to some proper clinical treatments, drugs or instruments, they might live but that is not possible as I'm sure you know.'

I could only nod in agreement. The squalor and stench of death inside the hut was appalling.

'What can you do for them?' I asked.

'Quite simply not a lot. I try and give them some hope if nothing else.'

He pointed with his boot at a chap sleeping and said, 'He's got ringworm. On his testicles. I'm surprised he's able to sleep. I've been applying a coating of wet clay to see if that helps.'

I nodded as he went on. 'It's easy for these men to give up and when they lose hope the fight just seeps right out of them. On countless occasions I have seen two men with the same symptoms and same physical state, and one will die and one will make it. I can only put that down to sheer willpower.'

I considered this for a moment and looked around the hut. You could tell the men who were dying by the look on their faces. Their gaze was lost before it reached their eyes and no amount of positive attitude and care from Dr Mathieson could change their destiny. It certainly was not the medical staff's fault – their hands were tied. No, blood was firmly on our captors' hands. I told myself right then and there that I would not stop fighting.

'Do you have anything for malaria?' I asked hopefully.

'Don't eat for a day. That may help for a bit. If you're still sick, crush up three spoonfuls of charcoal and get that down you. Apart from that there's very little I can do, even though the world's largest quinine factory is over on Java. I don't imagine any of it getting passed on to us, do you?'

He said, 'The Japs think that poor health is a sign of weakness of the spirit. They think that beating us only makes us stronger. That is the kind of people we're dealing with here.'

'What can you do for this?' I asked him, lifting a foot on to a bamboo chair.

'Tropical ulcers. A disease of food, filth and friction. Do you know what maggots look like?'

'Maggots?' I asked, frantically inspecting my foot, praying that I was subject to some sick joke.

'Yes, maggots. They'll fix you right up. Go down to the latrines, find yourself a handful of those wee white beasties and sit them on your ulcers. They will chomp through the dead flesh and before you know it you'll be right as rain.'

Almost as an afterthought, he added, 'Remember to count how many you put on carefully. You don't want to forget one and leave it in there to eat itself to death.'

I left the medical hut, shaking my head, still wondering if I were being had. Letting maggots eat my skin did not sound particularly appetising but I was willing to try anything. I knew I had to stop the rot that was devouring my legs.

The latrines were nothing more than holes in the ground but now with bamboo slats across them. A bunch of jungle leaves usually lay piled near by or you took your own foliage or toilet paper if there was no river water collected for the job. I did not have to go far to find what I was looking for. I gingerly scooped up a handful of maggots, watching them squirm and wriggle. Without thinking about it too much I found a quiet spot near by and sat down, placing just two or three on a nasty ulcer on my ankle. The maggots, which were about a quarter of an inch long, instinctively knew what to do. They started gnawing away at my skin with the most minuscule of bites. The sensation was of tingling, unearthly yet not altogether unpleasant, until the realisation that maggots were eating your raw flesh came racing back to the forefront of your mind. I can still feel that sensation to this day.

But to Dr Mathieson's credit it certainly worked. Within days the wounds had started to heal and new skin grew back. It was a trick that I persisted with throughout my time on the railway, passing it on to other men when I thought I could do so without being dismissed as a Jap-happy sicko.

No matter how much the Japanese increased our workload, or how hard they pushed us, we generally could not manage to progress more than twenty feet per day. After sixty straight days on the railway – with no days off; no public or bank holidays – we had reached the dreaded slab of rock that barred our path for the next five hundred or six hundred yards. The mere sight of that rock must have been enough for one prisoner, who made a bid for freedom.

I was unaware that anyone had escaped until one morning at tenko a sorry-looking chap was dragged before us. He had been beaten horrifically, his swollen and bloody features virtually unrecognisable. The interpreter told us, 'This man very bad. He try to escape. No gooda.'

Two guards threw down on the ground in front of us the battered wreck of a human frame and made him kneel. He did not plead for mercy or beg for assistance. He knew his fate and waited silently, resigned to it. The Black Prince, who seemed to have dressed up especially for the occasion, strode forward and unsheathed his long samurai sword. He prodded the prisoner in the back, forcing him to straighten up. Then the Black Prince raised his sword, its stainless steel glinted in the sunshine. It was a moment of such horror that I could scarcely believe it was really happening. I closed my eyes tightly. This was one of the many instances of barbarism on the railway that I would try to shut out of my mind. But I could not escape the chilling swoosh of the blade as it cut through the damp tropical air or the sickening thwack of the sword coming down on our comrade's neck, followed by the dull thump of his head landing on the ground. I kept my eyes firmly shut but swayed on my feet and felt a collective gasp of impotent anger and revulsion. It was a scene from another age. I thought of the French Revolution when the crowds went mad for the guillotine. But I thought it so macabre, so chilling, that I failed to see how anybody could find that an enjoyable experience, no matter how much you hated someone.

There was an undercurrent circling among us men, a desperate feeling of wanting to do *something*. But of course we were powerless. By the time I opened my eyes the body and head had been taken away and only a pool of dark red blood remained, leaching into the Siamese soil. I fought the impulse to be sick as I felt the pit of my stomach rising. A feeling of hopelessness overwhelmed me. We were at the mercy of a barbaric madman who enjoyed killing for the fun of it.

I had been witness to some terrible things as a POW and apart from the spread-eagled torture this was the worst yet. I just thanked my lucky stars that I was not part of the burial party because that must have been extremely traumatic.

Without any further ado our stunned work party was shepherded back to Hellfire Pass. We walked in desolate silence, each lost in his own thoughts until we arrived at the Pass.

It was part of a two-and-a-half-mile curved section of railway that required seven bridges and five arduous cut-tings. Ahead of us the Japanese took our sappers, the British Army engineers, to start blasting away at Hellfire Pass. They climbed on top of the rock with bags of dynamite, their job being to blast away sections of rock twice a day for the rest of us to pound and shatter with eight-pound sledgehammers. The Japanese never gave us any warning of an impending explosion and suddenly the whole ground would shake at the almighty bang. Brightly coloured birds of paradise would flee their roosts squawking and we would hit the deck to avoid the deadly spray of rock shrap-nel that would follow. The Japanese always made the British engineers light the fuse. On more than one occasion

the poor sod who couldn't flee fast enough over the treacherous ground would be blown up with the rocks – much to
the obvious delight of Dr Death, who found it hilarious.

Like the disposable and economical machines we had
become, we hammered away at drill pieces to bore holes
into the rock for the explosives and then smashed up the
boulders and rocks, making them as small as we could. It
was back-breaking work, made tougher by the harshness
of our natural and unnatural environment, pathetic diet,
and catalogue of diseases, illnesses and injuries, not to
mention our general fatigue, depression and broken spirits.

The rocks, once splintered into semi-manageable pieces,
would be picked up by hand and loaded into baskets.
Other prisoners would then haul these away and dump
them beside the railway, where the rocks had to be broken
up further to be made into ballast for the railway sleepers. Eventually the guards pulled sick men out of hospital
huts by their hair and dragged them down to work on the
railway beside these piles of dirt and rock that needed
breaking down. Using small hammers with twelve-inch
handles they had to sit there and tap feebly away all day
in the blazing sun. Nobody was immune from work.

I spent seven or eight months hammering away at that
bloody rock. On top of the cutting Dr Death sat gloating
and occasionally relieving his boredom by hurling stones
and boulders at us slaving down below. Once again, failure to meet our daily quotas meant working on into the
dark by firelight and the eerie glow of lamps, making the
place look like hell. Until finally the only damage done by
our falling sledgehammers was that caused by gravity

rather than the force of our swing. We could not take any more and surprisingly the Japanese recognised that. Now just skin and bones we were so skinny that a scrawny guard could lift each of us with one arm.

If an exploring anthropologist had stumbled upon us in that jungle, he would have imagined that he had made a sensational new discovery: a prehistoric tribe, uniformly filthy with long hair and beards covering clapped-in cheeks and framing sunken eyes. He would have observed in wonder the curious tottering gait unique to the half-starved tribesmen who worshipped and sacrificed their number on a giant slab of rock. And he would have been baffled by the absence of the female of the species.

Kanyu I and II, under the iron fist of the Black Prince, were among the worst of all the camps on the railway. The Japanese had reduced us to the stone age. There were no positives. No haircuts or pay, no days off, no trading, no vegetable stews or fried duck eggs, no pantomimes or song. There was not even a single book in the entire camp. It was work, work and more work. Speedo! It simply could not have been any worse.

Not through any sense of pity or guilt, certainly, we were to be moved to a camp further up the railway. It was named, predictably, Kanyu II, almost identical to our original camp – just further down the river.

At roll-call they told us, 'All men march.'

The same thoughts went through my mind. *We have been used up, we're no use to them any more. We're all going to be massacred. Whatever it is it's not going to be better. It certainly won't be a holiday camp!*

Towards the end of April 1943 the Black Prince and his merry band of psychotic villains marched us into the jungle again. It took a solid day to reach our new camp and I heaved a sigh of relief to see that we did not have to build our own huts; presumably the POWs who had been there before us had been moved forward as well, on to Kanyu III. I would later learn that Australian POWs took our place at Kanyu I and with it the deathly task of completing Hellfire Pass. They were to pay a terrible price.

Six

Bridge on the River Kwai

The Japanese put us straight to work. This section of railway, further north, would eventually join up with that of our earlier handiwork at Hellfire Pass. We began clearing jungle, just as we had at the first Kanyu cutting. The work was certainly easier than gouging our way through the rocks and boulders of Hellfire Pass but it was still horrendous. With the same guards and Japanese officers hovering around us it was the same torment. Brutality, disease, starvation and death stalked our every step.

On the first evening of our arrival, still barefoot and naked except for our Jap-happies, we did some remedial work on the huts, some of which leaned at crazy angles like jungle versions of the Leaning Tower of Pisa. The roofs all needed replacing with fresh atap leaves. Whether by design or otherwise, we reverted to the same sleeping

179

arrangements as at the first camp, taking up the same places. Men took a lot of comfort from routine and familiarities, no matter how fickle or fleeting they may have been.

After a few weeks of steady progress we were nearing the river Kwai, across which the Japanese intended us to build two bridges, the first to be made of wood and bamboo, the second to be of steel and concrete. It was going to be a major engineering operation and I doubted that we would manage it in our state and with the pathetic tools we had to hand.

We carried on clearing the path for the track of the railway, while work parties went into the jungle felling trees for the bridge and bamboo for the scaffolding.

Then disaster struck. One night I awoke with dysentery calling. Holding my aching stomach I raced to the latrines in the dark but on the way back to my hut a Korean guard stopped me. He had come out of the darkness and caught me by surprise. He yammered in my face. I had no idea what he was on about. At first I thought he was admonishing me for failing to salute him but I had never noticed the bugger. He was still talking frantically and pointing down at my midriff. To my horror I realised he was becoming frisky.

'Jiggy, jiggy,' he was saying, trying to grab me.

'No!' I shouted at him.

'Jiggy. You me, jiggy.'

I told him 'No' again, firmly. He carried on trying to grab me so without hesitating I kicked him as hard as I could, barefooted, square between his legs. He collapsed, groaning in agony.

I bolted for my hut but his roaring had summoned hordes of other guards. Unfortunately I ran slap bang into one of them. He seized on to me and before I knew it they were coming at me from all quarters. Rifle butts and fists sent me to the ground. Someone stabbed me in the back-side with a bayonet. Boots and fists flailed into my body before they hauled me up and dragged me to the front of the Japanese officers' hut. Bleeding from the blows to the head and face, I waited for the interpreter, who had been summoned. As I swayed an NCO kept beating me, knocking me to the ground. Each time I fell he made me stand up again. Eventually the interpreter was raised, along with the camp commandant, the dreaded Black Prince. This was a moment of absolute terror. Throughout my captivity I had tried at all times to stay out of range of the brutal Japanese guards and now here I was receiving the personal attentions of the camp's sadist-in-chief. The guards all stood to attention as the commandant asked the Korean for his side of the story. No doubt he left out the bit about making sexual advances towards me.

When he was done the commandant asked why I had assaulted the guard. I told them the truth. The interpreter relayed my story and when he had finished the Black Prince started screaming at all and sundry. I had no idea what was going on. I just knew I was in serious trouble. They took the Korean guard away and marched me to the front of the guardhouse, where I was forced to stand to attention. Racked with pain and suffering from broken toes, I wobbled and wilted. Any sign of slumping over brought a flurry of rifle butts to the kidneys to straighten

181

me up again. Every minute of every hour throughout the night was pure torture. On top of the pain came the constant buzzing and biting from the camp's abundant insect life.

At sunrise the men assembled for breakfast and roll-call before going out to slave on the railway. The guards kept me behind. As day broke I was a hopeless mess. The rising sun bore down on my defenceless body and when I lost consciousness my personal minders threw buckets of water over me and kicked me to attention.

And so it went on hour after endless hour. It was relentless. My bashed eyes had now closed and my face felt swollen as blood seeped from my head, body and feet. My body burned in the unforgiving sun and the only water I got was sloshed from the bucket as they revived me after I collapsed from heat exhaustion. I prayed that it would end, prayed for a bullet through the brain. But no, they continued to play out their game of torture like a cat with a mouse.

Sunset came. The men returned and averted their eyes – a sure sign that my predicament was serious. Nobody showed any signs of sympathy or concern, to do so was to risk reprisals on themselves. The rest of the chilly night passed in a blur of kicks and beatings. I hallucinated and felt as if I were going insane. Those bastards did not deserve to live – not in my book. Throughout the night I was more often on the ground and being sloshed with river water than I was at attention.

Come morning my officer went to the Black Prince to protest on my behalf. He was a very brave man and predictably got slapped savagely for his troubles. After the men left for work the Black Prince instructed two guards to haul me off to the black hole. My heart sank. I knew that most men kept in there, usually for three or four weeks, did not come out alive. And if they did they had been reduced to crippled wrecks who never fully recovered. The guards threw me into one of the bamboo cages. With bent knees, I leant with my back raised and arms at my sides as they squeezed its door shut. Darkness and the filth of the previous occupants engulfed me. I knelt and sobbed, falling in and out of consciousness.

The corrugated iron covering the semi-submerged cage intensified the stifling heat. In the darkness the sense of isolation was devastating and I became half out of my mind with pain and exhaustion.

Days came and went, the only notion of time provided by the arrival of a watery bowl of rice once a day. The next few days were the worst I had experienced on the railway, like a culmination of the extremes of temperature from the steel carriages on the way up to the railway, along with the death march and every other ounce of suffering endured since, all crammed into that tiny, back-breaking black hole. Malaria struck me down, causing uncontrollable shivers and pain that was diverted only when tropical ulcers and kidney stones reared to the fore. My hair matted, dirty and unshaven, lice crawling all over me, no soap or water, no drugs or hope, my degradation was complete.

I had counted six or seven bowls of rice by the time they allowed me out. As I crawled out of the dark cell and back to my hut, I deemed myself lucky to have spent such a short period in the black hole. I had been in for a week and it could easily have been a month. To me it felt like a century.

I reached my hut on all fours and Dr Mathieson and his orderlies got to work on me. Slowly they brought me back to life with lime juice, water and scavenged food scraps, a little milk and some duck eggs. Within a week, even in my feeble condition, I was passed as fit and sent back to work on the first railway bridge over the river Kwai. Happily I never saw that Korean guard again.

We marched back along the track we had been clearing until it opened up at the river. What I saw stunned me. During the fortnight of my imprisonment and convalescence the outline of a bridge had grown out of the water. It was a truly amazing sight. The bridge stood encased in a great bamboo cage of scaffolding and hundreds of prisoners teemed all over it like ants. It was astonishing to think that this had been built with little more than bare hands and primitive technology. The general opinion among us men had been that the undertaking was impossible. But then again we had thought the same of Hellfire Pass and we somehow managed to do that too.

Two Japanese engineers, who were always officers, stayed on site at all times. Though many were English-educated, most of them dictated their orders through interpreters. Their working methods were haphazard to say the least. Where we would have used tapes to measure distances, they guessed. It didn't seem to bother them if some railway sleepers jutted out a foot more than others. But they were very demanding and prone to strike out with the four-foot iron bars that they carried. No doubt they were under enormous pressures themselves to get the bridge done but the way they treated the men, like animal slavers, was unforgivable.

The men used an antiquated rope-and-pulley system to drive teak piles deep into the river floor. The pile driver had a huge rock on the top of it and the prisoners raising it heaved on the ropes as if in a game of tug o' war, while a Nippon engineer would keep them in time with a rhythmic count of 'Ichi, ni, san, shi'. On his command they would suddenly all let go of the rope sending the rock crashing down on the pile below. Simple but effective, I thought. The laboured chanting and heaving, which went on for up to eighteen hours a day, made me think of the ancient Pharaohs and how their slaves had achieved the seemingly impossible by constructing the pyramids. There was certainly something biblical about our plight.

For those working in the muddied river, sometimes up to their necks, life could be much more difficult. The filthy water infected cuts and sores. It was also impossible to see where you were treading and many more injuries occurred that way. The additional danger of falling objects, including logs and struts, meant that mortality rates among these men were extremely high. Making the most of my climbing skills and head for heights, I tried to work as high up the structure as possible. Some men hated working aloft but for me it meant I could work at a more sedate pace to recover from the black hole and I was out of reach of the guards and their flailing sticks.

While the piles were driven into the river bed, prisoners made sections of the bridge on land, mostly from bamboo and teak, in a basic fabrication yard. Once they had finished a twenty-foot section elephants manoeuvred it down to the river and men built it on to the piles. After a stint on the bridge I moved to the yard and spent most of my time drilling holes, using an awl. It was a real production line: against a backdrop of shouting and hammering from the river, the logs were rolled in and hoisted on to trestles for me to drill holes into. Most of the time the logs would be too thick for the awl and I would have to drill halfway through the log, turn it over and drill in from the other side, hoping that the holes met in the middle. The metal bolts destined for the holes were already rusting and I doubted whether they would last very long. It was tough, tiring work boring into those hard jungle woods but at least I could work on my own. It also meant that I could slack off a bit and do very little, whereas those working in a group found themselves watched constantly and could not afford that luxury. When I went down to the river it was a marvel to watch the men working. To see the bridge rising from the Kwai, being built in the midst of the jungle, with no machinery or sense of civilisation, was unreal.

Building the bridge was probably the easiest time I experienced on the railway. The work was more about craft and guile than brute strength and physical labour.

But it never stopped the guards from making us work at double time or administering beatings for little or no reason whatsoever. On one occasion I received a severe beating after failing to drill a half-inch hole through a twelve-inch-diameter log. It sounded like a simple job but the awl I had been given reached only halfway through the log. Once I had drilled as far as I could I turned the log around and started drilling from the other side, hoping that it would join in the middle. But of course this time that was too much to ask. Even though I had been given an almost impossible task, a rotund Korean guard, whom we nicknamed 'Musso' because of his similarity to the Italian fascist dictator, noticed and went berserk. He screamed in my face, telling me what I had done wrong as if I had failed to notice.

'Do it your bloody self then!' I snapped. I regretted those words almost immediately. Musso was a nasty piece of work and slammed his rifle butt into my face. It floored me and knocked out one of my front teeth. The tooth had snapped off at an angle, painfully exposing raw nerves. After several more blows and kicks I quickly recovered and scrambled back to work, just thankful not to have been beaten to death.

The broken tooth was agonising and hours later, after we finished work, I paid another visit to the medical hut. The orderlies breezily set about me with a pair of pliers as if they were a pair of mechanics working on a rusty old tractor. One held my head tightly while the other tugged and tugged, eventually managing to wrench out the offending incisor. It was excruciating but the orderlies had evidently become quite proficient as dentists and it was all over pretty quickly.

The building of the bridge on the river Kwai took a terrible toll on us and the depiction of our sufferings in the film of the same name was a very, very sanitised version of events. Unlike the well-fed extras in the movie, we did not whistle the 'Colonel Bogey' tune. Nor did we work alongside Americans, nor did we have any semblance of uniform. We were naked, barefoot slaves. And there were certainly no pretty and scantily clad local girls wandering through the jungle.

And contrary to the film, our real-life commander Colonel Philip Toosey did not collaborate with the Japanese. I was not alone in doing as little work as possible without blatantly shirking, which resulted in sadistic beatings. Energy, every ounce of it, *had* to be conserved for survival. To bust a gut on starvation rations was absolute suicide. We had long lost our dignity and working faster certainly would not have brought any back. In fact it would have resulted in the opposite with even more of us dying.

Instead we made constant attempts at sabotage. Men whispered orders to impair the construction of the bridge wherever possible. Some charged with making up concrete mixtures deliberately added too much sand or not enough, which would later have disastrous effects. We collected huge numbers of termites and white ants and deposited them into the grooves and joints of load-bearing trunks.

Out of sight of the guards I furtively sawed halfway

through wooden bolts wherever possible, hoping they would snap whenever any serious weight, like a train, was placed upon them.

We slogged on, starving and diseased, believing that things just could not get any worse – and then, in June, the monsoon arrived. For months the land mass of the Indian subcontinent had been heating up, creating an area of low pressure that now drew in mighty moisture-laden winds from the Indian Ocean. The rains flooded our huts, with rivers running through them – complete with small brown fish that some of the starving men succeeded in catching. We became permanently sodden. The camp ground transformed into a sea of mud and conditions around the latrines became unspeakable. Work on the bridge and railway turned even more hazardous, magnifying our misery, yet we were unprepared for the horror about to be unleashed upon us by the monsoon.

For the river Kwai and its tributaries harboured a killer even more lethal than the Japanese and our starvation diet. As an inevitable consequence of the lack of sanitation and the tens of thousands of bodies buried in shallow graves or dumped in the jungle, the river system was loaded with cholera bacteria and the monsoon season became cholera season. As the heightened waters of the Kwai flushed *Vibrio cholerae* throughout the land, this fearful disease cast a black shadow over the camp. Cholera arrived unseen and unheard but soon had us in its grip. I was slow to hear about it. But I sensed something terrible in the camp. More men were falling ill than usual and the Japanese kept their distance, leaving us alone. They were scared to death of catching cholera themselves. The Japanese Imperial Army had experienced the devastating impact of cholera among its troops in China in 1937 and again in 1940–1, and feared its swift progress like the Black Death.

Cholera outbreaks are related to standards of hygiene, food preparation and the quality of drinking water – all of which were undeniably horrific on the railway. Rats were also rife and had muscled into our lives to such an extent that we hardly shooed them away any more, and they are also carriers of the cholera bacteria, another parallel with the plague.

One of our officers gathered us together for an extraordinary general meeting. As serious-looking as I had ever seen him, he said, 'A cholera epidemic is threatening us all. We have set up a quarantine area and you are advised to avoid it wherever possible. Need I remind you all not to drink unboiled water? If you are unsure of its origins, find out or leave it. Understood? This is our biggest test yet.'

Cholera had infected a stream that ran past our camp. The Japanese had refused to build a bridge across it to stop it from spreading, so we had to use contaminated boats to cross the water. By the end of it all we would lose thousands on the railway quite needlessly to cholera. The conditions in the coolie camps were even worse and tens of thousands of native labourers, sometimes entire camps, were wiped out.

Overnight cholera struck me down. I woke up with explosive diarrhoea and violent, projectile vomiting. My ears were ringing and I felt dizzy. Cramps started in my bowels and soon spread all over my body as it rapidly dehydrated. I was drying from the inside out, shrivelling like a picked grape left out in the sun. The cholera bacteria burrowed into the walls of my small intestine producing toxins that sucked the vital salts and every ounce of water out of my body. I was unsure what was wrong but I knew it was serious – I did not want to finish up with the life drained out of me. I had always been extremely careful to drink only boiled water so at first I was doubtful that it was cholera. I did not know much about it but I knew that the first twenty-four hours were crucial. If you see through a day and a night, you would probably survive. Most men who succumbed did so in the first few hours, a horrible death and so quick. Men who threw the bodies of cholera victims on to funeral pyres in the morning could easily contract the disease, die and be thrown on the pyre themselves in the evening. They died in agony like crazed animals and it was dreadful to see.

I lay in my bed, unable to rise for the work party. By then I was semi-conscious and I thought this was the end. I was hallucinating. Vivid red flashes stormed my eyelids. I knew I had to seek help. After psyching myself up I managed to rise and wobble to Dr Mathieson's hut. As soon as I walked in he knew that I had cholera. It was a death sentence and he was reluctant to tell me. Instead he simply said, 'You'll have to be isolated. You'll be looked after.'

His orderlies led me to a cream-coloured bell tent, like we had used in the Scouts. As they peeled back the tent's front flap, a deathly stench leaped out. Unknown to me this was the 'death tent' and I was the unlucky thirteenth occupant of a dimly lit space already full of men. When I saw their state, their eyes rolled back, rasping, unintelligible voices, raised legs with knees bent – the bizarre telltale sign of a cholera sufferer – I knew that my number was up. The orderlies were putting me in here to die. The fight was fading from me and I lay down on the canvas floor with a sense of of complete and utter desolation.

I have no idea how long I lay there. I was no longer aware of those around me or if anyone came and tended to me. My mind drifted. I allowed myself some thoughts of home, even though they were jumbled and vague. I became upset when I couldn't picture the faces of my mum, dad and Aunt Dossie. I even struggled to remember what Hazel looked like. Feverish dreams rampaged terrifyingly through my mind. The walls of the tent seemed to move and expand like an inflated balloon, only to pop and come crashing back on top of me. A sudden death seemed as inviting as a warm bath.

Eventually, on what must have been the following day, some orderlies carried me out of the tent and back to the hospital hut. Out of the thirteen men in that tent, Dr Mathieson told me months later, I was the only survivor. His medical staff tried to keep me alive by giving me as many sips of sterilised water as possible. They also forced some coconut milk puree down my throat, as water alone was not enough. While treatment should have been relatively simple, the lost fluids needing to be replaced with a liquid mixture of sugar and salts, the Japanese refused to give us any extra supplies, even though progress on the railway had dropped off and the outbreak threatened to wipe out the whole camp – them included. I was only half *compos mentis* and just wanted to sleep. But the orderlies kept tapping my cheeks to keep me awake and engaged me in conversation to keep my mind and soul engaged. They found the dog-eared black-and-white photographs in my bed-space and asked about my family. I rambled on about Aberdeen and playing practical jokes on Dossie. They asked who the pretty blonde girl was – the photo more worn than others. The lovely Hazel. I thought of her and how we used to dance at the Palais de Dance, how she was the only girl who could keep up with my twinkling toes, now reduced to bloodied and mangled stumps. The orderlies tried to make me laugh, asking how far I got with Hazel, and I told them about our long walks through the dandelions of Duthie Park, how I would try to get her alone, those piercing blue eyes all to myself.

Florence Nightingale could not have faulted their patience and unwavering care. If I had given up hope, they never did. And by this time I had very little hope left in me. The idea of suicide was a constant threat, not just for me but for many men. Some gave in and threw themselves from the bridge or head first down the latrines. There was no doubt that clinical depression had muddied most of our minds.

I could have lain there for days or weeks. It was hard to be certain. A Japanese doctor visited the camp and inspected me. Eventually the medical officers persuaded him, along with the Black Prince, that I was of no further use. My days working on the railway were over, at least while in the condition I was. Permission came through for me to be sent down river to the mass hospital camp at Chungkai.

I was leaving a camp that had reduced us to animals, starved half-dead beasts of burden. It had brought out the best and the worst in us. My carers showed endless compassion but the camp was also full of men who would steal food from the sick and dying.

The next thing I knew I was being carried down to the river on a stretcher and loaded on to a forty-foot barge with a dozen or so other 'heavy sick', many with gaping tropical ulcers or recovering from cholera. As we were towed by a tugboat down the river, I was still so weak that I ignored everything around me and could not even bring myself to respond to the others making idle chitchat on the peaceful journey downstream. Calmly scything through the jungle I knew I was leaving the hell of camp life.

After an overnight stop, where we slept in a cutting on the riverbank, we arrived at Chungkai hospital camp. It was then that I realised how lucky I was. A massive place, it was located in a jungle clearing beside the Meelong River, near where the railway commenced and about a hundred kilometres from Bangkok. To think that all of the men in that square mile were either sick or recovering from illness and injury really tells a tale in itself. There were nearly ten thousand survivors gathered in the camp in various states of decay. It was the first time that I could grasp the vast, industrial scale of the railway.

On arrival at Chungkai British orderlies met us at the riverbank. Our state horrified them. They carried me by stretcher to a hospital hut, where they categorised me and left me alone. Lying on a short bamboo cot with no bedding, I looked around. In the long, bright hut lay about thirty others all in much the same decrepit state. Cholera had been the final straw for my health and I could no longer walk. Dysentery, malaria, beriberi and gaping tropical ulcers that engulfed both ankles and lower calves had been enough but cholera finished me off. Mentally, losing control of my legs was too much. Either I was too damned weak or they were irreparably damaged, because no matter what my brain instructed them to do I could no longer even *move* my legs.

I was so devastated that I thought I may as well be dead. Having led such a full, active and sporting life, losing my legs was worse than going blind for me. I had real fears that I would never walk again and so depression set in. I could not see a glimmer of light at the end of tunnel – only blackness.

Some orderlies came into the hut and gave us all a liquid meal, which had some egg in it and milk – either goat or coconut, I could not be sure. If I tasted it now, it would probably be foul but at the time it was wonderful. The best thing I had tasted in over a year.

I lay in that hut for over a week with the black dog of depression nipping at my sorry heels. The cheery orderlies and doctors tried talking to me to lift my spirits but my mind was unresponsive. I could see that they were not trying to help me walk again so I felt that they were just

195

pacifying me. Like all of the patients I dreaded the nightly agonising round of the orderlies who scraped out our suppurating ulcers with a sharpened dessert spoon. The only highlight of my day was food. I was definitely a difficult and moody patient.

One of the doctors was a very tall Australian medical officer, and he conducted my general examination. I was greatly impressed by him during my brief consultation. A striking figure with an aura of authority and leadership, he seemed never to waste his words or actions – as if every single minute were utterly necessary and priceless. The orderlies all worshipped him.

They told me his name was 'Weary' Dunlop. He worked miracles at Chungkai and enjoyed the adulation of his men for taking numerous beatings from the Japanese to prevent sick men from being sent to work.

Shortly after his capture on Java in March 1942 he had personally saved the lives of four patients. The Japanese had stormed into the prison hospital and demanded that it be broken up. Their commanding officer ordered that four of the boys – two paraplegics and two blind lads – should be bayoneted. Colonel Dunlop put himself between the Japanese bayonets and a young British serviceman, Billy Griffiths, who had been blinded and lost both hands when he walked into a booby trap. In the tense stand-off that followed the Japanese backed down. (After the war Griffiths became a leading figure in the development of disabled sport in the UK and both men were reunited on the *This Is Your Life* television programme.)

Dunlop set a shining example of how officers ought to

conduct themselves and gave all too many a showing up. He was twice threatened with execution but intervened constantly on behalf of the sick men. He introduced order, fairness, record-keeping and above all hope to Chungkai.

Dunlop became a legendary figure both during and after the war, and was knighted for his amazing bravery and for saving countless lives. When Sir Edward 'Weary' Dunlop died in 1993, he was rightly given a full state funeral in Melbourne.

After a couple of weeks of feeding and rest they decided I was ready for rehabilitation. I took some amount of convincing but once they hoisted me out of bed and started carrying me from the hut, my protests were futile.

My admiration and respect for the medical staff would only increase with every day at Chungkai. Despite their mammoth task and the flood of sick men dumped at the camp every day, their dedication and patience were awe-inspiring. They had built parallel bars outside with a canopy over the bamboo apparatus for shade. Men used the gymnastic-type equipment to learn to walk again, holding themselves upright with their arms and upper body and retraining their legs. On my first visit the staff sat me down on a stool beside the bars and I watched a man struggle and strain, with beads of sweat streaming down his forehead, to walk the length of the bars, helpers waiting to catch him if he fell. I thought to myself, I'll never be able to do that.

But that was to come. First the orderlies had much simpler, allegedly more achievable tasks for me to tackle. As

I sat there on the three-legged stool they attached to my right foot a small bag with some sand or dirt in it.

'Try and lift your foot off the ground. Even an inch will do.'

I tried but nothing happened. My brain was willing but my foot refused to budge.

'Keep trying,' they encouraged. But no matter what I tried it wasn't moving. Within minutes I was exhausted and they told me to rest. They left me alone, stewing in self-loathing, and came back half an hour later.

'Try again. But this time I want you to concentrate with all your might from brain to foot. It's all about mind over matter.'

From an early age I had relished a challenge and I hated being beaten. I focused my eyes on the hairs on my foot and willed it to move. After a while the orderlies shouted, 'Yes, you did it!' Although I never saw it I must have raised my foot half an inch and for the next couple of hours I sat there trying to repeat it. I was sweating like a pig, the frustration oozing out of me as I made incremental progress. The old stubborn Alistair was returning. By the end of the session I could lift both feet an inch off the ground.

The staff carried me back to my hut, where I fell asleep exhausted. The next day they took me back and sitting on that stool I managed to raise my leg two or three inches. I felt ready for the parallel bars and the orderlies agreed. They lifted me up and held my shrunken backside as I dangled my useless legs. Being on my feet felt surreal, as if I had never walked before. They pushed me to try to move a leg.

'You moved your leg when you were sitting down so you can do it now.'

Try as I might, I couldn't get my legs to move.

'Don't worry about it if you can't. We'll try again tomorrow.'

I went back to the stool and tried again. Once I had mastered lifting one bag of weights I went on to the next heaviest. I gave up only when completely knackered, and they carried me back to the hut.

On the way back a young chap was walking towards me when he stopped suddenly and said excitedly, 'It's not you, is it? Is it you? Is it?'

I recognised him straight away. 'Yes, it's me, Freddie.'

'Awright mucker! It's been a while.'

Indeed it had. It was the first time I had smiled in months. Freddie Brind looked remarkably fit and well, considering. I was not surprised he struggled to recognise me, however. I had lost three or four stone and most of my dignity and self-respect.

One of the medical officers carrying me told Freddie, 'Alistair here has been learning to walk again. He's doing very well.'

As they carried me Freddie trailed alongside, talking at a million miles a minute. It was as if we had never been parted. At the hut the orderlies left and we were alone. We were so pleased to see each other. For me he was a breath of fresh air. I had constantly worried about him, his brother Jim and the other lad, John Scott. I still felt like I had let them down, abandoning them at Changi all those months ago. It seemed like a lifetime ago. I wanted to know everything but I struggled to get a word in. He told me he had been at Chungkai for almost twelve months, having arrived with his brother. He did not know what had happened to John, who became separated from them at Changi. But Freddie was more interested in telling me what I should be doing. He might only have been aged fifteen then but he was a truly inspirational figure.

Lying in my bed I must have looked a pathetic, sorry soul. He told me in no uncertain terms, 'This isn't you, Alistair. You need to pull yourself together. You can do it.'

He must have noticed the deep-rooted scepticism that lay behind my watery eyes.

'You can do it all right, mucker. I'll see to it. In fact I'll have you swimming across that river before you know it. I swim across it every day to collect dead bamboo for the cooks' fires and you can come with me, it's a breeze.'

'No way,' I said. I couldn't even walk – I couldn't see how I could ever possibly swim again.

'You wait and see,' he beamed. 'Wait there.'

He dashed off. Good old Freddie, I smiled. He had made it. The senior Gordon Highlanders officers must have pleaded with the Japanese not to send the boys to the railway and instead to the relative safety of Chungkai. I was surprised, though, that they had not been kept at Changi, which may have been safer. Still Freddie looked healthy and the glint in his eyes registered that he remained as cheeky as ever.

Freddie soon returned with some cake – and his brother Jim. It was great to see him too. He had lost some weight but still looked quite healthy. He was the same old Jim; it

200

was impossible to get a word out of him. Instead I devoured the cake, which he called 'Gula Malacca' and told me was made from the sap of a palm tree. It was extremely sweet and tasty – the first amount of sugar to pass my lips in two years. It was possibly not the best thing for me, as I had some bowel problems after that but it was so delicious that it was worth it. I stopped short of asking Freddie where he got it from; I didn't want to know. And if Freddie had been in Chungkai for a year without my supervision to rein in his unbridled curiosity and enthusiasm, he no doubt knew every nook and cranny of the place.

From then on I saw Freddie daily. He swam across the river every day to collect firewood for the cooks. All of the wood around the camp had already been pilfered so the best pickings were across the 150-yard-wide stretch of fast-flowing brown water. He would dash across, bundle together a load and haul it back behind him. For his efforts the cooks gave him extra food. The Japanese knew of his exploits but never stopped him. He was doing no harm and he always returned. Even they found it difficult to be mad with Freddie.

He was also embroiled with the Australians and their clandestine cigarette production and distribution racket. All of these activities were done at night and were so well concealed that the Japanese never shut them down as long as I was there. Freddie told me how they made the cigarettes. They used a flat wooden board, which had a thick parchment attached to it that rolled around a thin piece of bamboo glued through it. The tobacco, which must have been smuggled inside the camp through the wire, was placed on the parchment. Paper came from books – usually the Bible, which was the preferred choice as it best kept alight – and it was rolled around the bamboo stick, wrapping itself around the tobacco. Once licked and sealed it formed a perfect smoke. I was amazed at how professional the cigarettes looked. The Dutch, who mainly kept to themselves, had their own operation.

Freddie was the Australians' top salesman. A natural barrow boy he could sell fish to the sea. He sneaked from hut to hut, group to group – he was never caught – and flogged his illicit wares. After some time, he told me, he had established a large clientele and everyone knew him as the boy in the know. He was paid a cut from the earnings and always had dollars in his pocket. While I never approved of his occupation, I was always grateful for the food he purchased for me from the sanctioned canteen. The supplements to my diet, which included two-egg omelettes, molasses, coconut and papaya, assisted in my recovery and probably later helped save my life.

Meanwhile the medical orderlies told Freddie in no uncertain terms – which were often the only terms he fully responded to – not to interfere with my rehab. But after Freddie's arrival on the scene I approached my physical exercises with a renewed vigour. Through sheer hard toil I slowly started to make headway. Day by day my movement returned. I lifted all of the weights attached to my foot and progressed to the parallel bars. Once I could struggle from one end to the other with help from my arms, they gave me a pair of crutches. After a few weeks on them I graduated to just one crutch and eventually was walking unaided, albeit with a pronounced rolling, John Wayne-like gait.

Despite my weeping tropical ulcers and still faltering walk, I was recovering well. In the evenings Freddie and I would talk for hours, much like we did on top of the hill at Changi. I even took in several theatrical shows, which the men had organised themselves. They were always outrageous burlesque affairs, held on a rickety stage and with an improvised orchestra. There was a piano, trumpet, saxophone and drums, and always plenty of laughs. It was a real boost to the spirits.

Compared with the other camps this truly was a holiday camp. I hardly ever saw a guard, let alone a coordinated or even random beating or punishment. Men walked about freely, traded, smoked cigarettes, sang songs and even played sports.

Reading between the lines and picking up on snippets of overheard conversations, I soon realised just how unlucky I had been. The Kanyu camps, under the sadistic rule of the Black Prince, were by far the worst camps I heard about. Other men talked of earning weekly pay for their work on the railway, which they saved and spent in canteens in their camps or when they got to Chungkai. Others enjoyed days off and long weekends. Some Japanese allowed men to sing rousing songs as they worked. Other prisoners had chatted with native lassies as they strolled past and traded with locals.

As I ventured further from my hut, exploring the vast camp, I saw dozens of blokes hopping around with legs lopped off. They were mainly victims of gangrene brought on by tropical ulcers. A couple of the senior doctors at Chungkai had been doing an incredible number of amputations and with rudimentary equipment and no anaesthetics, had attained amazingly high success rates. One of these doctors, a Canadian called Captain Marko, had performed 120 amputations.

As my condition improved I was able to take in the amazing hospital camp operation. Artisans and tradesmen among the prisoners had made an astonishing array of medical equipment, adapting old Ovaltine cans, Japanese beer bottles and mess tins to become retractors, saline drips and anaesthetic masks. They employed bamboo to make shunts, false legs, a dentist's chair and even an orthopaedic bed. They set up stills to produce surgical alcohol and distilled water. Drugs were bought on the black market and smuggled in to the camp, I would later learn, by the heroes of the secret 'V' organisation – interned British businessmen in Bangkok, who also alerted the neutral authorities to our plight.

Chungkai was about rebuilding minds as well as bodies. Many of us had to relearn how to socialise and to overcome the trauma of the railway. Accordingly there were plenty of organised activities to keep my mind occupied in the evenings. We had so many talented and professional people in our ranks to give classes and talks. There were professors and lecturers in all manner of disciplines but one of the most popular speakers was a cockney burglar, who regularly entertained audiences with tales of how he had robbed his way across London. Chungkai had a great theatre too, a massive and fantastically well-organised place with concerts every Friday and Saturday night. These were of classical, jazz and popular music, along with cabaret shows of a professional level. The one I enjoyed most was called 'Wonderbar'. It included a can-can routine and the prisoners' favourite drag queen – Bobby Spong.

One afternoon when I was at the Thai-run canteen buying a coconut with some dollars Freddie had generously insisted that I take, I saw a notice on the message board that caught my eye. I recognised the name immediately.

The handwritten notice proclaimed, 'E. W. Swanton – renowned cricket commentator and observer to give talk on Test match cricket this evening after dinner at the hut beside the officers' mess.'

I went on my own, as cricket and especially talk of cricket was too boring an activity for restless Freddie. I had always admired the sport and enjoyed tussling with my brother Douglas on the green down from our house. Ernest William Swanton had been one of Britain's leading cricket writers and commentators before the war and even claimed to have been taken in his pram to watch the great W. G. Grace batting for London County. The hut was already crammed full when I entered, and pitched in darkness. Once the murmurs subsided a voice at the front began. I knew it was Swanton – he had a very distinguished voice and I recognised his impeccable accent from listening to Test matches on the wireless back in Aberdeen. Swanton, who had joined the Bedfordshires, was wounded during the battle for Singapore and was in hospital when the Japanese overran us. At Chungkai he could often be seen cradling his beloved 1939 copy of cricket bible *Wisden*, which he had convinced a Japanese censor to mark as 'Not subversive'.

He introduced himself with his own blend of pomposity and gregariousness and began talking on Test cricket. We stood in reverential silence. Such were his descriptive powers that you could almost hear the compelling crack of leather on willow. Listening to him I was surprised to hear that he was full of praise and admiration for the Australians. He was envious of their hardened attitude and the way they played without fear of reputations. To the harrumphing of some English chaps who stood near me, he proclaimed the Australian great, Don Bradman, as the best player he had ever seen. Bradman's powers of concentration, he said, distinguished him from his English counterparts, including Denis Compton. 'It's the blazing fire in their bellies,' Swanton recalled. He went on to describe a century that he had witnessed Bradman score, 'all along the ground, hardly a shot in anger, or an ounce of effort'.

Swanton had us lapping up every word he said. He told of his disappointment at being overlooked by his newspaper, the London *Evening Standard*, for the 1932–3 Ashes tour of Australia, which would become infamous as the 'Bodyline' tour. But he dismissed the furore over the series, in which English bowlers perfected a brutal and uncompromising tactical move of aiming deliveries at the head and body of the opposing batsmen, to thwart Bradman in particular, as media 'hype'. Despite some men offering their views on Bodyline and questions flying at Swanton from all quarters, he swerved the topic. Instead he spoke on the English greats he had seen, including the prolific Wally Hammond, Len Hutton and Mr Bodyline himself, Harold Larwood.

After a mesmerising ninety minutes Swanton wrapped up his talk and the men retreated to their huts. Some stayed behind to speak to him, no doubt raising their contrary views on Bodyline, and I hovered around for a while. I thought of shaking his hand and thanking him for one of the most enjoyable moments I had had in captivity but he seemed well tied up, so I wandered into the warm night air. I took a walk around the camp to stretch my legs that had been aching standing there listening for so long. My 'happy feet' were buzzing and so was my mind. The talk had enlivened me.

While it lifted my spirits, it was a stark reminder that there was a world outside this rotten jungle. Chungkai was proving an almost enjoyable period. The only downside for me was that I knew it wouldn't last. Always looming in the back of my mind was the notion that after my recovery I would be sent back to the railway. I knew that the Japanese periodically asked British commanders for so many men to go back to work on the railway. Obviously the fittest went first. If the required numbers were not provided, the Japanese stormed in and took men at random. Walking back to my hut from the Swanton talk finally feeling weary, I decided to stay put as long as possible. I would fake the state of my health, make it out to be worse than it was, lie to the doctors and avoid seeing them wherever I could. At least my ulcers were taking some time to heal and while they gaped open, surely I would be safe.

After six months or so, once my waddling walk had been ironed out, Freddie decided I was ready to swim across the river with him. I had my doubts but I wasn't going to let him know that, so I agreed.

Having once been a strong swimmer – one of the best at Bon Accord Swimming Club – I had to have faith in myself. I knew that I could at least keep myself afloat. Freddie reassured me that he was there to save me. 'I've got my lifesaving badge young fellow. I'm more likely to save you,' I grumbled, as I eased myself down the river-bank and into the water. I stayed by the bank and floundered around with some easy breaststroke until I realised I could float. Not having had a proper bath or shower for more than two years, being submerged in the water was so heavenly. It was amazingly refreshing and I splashed the water over my face as Freddie dog-paddled in circles around me.

'How does it feel?' he asked.

'Like I'm on holiday.'

'Ready to cross the river?'

'Maybe tomorrow,' I said. 'I'm happy enough here for now. Let me enjoy it.'

The next day we returned. We ventured upstream slightly so that the current of the river would be with us as we swam. I soon trailed behind Freddie, who was an excellent swimmer, and he treaded water until I caught up again. I reckoned it was about four lengths of an Olympic-sized swimming pool – two hundred metres.

However far it was, I was completely knackered when I got to the other side. I got my puff back while Freddie gathered some dry wood, and we swam back.

After that I joined Freddie in the river crossings almost every day. I enjoyed the task and it no doubt helped my rehabilitation. I also hoped that I was improving my stock and the wood-collecting duties would prevent me from being sent back to the railway. The thought of returning sent shudders down my spine and I tried not to dwell on it.

But of course I was right. One day the dreadful news came – I was being sent back to work.

An officer found me in the hut and said, 'Collect your things. You leave in the morning.'

'Where to?' I asked, already knowing the answer.

'Who knows? May God be with you.'

I told Freddie, who outwardly took it rather well. He shook my hand and vowed to keep in touch no matter what. I think I took the departure worse than he did, fearing for the both of us. What was next? I prayed to be spared from another railway camp – even one with a canteen.

In the morning I gathered on the parade square with a few hundred other men. After much waiting around with no information to chew over, we were marched into the jungle. Within a few hours along a narrow path we arrived at another camp. This was known as Tamarkan and was much smaller than Chungkai – it was more like a railway camp, although cleaner and, since it was a recuperation camp, more sanitary. Fears of being sent to work were soothed when the interpreter told us that we would be here only temporarily, before being sent 'somewhere else'. So for the next few days we kicked our heels. I walked about a lot, trying to keep my fitness levels up for whatever lay before me. It was extremely depressing to be there, especially after Chungkai. An air of resignation hung among us and after a few days we were almost glad to be moving again.

The guards loaded us on to trucks and drove us back to Bam Pong, where I had started my jungle trek all those months and tears ago. It took all day to get there, and we arrived choking with dust and thirst. I did not need to be told what to do when we stopped by a train: the steel carriages looked sickeningly familiar. My mind spinning, stomach churning, I was pushed inside, again with thirty or forty others. Thoughts of being disposed of returned, even though I knew they didn't need to take us far to do that.

The Korean guard was trying to close the door but desperate men blocked it with their bare feet. They pleaded with him, 'Leave the door open, please! Please!'

He looked confused, as if he were considering our frantic pleas. This ray of hope spurred the men on.

'We won't jump!'

'We'll close it at sidings and stops,' another said.

Unbelievably the guard allowed the door to remain open. It made a hell of a difference. As we got moving it provided an almost pleasant breeze. We could also hang each other outside bum first to do our business in a more sanitary, albeit more hazardous manner. I could not get over the fact of the guard allowing the door to stay open, about the first act of kindness or sympathy I had received from one of them. We all agreed to roll the doors shut when we came to stops so other guards wouldn't get wind of it and question why it was open. We still had some common sense left in us.

While the breeze helped, it was still a torturous journey. There was nothing to do but stand and wait it out. By now I could shut down my mind more easily than before and ignore terrible thoughts or happenings. But knowing that we had five days to go to get back to Singapore only made the journey longer. At least on the way up to the railway we always thought that the next siding, or next stop, would be our final destination. Now we just knew that it would go on and on, and on . . .

Seven

It's a Sin to Tell a Lie

As we straggled through the city of Singapore we presented a very different spectacle from the smart columns of wide-eyed and hopeful young men who had proudly descended in full Highland dress from the SS *Andes* when she berthed in Singapore harbour all those months before.

Our kilts and sporrans had long gone, so too the topees that protected us from the harsh tropical sun. Now we were a bedraggled ghost army of living skeletons, scarred with seeping tropical ulcers, limping and stumbling through the streets of what had been Britain's great Far Eastern fortress and clad just in our Jap-happy loincloths. Lice-ridden and clutching our meagre possessions we were a pathetic sight but we were determined to survive.

Our destination was the River Valley Road camp, in Singapore City, where a new chapter of slavery and

213

misery awaited us. Still we felt relieved to have survived the nightmare train journey from Thailand and pleased to be out of the jungle and back amid familiar surroundings, which served as a reminder that civilisation really did still exist even if our brutal captors remained strangers to it. And surely nothing could be worse than the disease-ridden camps of the Death Railway. Hellfire Pass and the bridge over the river Kwai with all of their horrors were behind us now. Or so we thought . . .

There were about a thousand men in the camp at that time. The Japanese were using it as a holding centre for prisoners destined to slave in their vast South-East Asian gulag, a network of prison camps linked to construction sites and industrial complexes vital for their war effort. With complete disregard for international law, starving prisoners sweated in the steaming jungles of Burma, Thailand, Borneo, the Philippines and Sumatra, and shivered in horrific and freezing conditions in coal and copper mines in Taiwan, Korea and Manchuria. By late 1943 acute manpower shortages in Japan itself led to the construction on the Japanese mainland of a system of prison camps adjacent to factories and mines operated by some of Japan's best-known companies.

The camp at River Valley Road was a little better than the camps on the railway. The accommodation remained very basic, made from timber, but its four walls provided more shelter from the elements than the open-sided huts on the railway. The trouble was this served only to make the huts a safer haven for the swarms of bugs that we had to contend with, now even more numerous than on the railway. They got everywhere: in your bed, in the rafters and buzzing around your head constantly. Of course we had no mosquito nets. Bed bugs were also rife, sucking precious blood from you as you slept. And then there were the rats that fought for space in the hut with thirty or forty prisoners. Regularly in the night men would angrily cry out to scare away rats that showed increasingly little fear of humans. Each man had only about two and a half feet of space to call his own. If one rolled over, we all had to roll over. You would lie on your back on the bare boards without blankets. With just your Jap-happy on it got very cold at night.

Thankfully it was not the monsoon season so at least we didn't have the rain and mud to put up with. The toilet facilities were basic, open wooden structures with a roof overhead, which was much the same as the shower block. The smell of the latrines was overpowering, as were the hordes of bugs and great clouds of disease-carrying bluebottles. People dreaded having to pay a visit.

A wooden fence surrounded the camp and had watchtowers stationed at intervals, manned by Japanese guards with machine guns. The security was not as tight as one might have expected. The Japanese knew that even if we did manage to escape the camp we had nowhere to go. And as Westerners we would have stuck out like sore thumbs.

Guards patrolled the compound ceaselessly, usually on solo patrols but always within shouting distance of another sentry. They were pretty sure of themselves. I used to struggle to sleep at night, often from the constant pain of beriberi, which mostly hit my legs but arms as well – any joints really. In the absence of painkillers I would often go for a walk around the camp. The guards never minded as long as you walked within your own space. I just wandered aimlessly to ease up my joints and in the hope that I would get so exhausted that sleep would overtake the pain. Quite a few men used to walk at night. I would recognise the same faces but always walked on my own – you were less likely to be challenged by the guards. If there were two or three of you together, they might think you were cooking something up and would give you a beating or punishment.

At River Valley Road I suffered from a recurring nightmare, always of the Death Railway. A Japanese guard with horrific bulging eyes filled with fury and evil would be beating me. All I could see was his enraged face, him just laying into me. I would wake up sweating, scared to death. And no matter what I did I could never get back to sleep.

Again I often slept on the ground just outside my hut. It was mighty cold but free of the bugs and the irritations of the other men and the old trick I had learned on the railway still worked – I got a better sleep. I didn't allow myself to think of home. All I could do was to think about the next day and how I would face it. I was psyching myself to make it through another day of hell and torture. To think of home was too much. It brought me down. Later when I thought my number was up I allowed myself to think of home – as a final, pleasurable treat because I thought I was going to die.

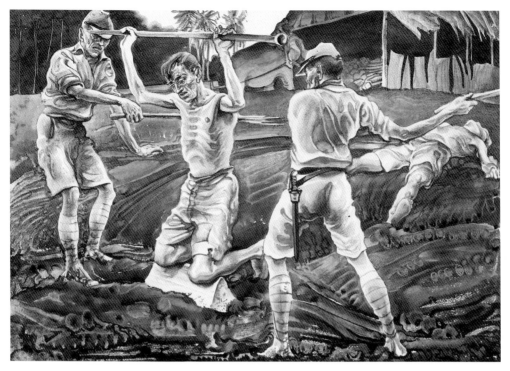

The guards on the railway continually found new ways to inflict punishment. Murray Griffin's depiction of torture, painted in 1946. (Murray Griffin, Australian War Memorial ART26525).

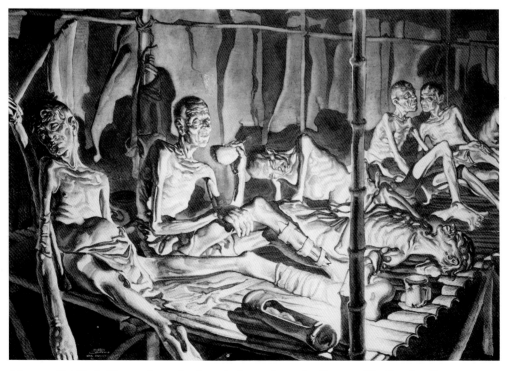

Murray Griffin's illustration of a hospital ward on the Burma–Thailand railway, painted in 1946. (Murray Griffin, Australian War Memorial ART25104).

This was the second bridge upstream from us on the Kwai – but you can see the bamboo scaffolding and the scale of the enterprise. (Australian War Memorial 118879)

The way we were: these skeletal prisoners, rescued from Changi, would have been expected to work eighteen-hour shifts on the Death Railway and to survive on a handful of rice. (Australian War Memorial 019199)

We lived in terror of Sergeant Seiichi Okada, also known as 'Doctor Death'. He enjoyed torturing prisoners. He was later charged with forcing sick POWs to work on the Death Railway but received only ten years imprisonment.
(Australian War Memorial P01433.033)

Lieutenant Usuki – the Black Prince. Also known as the Kanyu Kid, he was the psychopath who had me tortured and thrown in the black hole. He beheaded one of my comrades in front of us. Executed by the British in 1946 for war crimes.
(Australian War Memorial P01433.034)

The Mad Mongrel – I still bear the scars of my encounter with this Korean sadist who was hanged by the British in 1946 for war crimes.
(Australian War Memorial P01433.032)

Oil-covered survivors from the sinking of the hellships *Kachidoki Maru* and *Rakuyo Maru* are rescued by sailors from the USS *Sealion II*. (Bates Family)

Stunned by our ordeal, we clung for days to flimsy rafts and wreckage. The lucky ones, around 150, were rescued and the world learned for the first time of the horrors of the Death Railway. (Bates Family)

Suffering from claustrophobia I walked for many miles every day on my return home. (Urquhart Family)

With my young brother Bill. I was so shattered when I returned from captivity that I didn't know who I was. (Urquhart Family)

Top left: On the mend in 1946 but the battle against nightmares, depression and ill-health had just begun. (Urquhart Family)

Top right: The remarkable 'boy soldier' Freddie Brind on his wedding day. He should have been given a medal for keeping our spirits up in the camps but he never recovered from imprisonment by the Japanese and died tragically young. (Urquhart Family)

Right: Our wedding day. The nightmares persisted and I had to sleep separately for fear of choking my wife Mary. (Urquhart Family)

With Mum (left) and Aunt Dossie (right) on my wedding day. (Urquhart Family)

With my first child, Joyce, in 1949. (Urquhart Family)

Meeting veterans on my emotional 2008 trip to visit the USS *Pampanito*, the submarine that sank me in 1944. (Urquhart Family)

At home, 2009.
(David Martin/Fotopress)

The officers and warrant officers at River Valley Road had their own huts and kept themselves apart. But they really had no authority over us. They were now just the same as everyone else – slave labour for an enemy that regarded us all, officers and ordinary soldiers alike, as subhumans to be worked to death. The only difference was that the officers never wore Jap-happies, their khaki shorts easily distinguishing them. Just like us though, they had to slave at Singapore's docks. Only one officer was permitted to stay behind in the camp. The Japanese used to pick which would stay behind and if they thought an officer bolshie he would always be on the work party. Morale and discipline stayed rock-bottom in the camp and our commanding officer, Captain R. D. Wilkie, even suffered the indignity of being robbed of his own personal and company funds. There was very little respect for officers.

Riddled with dysentery, malaria, beriberi, tropical ulcers and disease, with bare, blistered feet and wearing just our Jap-happies, we paraded every morning shortly after sunrise. The sun would come up about 6 a.m. and by 7 a.m. you had to be up, have had your food and be ready to go out on the work party. The cook signalled breakfast by rattling a tin and everyone rushed to join the queue. One of the POWs served us – a cup of rice and a cup of boiling water, the same unappetising affair as on the railway, the rice again littered with all sorts of maggots, flies, lice, bed bugs and greyish weevils. Not that I was bothered. I was so hungry and so focused on staying alive that I devoured any food no matter what was in it or how it was contaminated. The cooks again had the advantage. They survived best, never doing hard labour and always better fed. With a bamboo ladle they would scoop up the rice and then skim the top of it using a paddle. Of course how much you got depended on how hard they pulled the ladle through the rice. As the men queued every eye fixed on that ladle, counting virtually every grain. I can see it still. We were in a desperate, horrible state.

Men would often try to call off sick. But it was the Japanese who decided whether or not you were sick enough to be off. You had to be very ill not to work. You were usually safe if you had tropical ulcers, coupled with dysentery or malaria. Yet having just one or the other would not be enough to save you from work. The tropical ulcers I had picked up on the railway were pretty much healed up. So despite continuing to suffer from dysentery and dehydration, during the three months I was at River Valley Road I was never allowed off work. Men died like flies but I never found out the fatality rate in my time there. You never knew how many were dying because you were away at work every day; they died in the so-called hospital wards and had been buried before you returned. There was a part of you too, to be honest, that didn't want to know.

After all I had been through I had decided to stay apart from everyone else and focus totally on survival. I lived a day at a time in my own little world, a private cocoon, and adopted the position of self-sufficient loner. To survive each day required maximum concentration and alertness. It also meant that you had to conserve every possible ounce of energy. If someone spoke to me, I replied but there was no memorable sense of community. I was so damned tired all of the time that it was an effort to do anything but survive. Self-preservation had become the name of the game for me.

After parade we had to walk three miles to the docks. On the way you could see some of the local Chinese or Malayans moving about – the usual cosmopolitan Singapore population. At Changi some Malayans had worked as guards but we had Japanese and Korean guards at River Valley Road. The Japanese treated the Koreans very badly and they in turn treated us even worse. We were always piggy in the middle, getting beatings from all sides. The Koreans were probably more brutal. They would hit you with anything they could lay their hands on and wouldn't know when to stop. The Japanese seemed more measured in the force they used and what they used against us.

We had no interaction with the locals on the walk to the docks – that was definitely taboo. The Korean guards walked in front and alongside you, and would beat you if you even looked at civilians. And even if you did manage to establish contact with the locals you had nothing to barter with anyway, so it was pretty hopeless even to try.

Once we arrived at the docks we were set to work straight away unloading bags of rice and sugar from various ships the Japanese had brought in for supplies. Whether they were Japanese ships or ones they had captured, I was unsure. We were always unloading, never on loading duty for some reason. We would pick up the heavy bags from the dockside and take them on our shoulders or backs to the warehouses known as go-down sheds. By now the sacks were heavier than us. I weighed less than a hundred pounds and our terrible, decrepit and weak physical state made the tough work that we performed without any shade from the relentless Asian sun unbearable. Every muscle, sinew and joint ached in the searing and relentless heat. Inevitably we would often drop the bags from our shoulders or backs. For the poor soul who dropped his load it was always a moment of terror when the sack burst open on the ground. All hell would break loose and you braced yourself for the inevitable beating, praying that it would be over with quickly. The Japanese would go mad and beat us with anything they had to hand. Blows would rain down from sticks, bamboo, fists and rifle butts.

There is no doubt that some of the guards enjoyed inflicting these beatings and vied with each other to see who could administer the most pain and suffering. I used to drop a sack at least once a week – sometimes twice a day. I remember thinking that the beating would never stop. They would usually last two or three minutes, which felt like an eternity. The guards could land a lot of blows in that time. Because I had been beaten repeatedly on the railway it was sort of commonplace to me. Yet every time your dignity really hurt more than the pain. It was the fact that you couldn't fight back that really hurt. If someone is hitting you and you can't fight back . . . it's just the worst. It broke your spirit as much as your bones. They would beat you right down to primate level very quickly.

When I witnessed other men getting beatings I was just glad it wasn't me. I had become anaesthetised to the suffering of others but I would feel sick when I saw someone in a worse physical or mental state than me getting the treatment. To see a grown man on the ground crying and howling, begging his tormentors to stop, was very hard to take. Your reaction to the beating meant a lot to the Japanese. If you caved in and showed fear, they would go at you harder. But if you showed that it wasn't hurting, they gave up. It seems the wrong way round – you'd think they would go easy on you if you were weaker. But the Japanese mind worked in strange ways.

We usually toiled until sundown – at around five or six in the evening, depending on which Japanese officer was in charge. If he were fed up, you might get finished early or alternatively they could make you work later under arc lamps until the ship had been completely unloaded. You tried to do the least amount of work possible while always looking busy. But the slower you went the more pain you had with the weight of the bags on your back – and the Japanese knew it. You would take the bag from dockside to the go-downs as quickly as you could and walk back as slowly as possible via a different route. You could go behind piles of other bags and hide for a bit. There was a lot of dodging of labour. Some men would do one journey to the go-downs and nip behind the stacks of sacks and stay there for up to half an hour.

After a long, ten-hour shift at the docks we were searched with our hands above our heads. You really had nowhere to hide anything, whether it was food or whatever. If they did find something on a worker, the man would be severely punished. He might be forced to stand with something heavy above his head all night and day or the guards might even call in the military police, the dreaded Kempeitai. It usually had to be something very serious in Japanese eyes for the military police to come. When they came and took people away the prisoners were never seen again.

I was utterly exhausted on the trudge back to camp. The only thing that spurred me on was the thought of getting a cup of rice. It was dark by the time you got back and after some food you went to your hut, which was in darkness from sunset to sunrise. Most of us just crashed out to sleep.

The days turned into weeks and then into months. There seemed no end to our misery. Then one day while working on the docks we were suddenly herded on to a large ship. None of us were given any prior warning, not even our officers. We were soon to find out why.

On 4 September 1944, nine hundred British POWs were rushed up the gangway of the *Kachidoki Maru,* a ten-thousand-tonne cargo vessel that had been named the *President Harrison* before it was captured from the Americans. Using sticks the Japanese drove us like cattle aboard the ship and down into the holds. We could never move fast enough for them. The liner had two holds, both quite obviously not made to accommodate human beings, yet they wanted around 450 of us in each. The lads below were shouting, begging and pleading for the Japanese not to let any more men in. But the louder they shouted, the more frenzied the guards became and down we went into the depths of hell.

Nothing in all of our suffering had prepared me for anything like this and even today I can scarcely find the words to describe the horrors of the *Kachidoki Maru*. By the time I got down to the hold I had nowhere to sit. It was standing room only, all of us packed like sardines, with no toilet facilities. Most had dysentery, malaria, beriberi and all manner of tropical diseases. Once inside and the hold crammed full, the Japanese battened down the hatches, plunging us into a terrifying black pit. At that moment the most fearful clamour went up as claustrophobia and panic gripped the men. Many feared they were doomed and began screaming and shouting. Yet a strange tranquillity overcame me. I felt resigned and just thought, This is it. I thought that we would never get out alive and would never see home again. You felt resigned to accept this as your last. I could only think that they were taking us out to sea to sink the ship and drown us all. Our captors were capable of it. I had seen that they were capable of anything.

We knew nothing about these ships, which would become infamous in the annals of Second World War history as 'hellships' – a fleet of dozens of rusting hulks used to shuttle supplies and prisoners around Japan's Far Eastern empire. Some of the most appalling episodes of the war occurred on these ships in which men driven crazy by thirst killed fellow prisoners to drink their blood. In some cases prisoners trying to escape from the seething mass of hysterical captives were shot by Japanese soldiers guarding the stairways from the holds. Some voyages took weeks with only a handful of prisoners surviving. Men drank their own urine. Sick prisoners were trampled to death or suffocated. The sane murdered the insane and wondered when it would be their turn to go mad. Cannibalism as well as vampirism was not unknown and even Japanese medics were shocked by what they found when the holds were finally opened. In the case of the *Oryoku Maru*, where insane prisoners killed fellow men for their blood, only 271 men survived out of 1619. The experience of one Dutch group was fairly typical: of 1500 men shipped from Java to Rangoon to work on the Death Railway, 200 died and 450 were unable to walk on arrival in Burma. Nineteen of the fifty-six hellships were sunk by submarines and aircraft and a total of 22,000 allied prisoners died during agonising voyages to the slave camps in Japan and Taiwan.

Down in the sweltering bowels of that ship we suffered for thirty-six hours before we got underway. The Japanese had been assembling HI-72, a tightly packed convoy of around a dozen ships with destroyer protection for the voyage to Japan. Unknown to us there was a second hellship in our convoy: the *Rakuyo Maru*, carrying around 1317 British and Australian prisoners.

There must have been at least one officer, a warrant officer or a sergeant major somewhere in the hold. But they certainly didn't make themselves known. Discipline had gone. Everyone, whatever their rank, was in the same situation. All of us just wanted to survive and were prepared to do anything to ensure that happened. It would have taken a very brave man to try and take command of the men in the hold in those conditions. It would have been suicidal.

The heat down in the holds was unbelievable. The longer the hatches stayed shut, the hotter it got. With all of the bodies tightly packed together temperatures quickly reached well in excess of one hundred degrees Fahrenheit. We began losing body fluid awfully quickly and dehydration became a big problem. As did stomach cramp. I was suffering from dysentery and dehydration, which were pretty much perpetual for me. In three and a half years I never really had a proper bowel movement.

I never thought anything could ever match the terror of the railway. Being in the hold was worse. At least while slaving on the railway you could move. And you had fresh air.

Air must have been coming into the hold from somewhere otherwise we would have all suffocated to death, though some men did. It felt like we were breathing in the last of it. When the ship began to move you realised within hours that anything was possible. Maybe we would be sunk deliberately and drowned as the Japanese had done to other prisoners.

Then another dread thought struck me. Submarines. The *Kachidoki Maru* had no Red Cross markings painted on it. I would later learn that none of the hellships bore any indication that POWs were on board, as they were required to do by the Geneva Convention. Red crosses were, however, painted on Japanese ammunition carriers. My fears that without markings we were a target for our own side were to prove all too justified.

As we sailed out of Singapore harbour on 6 September, in Hawaii signals officers of the US Navy's Fleet Radio Unit Pacific were listening in to Japanese radio traffic and intercepted messages relating to our convoy and its course. On 9 September orders were issued to three US submarines. Two days later on the night of 11 September, in the shipping lane known to American crews as 'Convoy College', the USS *Growler* broke the calm surface of the South China Sea, south of Hainan Island. As the crew of the *Growler* checked out the overcast skies that threatened rain on the horizon, the bow of the USS *Sealion II* was the next to emerge from the depths and sidle alongside the *Growler*. One and a half hours later the USS *Pampanito* joined the compact. The wolf pack was formed. The submarines were so close together, around a hundred metres apart, that the captains were able to shout to each other and forge their attack plans. As they separated to take up their positions in a stretch of water out of range of Japanese aircraft, the captains wished each other happy hunting and dived. They were in high spirits and had nicknamed their wolf pack 'Ben's Busters', after the *Growler*'s audacious skipper, Commander Ben Oakley. They knew each other well and had spent the previous month harassing Japanese convoys and sinking freighters in the South China Sea.

In the hold of the *Kachidoki Maru* the torment went on. The noise was constant and deafening, an awful cacophony of throbbing engines, moaning, coughing and occasional panic-stricken screaming the background music for this latest torture. The chilling screams of the mad and insane would stop abruptly. I didn't know how they were dealt with but I could imagine . . .

I was completely stuck where I was in the hold and could not move. No one could. You couldn't sit or lie down, you couldn't even go down on your haunches, there was so little room. You didn't really want to lie down anyway. It was a sea of human waste and you risked being trampled. You had your space and protected it with your life. Quite literally. You stayed strong, protecting your space with elbows and fists. By any means necessary. By this stage it was every man for himself. Each person had their own problems to resolve, their own life to save. Strangers surrounded me, all British but none of us knew each other. The only noise coming from outside the hold was the steady shudder of the ship as we crawled along. At least it felt like we were crawling. The noises inside continued getting louder as men kept panicking or shouting out in pain.

The smell inside the hold was indescribable, a repugnant stench. An overpowering mixture of excrement, urine, vomit, sweaty bodies, weeping ulcers and rotting flesh clogged the atmosphere. There was no way we could get any fresh air. Even when the Japanese opened the hatches it didn't really help that much – you were still breathing in what was already there.

In the darkness we had no way to keep track of time. But at some point on that first day of the voyage the battens were taken off and the hatches opened wide. I was stuck a long way from the hatch but could see the blue emptiness of the sky, a distant, tantalising beacon of freedom that from down there looked as close as I would ever get to it again. Some men, maybe forty or fifty or so, were allowed to go up on deck. Not the rest of us. That started a terrible mêlée. People climbed over each other, scratching and scrambling. It was sheer pandemonium. I supposed that the men allowed on deck could use the toilet arrangement that hung over the side of the ship. But letting fifty men use the toilet would have taken a long time and it would have been an especially long time for the impatient Japanese, so I doubt whether more than one or two were allowed to go. It did allow a lovely cool breeze to come inside the hold and ease some of the airlessness momentarily. While the hatches were open, the guards lowered down a single pail of rice. Even the most peaceful man alive turned into a real scavenger. We were fighting for our lives. When the men got put back down in the hold they found that their places had been taken over by other prisoners. Space was at such a premium. That caused more fights to break out. It is impossible to describe fully just how horrendous the conditions were. During the whole journey the guards opened the hatches just three times. I never got up on deck. I suspect that some allowed up managed to hide somewhere on the deck. I know I would have. It would have been worth the risk. Anything was better than being down in that dark hold. If anyone got caught, they would in all probability have been killed. At the very least they would have had a serious beating.

When the guards closed the hatches again, plunging us

back into darkness, the feeling of complete desolation, total resignation, returned. Thirst became our biggest problem. People don't understand what real thirst truly is. You start to hallucinate and see mirages, and that is the most dangerous thing. People died down in the holds from suffocation or heart attacks. The men who died were not taken away. Their bodies lay among us.

The second time the hatches opened the bucket of rice came down nearer to where I was. Someone threw a lump of rice and I managed to catch it. I wolfed it down. Rice becomes water and that is what I needed to abate my thirst. At no time during this terrible journey did the Japanese give us water; we relied on the occasional rice ball for it. The terrible stomach cramps induced by the lack of food and water defied belief. The pain doubled me over. This was a slow and painful death.

Six days out of Singapore I wondered how much more I could take. Then in the distance came a muffled explosion. Right on cue we had sailed into the trap set by the American submariners, who were determined to sink as many of the vessels they believed to be carrying oil and rubber as they could. At two in the morning the USS *Growler* had fired at the convoy sending our escorts fanning out. Then in one of the most daring manoeuvres in American naval history the *Growler* took on the Japanese destroyer *Shikinami* bow to bow. At a range of a thousand yards, Commander Oakley slammed three torpedoes into the *Shikinami*. She was only two hundred yards from the *Growler* when she sank. Oakley hit another two vessels before withdrawing to rearm.

Next the *Pampanito* and the *Sealion II* moved in for the kill. On board the *Pampanito* Lieutenant Commander Paul Summers had just taken up a perfect position to attack the scattered convoy when several large explosions unexpectedly rocked his vessel. To the west of Summers the *Sealion II* had fired two salvoes of three torpedoes each at the frantically zig-zagging convoy – and met with spectacular success. Three torpedoes smashed into a large oil tanker that exploded into flames, lighting up the sea like a giant flare. Out of control the burning tanker collided with the *Kachidoki Maru*. We had an amazingly close escape as it screeched along the side of our hull. When the *Kachidoki Maru* suddenly listed dramatically, pandemonium broke out afresh as men screamed in terror and begged to be let up on deck. It was terrifying; we expected to be torpedoed at any moment and drowned like rats in those stinking holds. We all fixed our eyes on the narrow stairwell to the decks, wondering how the hell we would ever get out.

But the burning tanker had illuminated a second target, the *Rakuyo Maru*. The poor prisoners in the holds knew what was coming and braced themselves for the inevitable. At 5.25 a.m. Lieutenant Commander Eli Reich steadied the *Sealion II*, a modern Balao-class submarine that had been commissioned just six months earlier, and fixed the *Rakuyo Maru* in the sights of his periscope. The thirty-one-year-old skipper took careful aim at the 9500-tonne vessel silhouetted against the night sky by the burning tanker. He was not going to miss. Earlier in the attack he had fired in support of the *Growler* and missed and been forced to flee Japanese escorts. And he had a personal score to settle: the first USS *Sealion* had been sunk in a Japanese bombing raid on the Philippines at the outbreak of war and Reich had lost four of his crew. There would be no mistake. As he gave the order to fire three steam torpedoes at ten-second intervals, the young New Yorker had no idea of the carnage he was about to cause. All three tin fish hit the *Rakuyo Maru*. The first struck the engine room, another hit amidships and the third torpedo hit the 477-foot ship in the bow area. Amazingly none of the 1317 prisoners were killed by the explosion. The ship started to list and the Japanese guards and sailors immediately deserted the sinking ship in ten of twelve available lifeboats, leaving the prisoners to fashion makeshift rafts and take to the water with what little food and water they could find on board.

Tragically 1159 men, survivors of the Death Railway and all of its hardships, either drowned or died of exposure after days floating in the sea. It was a colossal loss of life and as the *Sealion II* dived to avoid depth charges the young sailors who celebrated their kill had no idea of the catastrophe unfolding above them.

While the *Sealion II* dived to safety, the *Growler* and the *Pampanito* set off after the convoy, and when Commander Oakley caught up with it the survivors in the water found themselves in the middle of a fierce naval battle. The *Growler* fired its torpedoes on the Japanese frigate *Hirado* and scored a direct hit. Some men in the water cheered while others saw all chance of rescue disappear. The shockwaves from the *Hirado* explosion killed some prisoners, others died when the Japanese retaliated with depth charges or were killed by the propellers. The *Growler* got away unscathed. (It was Oakley's last major triumph, two months later he and his crew were killed when the *Growler* succumbed to Japanese depth-charging.)

Darkness had once again fallen and the *Kachidoki Maru* steamed north towards Taiwan, making a dash for protective air cover. But by eleven o'clock that night the *Pampanito* caught up with us and thirty-one-year-old skipper Paul Summers was planning a very special celebration of his birthday, which had taken place just a few days before on the day we sailed from Singapore.

Any hopes we had that we had outrun the wolf pack or that the attack was over were about to be dashed. Summers prepared to mount a surface attack on the *Kachidoki Maru* but had to abandon it because of technical difficulties. His crew worked feverishly to fix the problem and Summers resumed the attack. We were the biggest vessel among the group of small ships and made a juicy target. As the *Kachidoki Maru* steamed into the crosshairs of *Pampanito*'s periscope, Summers gave the fateful order to fire. Four minutes later we suddenly felt a tremendous blast and an explosion tore through the hold. The whole structure shuddered and water flooded in from above. I knew then as the water crashed on top of me that my worst fears had been realised. We had been hit and I knew that the torpedo had struck very close to us. It was in fact the first of two torpedoes that would send the hellship to the bottom within fifteen minutes.

The ship tilted. We were going down. Up above the Japanese began shooting their wounded men in the sick bay in mercy killings. Down below men shouted and panicked and scrambled madly for the single ladder up on to the deck. The noise was horrendous. But the pressure of the water must have pushed the hatches wide open. Either that or someone on deck, whether one of the stowaways or one of the POWs up there at the time we were hit, gave us a chance. Water rushed into the hold straight away with incredible pressure. It pushed me up as the ship continued to tip over. The hatches became parallel with the sea now and by some miracle the water washed me out of the hatch, and I floundered into a stream or strong current that rushed me out into the sea. It all seemed to happen at once. I popped out of the ship like a cork out of a champagne bottle.

After the extreme heat of the hold the water felt very cold. The sea was just a mass of thick oil as a total of twelve ships in our convoy were sunk that night. I knew I had to get as far away from the ship as possible as soon as I could, to avoid being dragged under with it, but it was like swimming through treacle. Those of us who could swim were the only ones who had a chance. I knew from my Boy Scout training that I had to swim away to avoid getting pulled down by the suction.

I swam for my life, as hard as I could, away from the waves created by the pull of the ship going down. I put my head down and powered with desperate overarm strokes, dodging debris as I went, all the time gulping down oil. It was like drinking fire and burned all the way down, doing irreparable damage to my vocal chords.

When I was fifty yards away I felt safe – for the moment. I turned to look at the ship. Treading water I saw it tilt and then in just a few seconds the stern silently and gracefully slipped under the waves. The sea was now aflame as the oil burned, and a torpedoed oil tanker was well ablaze. Like a scene from Dante's *Inferno*, smoke filled the night sky and shouts and screams came from all directions. As the flames got closer I feared that I might be burned alive. Luckily they spluttered out before reaching me and then I was very sick, bringing up a horrible mixture of crude oil and salt water.

Even after the sinking the killing went on for those of us who survived and got on to rafts. Anyone starting to panic was thrown off into the sea. When they scrambled to get back on they were kicked away. Men pushed under and held under Japanese survivors. Fighting broke out as the animal instinct to survive asserted itself, making some survivors try to capture more seaworthy vessels and shove others off to their deaths. Many gave up, already so weak, dangerously dehydrated and ill. Frequently they had been injured too in the sinking. Many gulped salt water and quickly went stark raving mad, drowning themselves to end the torment. Horrible as it may sound, as men became mad they had to be shoved off the rafts or boats or the remainder might have perished.

There was a lot of shouting and screaming. Cries of 'Get off, you bastard!' or 'I'll kill you!' made me close my eyes in distress. Most of the shouts were in English. There were not many Japanese, the majority of whom had got off early in lifeboats. Drowning and dying men called for their wives, their children or mothers. Men said things like 'Daddy will be home soon' and then disappeared beneath the waves. It was harrowing to hear. By that stage most of us were treading a very fine line between sanity and madness. It didn't take much to put people over the top. I couldn't see where it was coming from but a group of men started singing. First to keep their spirits up they sang 'Rule Britannia'. After the Selarang Incident we had been banned from singing this stirring anthem with its line about 'Britons never, ever, being slaves'. But this was a strange freedom and as the situation worsened the song changed and the poignant words of the great hymn 'Abide with Me' drifted across the South China Sea. It was very moving and I still cannot bear to hear that hymn in church.

I felt horrendous and wondered if I would last the night. How little could a human being survive on? I was about to find out. In the water with bedlam all around, a great urge to be on my own engulfed me. It felt like the safest tactic.

Two hundred and forty-four of my comrades on the *Kachidoki Maru* died that night. It was tragic beyond belief that having survived the Death Railway they became prisoners of the deep.

Suddenly the thought of sharks came into my mind. I knew that I must have suffered some cuts on the way out and that sharks were attracted to the scent of blood – I had to get out of the water as soon as I could.

My prayers were answered when a single-man raft came floating past. Exhausted and covered in thick bunker oil I hoisted myself into it. It was oval-shaped like a big dog's basket, made of a cork-like substance and just big enough for me to sit in with my legs out in front. It had no provisions in it. With so many dead bodies floating in the water the sharks must have had a field day. From the sea I picked up shreds of string and rope, as well as bits of wood that I thought might be useful later. I also managed to find a few scraps of canvas to shield me from the sun if I lasted that long. I looked for any-thing in the water that might do for a paddle but it was pointless anyway. I didn't know in which direction to paddle. It was amazing how quickly I drifted away from the rest of the shipwrecked men. I could soon see outlines of people in the water in the distance, all of them covered in oil. I had no way to know who they were, whether Japanese or POWs. It was easy to mistake a Japanese for one of my own. I made up my mind that if it came down to me or a Japanese, he would be going to meet his ancestors.

The position I had drifted to must have been in the opposite direction from the bulk of the flotilla. A strong current took me even further away.

The noise from everyone else in the sea started to fade anyway. Soon I was alone and bitterly cold in the night air. I tried to use the rope I had picked out of the water to lash the raft together more sturdily but it was very diffi-cult in the dark and with my lack of energy. Yet I busied myself, knowing that I had to stay awake to stay alive.

When light came in the morning I was utterly alone. There was not a thing in sight. Just the vastness of the blue sea, the infinite blue sky and the scorching yellow sun. Whether it was because of the heat, thirst or oil, my tongue had begun to swell. My eyes stung from the oil. When the sun had been up a couple of hours I had still not seen or heard a thing. I started to think of home, of my family and friends, and of happy times in Scotland.

Castaway and dreaming of home I was shocked to suddenly hear a shout from behind me.

'You will be picked up soon!' a voice called out. My spirits soared at the thought of a companion to share the ordeal but my joy was short-lived. I turned around full of expectation only to be confronted by a Japanese officer in a one-man raft similar to mine. Immediately I thought, Right! Here we go. I couldn't see if he still had his sword or not but prepared myself for a fight. There was no way to fight from the raft, I knew it had to be in the water. I knew that my swimming ability would give me the edge. I had my lifesaving badge and I could control a frantic person in the water. He was also fully dressed in a tunic, trousers and boots so I was confident of beating him. It was incredible that even in the extreme circumstances we were in, the need to defend yourself from another human being was uppermost in my mind.

He was using a proper paddle to come towards me. I steeled myself but he stopped five yards or so away and shouted, 'Here', as he threw me a tin. Despite my oily hands I managed to catch it. The Japanese officer then paddled off without saying anything more and it was the last I saw of him.

The top on the tin was sealed and waterproof. I clawed at it frantically, eager to know what was inside. It seemed to take for ever. When I finally managed to prise the top off my heart sank. The tin contained chocolates, something we could have only dreamed of in the last two years but a death sentence for me now, dehydrated and adrift in the tropical ocean. I would have loved to have devoured those chocolates but I knew that afterwards they would have sent me mad with thirst. Eating them may have even killed me because I had eaten nothing like that for such a long time. Immediately I threw the tin and its lid in the water. I watched it sink and realised I probably should have discarded the chocolates but kept the tin to catch any rain water. It was a cruel moment.

I was alone again, and so tired, completely unable to do anything. All I could do was lie there and use my brain and imagination to keep me awake. One of the things I did was to go back in my mind to the plumbers' merchant in Aberdeen I worked at before the war. I did a mental stock-take through the bins and warehouse, memorising all of the stock. Going through the drawers of pipes, fittings, couplings, screws, nuts and washers took a long time and I enjoyed it. I even made up imaginary orders for customers in the 'big houses'.

It was so hot out on the open sea with the unrelenting glare bouncing off the water. My burning skin was dissolving into salt-water immersion sores, made even more painful when crude oil got into the fissures. It felt like being cooked alive. When one part of my skin could take no more of the blow-torch heat I would move my little pieces of canvas around, feebly trying to gain some protection. I began to think of the cold and bitter winters back in Aberdeen, almost willing myself cool.

I recalled childhood days of making slides and organising snowball fights and smiled as I thought of our sledging expeditions to Auchinyell Brae, where we would toboggan from early morning until late at night, returning home with ears and fingers frozen numb.

Images began flooding back. I could see the fantastic sight of the mighty carts that belonged to Wordie and Co. picking up goods from the warehouse to take them down to the railway goods station. It was amazing to see the giant Clydesdales struggling in pairs up frosty braes, hauling huge loads with their masters whipping them on and shouting out obscenities. The carters were a 'gallus' lot, really rough and ready.

I laughed to myself as I thought of the rag and bone man too. At the sound of his bugle we kids would swarm behind his cart like a plague of locusts, hoping to be given a balloon or to pick up the steaming horse dung to take triumphantly back home for Mum to put on the garden. There were some real fights over that dung!

When the sun went down again it was bitingly cold. A full moon on that cloudless second night made it feel even colder for some reason. I had the bits and pieces of canvas draped over me but I was so cold. Terrified of rolling off the raft, I still had to stay awake. I was at my lowest ebb. The light from the moon struck the water and reflected bright in my eyes. I started to see things that weren't there. Imaginary bits of wreckage or a boat would suddenly come into view. I began to lose my senses, saying to myself, 'Come on, let yourself go. Go to sleep.' It was always an inner battle. Half of me wanted to give up. The other half refused. And so it went on.

Alone with no sight of land, birds, dolphins or life of any kind, I sang songs to keep my mind occupied and awake. No words would come out of my parched throat but I sang them in my head. I went through all the pre-1940 dance songs I knew and always returned to my favourite: 'It's a Sin to Tell a Lie'.

It was a hit for Fats Waller and I sang it over and over and over in my head.

> *Be sure it's true when you say I love you*
> *It's a sin to tell a lie*
> *Millions of hearts have been broken*
> *Just because these words were spoken*
>
> *I love you, yes I do, I love you*
> *If you break my heart I'll die*
> *So be sure it's true*
> *When you say I love you*
> *It's a sin to tell a lie*

Unknown to me over 650 survivors of the *Kachidoki Maru* had already been picked up by the Japanese and the *Pampanito*, which had returned to the scene of the original attack to make a horrible discovery. As the submarine surfaced amid the debris and wreckage of the *Rakuyo Maru*, the crew saw survivors who had been in the water for three days and were horrified when weak voices started shouting. At first the young Americans could not understand the British and Australian accents, until one of the sailors made out the words 'pick us up, please!' Then the awful reality dawned. These oil-covered survivors were not Japanese but English, Scottish and Australian. The wolf pack had sunk two hellships packed with prisoners of war. One thousand four hundred and three allied servicemen had died as a result of the failure of the Japanese to observe the Geneva Convention and apply red crosses to our hellships.

Pampanito promptly radioed for assistance, and the *Sealion II* and two other American submarines returned to the scene. With survivors too weak to clamber aboard the subs, American sailors dived into the sea to pull men out, rescuing a total of 159 men. A handful died on board and the Americans were horrified at the condition of the survivors and to hear about the Death Railway and the privations we had endured. Incredibly the evidence gleaned from these survivors allowed the allies to discover for the first time the true extent of the horrors on the Death Railway and simultaneous announcements were subsequently made to stunned Houses of Parliament in both London and Canberra.

The men picked up by the subs were the lucky ones. Joe Bates, communications officer on the *Sealion II*, later told how his captain angered the crew by ordering the submarine to dive after rescuing just fifty survivors, leaving behind dozens of others frantically calling out, 'Over here!

Over here!' It was a heartbreaking decision but Lieutenant Commander Eli Reich feared for the safety of his vessel. The cries of the men left behind haunted Joe Bates and his shipmates for decades.

I was still drifting alone. By the time the sun came up on the fifth day I could no longer see; my eyes had been seared by the dazzling sun and sparkling sea. I had no eyebrows or hair on my head; I think the sheer shock of what was happening to me had caused my hair to fall out. I kept moving around in my tiny raft the best I could and prayed for rain. I sang to myself and vainly tried to croak out loud, urging myself: 'Hang on in there until you can't hang on any longer.'

Badly burned by the sun, my tongue swollen, gripped by a maddening thirst, effectively blind and completely hairless, I fell into a trance-like state. I was on the very edge of death. At some point on that fifth day there came a lot of shouting around me. I was lifted into a small boat and then on to a Japanese whaling ship. I must have been left on deck but from there on I have no real recollection. I don't know what the Japanese on board that ship did for me. As far as I was concerned they just left me alone but they must have at least given me some water. I was as close to death as I had ever been.

The next thing I knew I was being dropped off at a port, which I later learned was on Hainan Island. Congregated there were other shipwrecked POW survivors. As a punishment we were paraded through the village stark naked. One man shouted out, 'If we work like horses, we may as well look like them.'

I was so burned and emaciated and ill that I staggered through the streets like a drunk. Some of the locals turned their backs on this terrible procession but others jeered and spat at us. I was past caring. There must have been at least a hundred of us, and then came an incredible and inspiring episode. As we stumbled along in the pouring rain someone started singing. It was 'Singin' in the Rain', and slowly we all took up the song and joined in, singing a very rude version of the hit – complete with altered lyrics crudely deriding our Japanese captors. Even in this terrible condition and after all we had been through, my comrades, ravaged by exposure, naked and in slavery, were defiant, their spirits unbroken.

Eight

Sentimental Journey

The effects of the exposure I suffered during my ordeal in the South China Sea had led to a complete collapse in my health. At the camp on Hainan I hovered at death's door, drifting in and out of awareness, but out of it for most of the time. Eventually on 18 September I was stretchered on to another hellship and lowered into the hold. As our ship made a dash for the Japanese mainland, dodging prowling American submarines, I lay blissfully unaware of the grim conditions in the bowels of the vessel.

It was another terrible journey and must have been full of angst for the conscious survivors. We were on board for eleven days with no drugs or medical assistance whatsoever for 120 ill men in our contingent. Terrified of further attacks the Japanese had commandeered all of the life-belts and despite the protests of Captain Wilkie had two or three each, while there were none available for prisoners. In fact our convoy was attacked again and a destroyer sunk. We were lucky to escape being sunk for a second time and it was nothing short of miraculous that only five men died in the holds during the voyage. Unknown to me I was lucky and had a guardian angel – Dr Mathieson was tending to me.

I came to my senses as we arrived in Japan and found myself being driven into the middle of a barren, almost desert-like landscape to a bleak prison camp surrounded by a ten-foot-high wooden fence, with barbed wire on top. Along with others I was slung into a timber hut, where we slept on the floor Japanese style. Exhausted I did not wake the entire night. Next morning I struggled to make it out of the hut for roll-call. We were issued with Japanese-green, all-in-one boiler suits with zip-up fronts, and rubber boots like the Nippon soldiers wore. I had to roll the sleeves up on my overalls, which struck me as being strange since the Japanese didn't have long arms.

A Japanese officer told us that we were in a place called Omuta and that our camp was designated Fukuoka Camp 25. It was a few miles from a seaport that owed much of its modern prosperity to the efforts of an Aberdeen merchant called Thomas Glover. He had opened Japan's first coal mines and developed the country's first dry-dock in the city. Its only other claim to fame was as the setting of Puccini's *Madame Butterfly*. That seaport was called Nagasaki.

We were being put to work immediately. This time labouring in a nearby open-cast coalmine. I was still in a terrible state; I barely knew my own name and could hardly stand. I dreaded hard labour. We marched for half an hour along a dirt track to the coalmine, which was quite small, much smaller than the ones I knew of on the east coast of Scotland. We saw very few locals and when we did they never gave us a second look. Vegetable plants grew on the roadside verge. The Japanese mainland was literally starving and food was being grown on every available scrap of land. There was of course no improvement to our rations.

We filled coal carts with our bare hands and sometimes shovels, and then in groups of four had to push the laden carts along a small railway, fifty yards or so up a slight incline to a point where we would tip them over and the coal would fall on to a large mound that trucks would take away. It was quite an effort to get the carts moving, even with four of us hard at it. But I doubt I was much use to anyone – I was completely worn out. It was nothing short of miraculous that I was still alive and I was a husk of a man, certainly unfit to work. I could do no more.

There were several of these mines scattered around Omuta, one of which was owned by a family called Aso. For decades after the war the Japanese government denied that allied prisoners had been used as slaves in any of these mines and factories, and it was only recently when researchers proved that the family of Taro Aso, the former Prime Minister of Japan, had personally profited from the labour of 197 Australian, 101 British and two Dutch prisoners that we received any kind of grudging recognition.

In January 2009 Mr Aso finally acknowledged for the first time that about three hundred allied POWs had indeed been forced to work at the Aso Mining Company's Yoshikuma coalmine in Fukuoka. Mr Aso would later become president of the company but until 2009 he maintained that the claims about POW labour could not be substantiated and because he was only four or five years old at the time he had no personal knowledge of it.

After a couple of days at the coalmine I went to the hospital hut to sign off sick. In the long room were half a dozen beds filled with acute dysentery and malaria sufferers. A doctor saw me enter and walked down the centre aisle. As he approached I thought I recognised his strut and ruddy complexion. When he got closer I could not believe my eyes.

'Doctor Mathieson, I presume.'

He grinned and shook my hand in true, reserved Scots fashion. But I was unsure that he had recognised me so I nudged his memory: 'Kanyu?'

'Good to see you, Alistair,' he said and genuinely seemed to mean it too. I was sure glad to see him anyway. He had already saved my life more than once.

Our quick catch-up chat did not dwell on the railway or the hellships – we just wanted to forget that lest it sap what little energy and will we had left. He did not even mention at this stage how he and his orderlies had nursed me on the second leg of our voyage while I was delirious. He signed me off work at the coalmine and reassigned me to camp duties once I had rested up. A few days later I reported to the orderly officer, a lieutenant who gave me all manner of duties to carry out that day. I was the general dogsbody of the camp and relished the role. I started off helping in the cook house, before emptying the contents of the Japanese latrines on their rows of tomato plants. I very rarely saw any Japanese in the camp, even during the day, and that suited me fine. They lived off-site and came in only when there was something serious going on. Usually we just had Korean guards and even they didn't bother going to the mines with the men, so most of the time everyone got on with things. It was a pleasant change in circumstances. I spent my afternoons tidying the yard with the besom-style brushes the Japanese favoured and I would be finished by the time the work party returned.

From then on I spent most of my spare time and evenings at the hospital hut. Dr Mathieson and I spoke for hours on all topics. It transpired that he also loved the outdoors, especially hill-walking, and had played rugby at high school. He was well educated and very capable. It was good to have some intelligent conversation. We were on the same wavelength and as fellow Scots often talked of home. Much of the chatter among the men could be pretty banal and boring. But Dr Mathieson took me under his wing and imparted a lot of his medical knowledge and wisdom.

He played a big part in bringing me out of the protective shell that I had retreated into during my time on the railway and the slavery of Singapore docks. I began regaining my personality.

Eventually the good doctor convinced our orderly officers as well as the Japanese to allow me to help out at the hospital as an orderly. My elevation had the blessing of Sergeant Fergusson, who was in charge of the hospital alongside Mathieson. He was very laid-back and quiet but brilliant at his job.

I had the task of ensuring that patients were as comfortable and disease-free as possible. By turning and bathing them, and conducting basic massages, I made sure that they did not get bedsores. Generally I tried to keep their spirits up. I also fetched their meals, made at the cook house, and carried them back on trays.

Dr Mathieson spent most of the time thinking up new ways of helping the sick. He was every bit a doctor – there was no mistaking him. Most of our patients could prove rather difficult – they often got angry and even physical, hitting out for no real reason. But Mathieson was extremely caring and never once got annoyed himself. He had a presence that even the most difficult patients seemed to accept. He became an inspirational figure to me. We had no real equipment or drugs so had to be resourceful. Then Dr Mathieson had the brainwave of bolstering the sick by injecting them with distilled water just under the skin. A placebo, it seemed to really rejuvenate the men whether it was all in the mind or not. Alas we could still do nothing for their pain; we did not even have aspirin. All we could do was offer some consoling words.

The dedicated and compassionate care provided by Dr Mathieson and Sergeant Fergusson ensured that only four men died during our time in Japan. They all died in October 1944 and three of these deaths were due partly to the effects of exposure after having been torpedoed on the hellships. One of those who died was a young Gordon Highlander, Private Henry Elder. He came from the tiny fishing village of Gourdon, a few miles south of Aberdeen. I did not like to dwell on the tragedy of a young lad from this tranquil village famed for its lobsters, who died alone so far from home after having survived so much.

Another victim, a young cockney called Tommy Taylor, died because we had no drugs to give him. He was survived by a twin brother in the camp. It was just too much to hope that both boys could survive the Death Railway and the hellships.

We cremated the four men and hid their ashes in a Buddhist temple for safekeeping.

Dr Mathieson was a good teacher. He patiently explained how beriberi was the result of vitamin deficiencies and how to diagnose other tropical diseases. Perhaps the most important piece of advice I received from him was delivered almost as an afterthought, as if I should know it already. He warned me that when I got out of camp I would have to be careful what I ate.

'You'll never be able to eat what you used to,' he said. 'Your stomach has shrunk so much that you'll have to be very careful. Anything too substantial, eaten too quickly, could kill you.'

It would prove life-saving advice.

The food at the camp had already caused a near fatal encounter when the Japanese gave the cook house some contaminated seafood. It caused havoc. While deliciously salty, and one of the finest culinary moments of my life, the pleasure was short-lived. All of those who ate the food, including myself, became seriously ill with food poisoning. It struck within hours – we suffered debilitating vomiting and diarrhoea, both ends going at once. The mess and stench was out of this world. Men lay doubled over screaming out in agony. Dr Mathieson, who was also a victim, proved wonderful on that occasion, working day and night to save dozens of lives. Within twenty-four hours the nightmare was over and incredibly nobody had succumbed.

There were still instances of Japanese tyranny. Whether or not they gave us the seafood knowing that it was contaminated, I could not be sure. But when someone stole some sugar from a storeroom the Japanese felt it was time to stamp their authority back on us. The whole camp, including us medical orderlies, was made to kneel erect on the parade square all night. With temperatures dropping below zero it was a long stretch. If you faltered from your position, the Japanese hosed water on to your legs, which in the sharp frost froze. The pain was something else. The punishment didn't freeze out the thief and it ended at 5 a.m. when the work party was gathered to go back to the mine.

During this time I acquired so much patience, understanding and caring that I began to feel better about myself even though I was skin and bone. My eyebrows started to sprout, as did some fuzzy clumps of hair. I had thoughts of training as a doctor if I ever got back to Scotland. I thought I was capable enough and I had decided that I really wanted to help others. One night in my hut I made a silent vow to spend the rest of my life bettering the lot of others.

Being in Japan, on the mainland, I felt slightly more optimistic, closer to civilisation, away from the arena of war. On the railway you felt forgotten, left to die and never to be heard of again. The jungle eroded any thoughts of rescue or going home. While Chungkai was comfortable, the fear of returning to the railway remained ever-present. But in Japan, and cooler climes, we always thought someone could come and save us. The only danger was that the 'saviours' would arrive too late, after the Japanese had killed us all.

After six months at the camp I could sense that the allies were winning the war in the Pacific. You could tell by the demeanour of the guards that it wasn't going well for them. They seemed to be extra glad to get out of the camp and return to their families when working parties returned. I saw some actually running through the gates. We were gaining the upper hand and both sides in the camp knew it. In one incident during the summer of 1945 Captain Wilkie threatened a bullying Japanese sergeant that he would have him shot after the war – something that would have been unthinkable on the railway. He also rejected repeated Japanese attempts to persuade us to make statements blaming the Americans for sinking us, which they could use for propaganda purposes.

Increasingly they left us alone. As the noose tightened around Japan the guards reduced our meagre rations even further; men developed boils and abscesses and instances of prisoners fainting at work increased. But subsisting on a diet of rice and occasionally beans, we started to receive the remnants of Red Cross parcels looted by our captors. We tasted raisins and cheese for the first time in years. It was the first evidence I had seen of the Red Cross during my entire captivity. At Christmas 1944 the Japanese had allowed us to celebrate with a day off. I had thought of home and it had suddenly struck me that it was six long years since I had celebrated Christmas there, back in 1938.

By the summer of 1945 bombing raids were becoming more frequent too. We saw scores of B-29 Superfortresses flying over us to paste Japanese cities and towns, including those close to us.

The ninth of August 1945 began like any other boring day in captivity. At dawn we turned out for tenko and the work parties marched out to the factory where our men now slaved. They were quite glad to be under guard. Since the incendiary bombings of Omuta and Nagasaki, Japanese civilians had taken to stoning POWs and there had been several vicious incidents with civilians in the factory. I began my daily chores around the camp prior to reporting to the hospital for orderly duties.

On an air-base thousands of miles away in the Mariana Islands a young US Air Force officer, Captain Charles Sweeney, aged just twenty-five like myself, was beginning a day that would be anything but normal. He and his youthful crew had already undergone a briefing and enjoyed the traditional early morning breakfast before any bombing mission. The chaplain's prayer had been a

little bit more emotional than usual and the escort for
Bockscar, his B-29 bomber, carried press men and pho-
tographers.

Three days after the bombing of Hiroshima fascist
hardliners in the Japanese government still wanted to fight
on. Stalin was already ripping apart the Japanese army in
Manchuria and the outcome of the war seemed obvious.
But the diehards wanted to fight on in the Japanese home
islands and among their plans they intended to massacre
all allied prisoners of war. 'Little Boy' had wiped out
Hiroshima and 140,000 of its people but had failed to
persuade Japan's rulers of the hopelessness of their cause.

Now US President Harry Truman decided that another
message must be sent. Sweeney's bomb hold contained
just one huge bomb: 'Fat Man'. Millions of man-hours
had gone into designing this implosion-type plutonium
bomb. Over ten feet long and five feet in diameter it
weighed in at 10,200 pounds and was designed to be
burst 1800 feet above its target.

But the initial target for Sweeney and his twenty-four-
year-old co-pilot, First Lieutenant Charles Albury, was
not Nagasaki but Kokura, the port city where we had
landed in the hellship from Hainan. The young pilots
made three passes on Kokura but found it clouded over
and were unable to comply with orders to drop the bomb
visually if possible. Running low on fuel and fearing they
might have to ditch Fat Man in the sea, Sweeney and
Albury turned their attention towards nearby Nagasaki. It
was covered with cloud too. But suddenly from thirty
thousand feet up *Bockscar*'s twenty-seven-year-old

veteran bomb-aimer Kermit Beahan caught a glimpse of the Nagasaki stadium and pressed the button that released the bomb.

It was around midday and I had finally plucked up the courage to undertake my most hateful task. Emptying the latrine cans on to the Japanese officers' tomato plants always made my stomach turn. But I did have to marvel at the spectacular effect it produced in the plants, which boasted tomatoes the size of apples. Earlier in the morning I had heard the drone of an aeroplane flying overheard. I looked up and saw it was flying quite low – in fact low enough to see its American military markings. I looked up open-mouthed as it flew directly over us. Since March 1945 we had seen growing numbers of American bombers flying above us to pound Japanese targets. Yet I was amazed this plane was flying so low and unchallenged. It made me think for an instant that the war might be over but as it disappeared my optimism went with it. We were unaware that Japan had been plunged into chaos at the top with the dropping three days earlier of Little Boy.

I was taking as much care as possible to avoid being splashed with the revolting contents of the cans as I moved up and down the drills of tomato plants behind the huts. The job always made me gag but was lighter work than the mines and furnaces. Halfway up a drill there came a tremendous clap of thunder from the direction of Nagasaki. I didn't think too much of it and had just finished watering the plants when a sudden gust of very hot air like a giant hairdryer blasted into me. It knocked my shrunken frame sideways and I had to use my bamboo ladle to prevent myself from falling over completely. I wondered where the freak wind had come from. I had never experienced anything like it. It came and went so quickly. But I didn't give it too much thought. In fact when I went into the hospital hut I didn't even mention the hot air to Dr Mathieson; instead we discussed the low-flying plane. Like me he couldn't understand why it had not been challenged as all previous raiders had.

Then the men came back from the factory and began to talk of a massive raid on Nagasaki and a huge direct hit on the armoury at the naval base. Massive clouds of smoke had been seen. But we had spotted no planes from the camp. Some men claimed to have seen dozens, even hundreds of planes, others none. As usual the camp generated abundant rumours and great speculation. We knew that something big had happened down in Nagasaki.

One Gordon proffered hopefully, 'They're bombing the shit out of the place. It's the final push. We'll be out of here in a week.'

But the low-flying lone plane attracted equally frenzied speculation. One of the lads suggested, 'It's high-ranking American officials, Winston Churchill himself maybe, coming to talk the Nip bastards into surrender.'

I remained less optimistic. There had been so many setbacks that I refused to allow myself to contemplate something as dramatic as the end.

On the hospital rounds Dr Mathieson was puzzled too. 'Why was there no opposition to those American planes?' he queried as I shadowed him.

'Never saw a Jap plane. Neither did anyone else,' I said, not knowing what to think.

Starved of news in the camp, our imaginations were nothing if not fevered. But none of us could have dreamed up what had happened at Nagasaki. The strange gust that had knocked me over was the hot breath of Fat Man, a nuclear weapon with even more destructive power than its cousin Little Boy. Unknown to us we had entered the atomic age.

Temperatures at ground zero in Nagasaki had flashed to between three thousand and four thousand degrees centigrade. The entire city had been flattened and thirty-nine thousand people had been vaporised instantly by this single bomb. The world had changed for ever.

Only the presence of large tracts of water within the city had prevented a fierce firestorm from developing and causing even greater loss of life. The undulating landscape had saved us from the worst of the blast but one of the camps nearby had been hit and six prisoners were killed.

As we finished the rounds Dr Mathieson's brow furrowed, 'If this is the end, hypothetically speaking of course, what will the Japs do with us?'

Having seen their appetite for wanton cruelty and death, and knowing their stance on the dishonour of surrender, it was a gut-churning question. Indeed we later learned that the Japanese Emperor had issued strict instructions to murder any POWs on the mainland, should it ever be invaded. Looking back I'm glad not to have known.

I told Mathieson that if the Japanese stormed our camp with the intention of massacring us all, we should fight to the death. Hopeless as our position was, with no weapons or means of fighting back, I wanted to make sure I took a few of the buggers with me.

'That's the spirit,' he replied much too unconvincingly.

For several days it was business as usual. Then on 15 August the men came back from the factory and said that its manager had spoken to a mass meeting of the workforce and broke down crying during his speech. The fifteenth of August, we were told, would be a big day of mourning for Japan. By now we felt sure that the war was over. Finally on 21 August we were paraded and the Japanese commander read out the declaration of the cessation of hostilities that had been called six days earlier.

Gradually the British took over the running of the camp but in the absence of the Japanese our food rations were diminishing rapidly. Leaflets promising imminent food drops came from above but the men were becoming hungry and restless. To appease them and their growling guts the officers allowed the slaughter of some pigs and chickens, which had been kept by the Japanese officers. The animals were killed unceremoniously in the parade square, their blood darkening the dirt. Our portions were minuscule but the chicken was delicious and the pork was simply divine. The latter was also especially good for the patients, said Dr Mathieson, because of the high salt content. At least that was the argument he put forward on behalf of the sick patients for extra rations.

On 25 August we received our first food drops. While most Red Cross supply crates and canisters came parachuting lightly to the ground, others thundered into the earth, huts, dining halls, latrines and trees like bombs. One man was slightly injured by flying splinters of wood when a canister landed on a building. Another thought he was covered in blood but it turned out to be tomato puree. Others, Japanese natives, were reportedly killed by the falling canisters. The parcels contained messages ordering us to remain inside the camp and wait to be liberated. Army discipline stood firm.

The life-saving canisters were filled with relief foodstuffs – sugar, milk, rice, as well as cigarettes and matches. Dr Mathieson ensured that the sick got first choice of proper food and insisted that the cook house did not produce any rich meals, which would have devastated our stomachs. Penicillin and aspirin also came in the drops, along with bandages, dressings, ointment, soap, sheets, towels and pillowcases. Finally our makeshift hospital was almost looking like the real thing.

As the weeks wore on our wait for rescue became incredibly frustrating. I never even contemplated leaving the camp until, one day early in September, a frantic Japanese man came running to us. Directed to the hospital hut he found Dr Mathieson and myself. In stilted English he managed to convey that his daughter was sick.

'Very small,' he managed, indicating with a grubby, weathered hand at his waist to show us her size.

'You help,' he said.

'But no drugs,' replied Mathieson.

'You come, you come,' he pleaded. He grabbed my hand and pulled me out of the hut. Mathieson grabbed some of his rudimentary medical implements and came with us. We trotted behind the urging father, his wooden sandals clack-clack-clacking along the dirt track. After about ten minutes we arrived at a modest, low-slung Japanese house. We removed our rubber boots and entered. It was the most bizarre house I had ever been in, with everything on the floor and a distinct lack of seating. Dark and cool inside, a woman in black silk trousers and a gaily coloured blouse, whom I took for the man's wife, waved at us and pointed to a murky corner. A young girl of about nine or ten lay curled up on the floor, shivering and barely able to offer a wave. Dr Mathieson saw to her and quickly realised she was running a dangerous temperature. She had a smattering of English and the Paisley doctor managed to ascertain she had stomach pains. We sponged her down, trying to relieve her fever, and then asked for some boiling water. I tried to explain that she should just take small sips.

We got her temperature down but nothing much else could be done. Dr Mathieson said, 'Two days', and held up two fingers to indicate she would be OK in forty-eight hours. He tried to explain the importance of light foods and was doing chicken impressions, which made all of us laugh.

While we had been attending to the girl, the woman, who had a mouthful of gold teeth that glinted in the dim light, had been preparing hot dishes and insisted we stay and eat with them. We sat on the floor and she lined up rows of bowls in front of us. Knowing the dangers in suddenly plumping for rich food, I chose a bowl of boiled rice, which was heavily salted and peppered. I tucked in and got a nudge in the ribs from Dr Mathieson urging me to take it easy. We ate as little as we could without offending our gracious hosts. They were extremely grateful and obviously had nowhere else to go. To my surprise I felt no animosity whatsoever to this family despite what their countrymen had put me through. The young girl deserved treatment as much as anybody and Dr Mathieson was of the same mind. As a true professional he had even treated the Japanese officers while on the Death Railway. It made me feel rather good inside to have been able to help them.

The woman disappeared again and returned with two bolts of Japanese silks, one for each one of us. They were gorgeously made, with extraordinarily colourful patterns, which I guessed would have been crafted into a kimono. I thought they were beautiful and I was extremely grateful. In fact I ensured my silk was kept safe. Years later I would give the piece of silk to my sister Rhoda, who made it into a housecoat.

A few days later while working in the hospital I heard a commotion outside. As I stepped out I caught my first glimpse of US marines. They had driven into camp on seven or eight lorries with white markings. For a stunned moment I gazed at them. It was so long since I had seen a white man who did not resemble a skeleton. I shouted for Dr Mathieson to come out.

We stood and watched in amazement. Smiling and strapping Yanks in pressed khaki uniforms were dispensing cigarettes by the fistful, hugging rag-and-bone strangers. Men were shouting and screaming, throwing things in the air, weeping and kissing the earth, lost in emotion. Some of the Americans were visibly upset at the sight of us and the pathetic state we were in. They lifted up men's shirts, shocked by the angular and protruding ribcages, bloated bellies and infant waistlines.

I shook hands with Dr Mathieson. We shared a silent moment taking it all in, before I went back to my hut to collect what few things I still had with me. Technically I wasn't in the medical corps so I went back with the troops. I jumped on one of the first trucks to speed out of the camp. It ferried us to Nagasaki harbour, where a ship was waiting to escort us to freedom. The Americans no doubt had to make several journeys to pick every one up from the camp so I was glad to be one of the first out.

The American driver was obviously off his rocker, not bothering to dodge boulders. He careered on lifting us high from our pews and bouncing our heads off the canvas. I stared at the countryside from the rear of the lorry. While it had been relatively bare before, the hedgerows and trees now appeared to be dying. As we thundered on the greenness of the hedgerows faded. Reddish-brown leaves turned brown, grey and then black. Fairly soon nothing was left. No birds sang, nothing lived. Trees had been reduced to knee-high ashen stumps. The area looked like the aftermath of a mass, blanket-bombing raid. Soot, ash and dust lay piled deep like fresh snow along the verge.

The truck kicked up great clouds of fine grey dust as it sped along. The stour had us all choking and lent us a ghostly demeanour as it settled on us. The Yanks told us proudly that they had dropped a 'special bomb' on Nagasaki but I knew nothing of radioactivity or of the near fatal consequences my exposure to it would have. We searched in vain for bomb craters unaware of the atomic airburst that had flattened Nagasaki and extinguished the life of 35,000 of its residents. You could not tell it had once been a city with a pre-war population of 195,000. It looked more like the dark side of the moon. I spotted just one remaining concrete structure that looked like a building. It was difficult to comprehend.

Yet it would take more than this strange sight to spoil our party. Covered in radioactive dust the boys were laughing, crying and singing. The words that rang out across the shattered ruins of Nagasaki were never sung with more conviction and passion.

Rule Britannia!
Britannia rule the waves!
Britons never, never, never shall be slaves!

But I remained detached, unsure of what to think. In fact I was still terrified, a reflection of how traumatised I had been by years of living in the shadow of the sword. Every rock we ran over, every clang and start, scared me. *How safe are we? Rogue Japs could be hiding around the corner, waiting for us.* My mind suddenly turned to home. *Will I really make it? Will Mother and Father still be alive? Whatever happened to Douglas? Was he killed in action? And Eric? God, I hope Hazel doesn't have a boyfriend!*

I was disturbed by the sight of the devastation but felt no sympathy for the Japanese. Serves them bloody well right, I thought. How else was it going to end?

After forty-five minutes or so we arrived at Nagasaki harbour. While the quayside still showed the effects of the bomb, with blackened patches and blasted buildings, it had been somewhat patched up. A gigantic US Navy aircraft carrier, the USS *Cape Gloucester,* stretched the entire length of the docks, blocking out the sun. I had never seen anything like it. In its vast shadow the Americans had engineered some makeshift open-roofed showers with partitions. I was given a bar of pink soap and ushered to a space. I undressed and stood straight under the jets of bracing water. Despite the chill it was the finest shower I had ever had and my first proper wash in three and a half years.

I scrubbed frantically, working up the thickest lather possible, rubbing it into all my forgotten nooks and crannies. I had been filthy for so long and the grime was so engrained that very little dirt actually came off. But on the inside it had extremely therapeutic powers. Ignoring the soldiers telling me to hurry up I savoured every moment, just letting the water bounce off my head and neck.

After half an hour they practically dragged me from the showers to be fumigated and de-loused before being placed on the scales. When I left Aberdeen I had weighed a healthy 135lbs but here in Nagasaki on the steel-yard scales – very accurate contraptions similar to those I had used at the plumbers' merchants – I was reduced to a skeletal 82lbs.

New arrivals, men from the vast industrial gulag the Japanese had created in Fukuoka, flooded the quayside and lengthened the queues for showers. Sadly at this final hurdle some men did not make it and died on that quay. This distressed the Americans immensely and they were shocked by the matter-of-fact way that the other prisoners accepted the deaths of their mates. We had seen so much, too much.

As I stepped into my tan boiler suit issued by the Americans, I was pleased to have arrived early. A marine band from the *Cape Gloucester* started playing 'Anchors Aweigh' on the quayside.

Men went bananas, bursting into song and dance, waving their arms in the air to 'The Two O'Clock Jump'. With sailors giving me a helping hand my spindly legs struggled up the rickety gangplank to the hangar deck, where row upon row of camp beds had been arranged. There must have been hundreds of them and I took the first space available and sat down. Streams of men poured in, some nervous and wary, others delirious with happiness, while some were just plain delirious. The chap beside me, Denis Southgate, was from Cornwall and a survivor from HMS *Prince of Wales*, which had been sunk by Japanese bombers off the coast of Malaya at the outbreak of the war. We got chatting. He had also been at Fukuoka Camp 25 but we had never met.

All of our spirits lifted later that first balmy night when music was played over the tannoy system. The first tune, a new one to me, was 'Sentimental Journey' by Glenn Miller. It remains to this day my favourite song. We were allowed up on the main deck in batches. It was a terrific evening, no clouds in the sky, as another Glenn Miller song, 'Moonlight Serenade', blared out scratchily from the speakers.

As we sailed out of Nagasaki I looked back at the devastation the militarist rulers of Japan had brought on their country. Surveying that atomic wasteland to the big-band sounds of Glenn Miller was the defining moment of my life.

Nine

Back from the Dead

That night on board the USS *Cape Gloucester* I slept peacefully for the first time in years. It was the only time since our capture three and a half years earlier that I had gone to bed without the terrible sleep-depriving companion of fear.

The next morning I went to the galley for breakfast. When I arrived I thought I had taken a wrong turn while negotiating the maze of steel corridors that snaked through the innards of the massive ship – it felt like I had intruded on a wild party or stepped into a carnival. Men were whooping and hollering, clapping and singing like enraptured evangelists. The catalyst for the furore centred all too predictably around the long stainless-steel canteen. Men lined up impatiently in a long, disorderly queue to the serving area, where immaculately attired Americans (I still could not get over how *clean* and *healthy* they looked compared with us) were dishing out mountainous servings.

A bulky Afro-American cook greeted us all with a beaming broad smile and urged us to get stuck in.

'Tuck in boys! It's all you can eat.'

We felt like kids in a sweet shop. I had never seen so many boiled eggs in my life, piled high in vast rows of gleaming white pyramids that made me wonder if the ship was carrying the world's entire supply. Men loaded handfuls on to their plates, adding liberal dashes of milky cereal, soft white bread and maple syrup. The smell of the cooked food sent my head spinning and I had to actually clamp my mouth shut to stop from drooling. The temptation was too much for most of the lads but I recalled Dr Mathieson's earlier advice and steered clear of the most exotic and tantalising delights. Instead, with the greatest reluctance, I plumped for half an egg, a single slice of lightly toasted bread with a thick layer of margarine and a cup of tea. It required immense willpower not to eat more but once I had finished and sat for ten minutes I did feel full. I was telling guys around me to be careful, that their stomachs had shrunk to dangerously small proportions. The response was resoundingly and emphatically in the negative. No frugal and canny Scot was telling these starving boys to watch what they ate.

After my protestations were overruled I went searching for Dr Mathieson. I finally found him in the officers' mess. I pleaded my case to the officer on the door and was allowed in to speak to the doctor. I told him what was happening in the galley and in his usual considered manner he replied, 'I've already spoken to the Captain and explained the medical situation. Keep telling people though.'

I went back to the galley, which had not calmed down. Already some men were feeling sickly, their deprived stomachs at bursting point. I kept passing the message on but generally got told to bugger off and mind my own business. Sadly several men fell critically ill from over-indulging – not that anyone and certainly not me could blame them. But I felt a terrific sadness when I heard that a man had died from gorging and the subsequent damage it caused to his innards. Here we had survived three or four hellish years, undergoing some of the greatest atrocities and human sufferings of all time, and men were succumbing on the journey home. Those smiling American chefs and their huge hearts had inadvertently killed men with kindness.

After that they reduced the portions greatly and stopped the buffet altogether. I spent a lot of time on my bunk, composing in my mind a letter to my mother. It took some time and many miles before I could bring myself to put pen to paper. We soon arrived at Okinawa – site of the last pitched battle in the war just months earlier – where we transferred to a troop ship, the USS *Tryon*, and set sail at once for Manila in the Philippines.

Once back at sea the Army insisted that we each sign a document that stated that we would refrain from speaking about our wartime experiences. I was outraged and felt uncomfortable with the notion so I signed as 'George

Kynoch', using my father's Christian name and my mother's maiden name. I employed the same backhand style that I had used during the Selarang Incident, knowing full well they could never produce it as evidence. I felt that the British government wanted to suppress the true horrors, hide the facts and appease the Japanese. I wanted nothing to do with a cover-up.

I finally penned a long and rambling letter to my mother that I hoped to mail from Manila. I was coming home, my thoughts ran away from my pen. Trying to condense three and a half years of hell into a bite-size chunk that was palatable for my family proved incredibly difficult. My mother kept my letter as a treasured possession and I have it still.

> Hello folks, this is your old son, aged 26 years, coming to you by 'courtesy of the once Imperial Japanese Army'. That's what they told you if they ever gave you anything. Well, I hope you are all well and happy and I hope looking forward to my homecoming as eagerly as I. It has been a long troublesome and heartbreaking period those last six years but you and I have at last got a break and well deserved I think. There is little need to tell you as some of the stories are already in print, that we have been treated worse than pigs, but thanks to God, I am spared. At this point let us pause for a few moments in memory of so many of my fine pals who helped me through in those days of torture in Thailand, but who were lost at sea on the journey to Japan.

We left Nagasaki on the aircraft carrier 'Cape Gloucester' and were transferred on to the ship at Okinawa, where we are en route for Manila, where we should arrive on the 29/9/45. The experience of the last three and a half years has taught me many lessons and hard ones. The crowning joy will be my arrival at the station at Aberdeen.

Please give my kindest regards to my relations and if any to my friends of the pre-war years. Gee, it's going to be embarrassing trying to pick up the threads again especially in my future job, whatever that may be.

Mother there is one person you have to thank more than anyone else in the world for my presence here now, and that is Hazel Watson. It appears that while I was lying in hospital at death's door very ill with dysentery and beriberi, my pals had done everything they could do to make me buck my spirits up and make a fight for it, but I must have been in a coma, I cannot remember much of what happened. However, they raked out my photographs and as Hazel was the most prominent and most likely my girlfriend, they kept repeating her name and showing me her photograph. They said it was not till three hours later, that I seemed to recollect and began repeating her name over and over again, which was the turning point, as I gradually grew better day by day, weighing approximately five stone at that time. But, please mother keep this to ourselves as I do not wish her to know, as it puts her and myself in an awkward position. I believe she is married but am not sure. I have never managed to determine my feelings for Hazel, but it is sufficient that the thought of her pulled me together at the critical moment.

I only wish that the fellows who looked after me then and gave me what little supplies of milk and eggs they risked their lives to steal off the Japanese guards, had been spared for this day.

Well mother that is the terrible price of the war, and we can only hope there will never be another. Hoping this finds you as it leaves me. All the best, love to all at home, hoping to see you soon. Cheerio, your ever loving son, Alistair XXX.

Denis Southgate, who preferred to be called 'Tiny', even though he was larger than me, asked what I was writing. I told him but he just shrugged.

'You should write home too,' I said. 'Your parents would be thrilled to hear from you.'

'I don't think so,' the twenty-two-year-old marine replied, sounding defeated.

'Nonsense man. Here.' I shoved a pen and paper in his lap. I sat beside him on the camp bed. 'I'll help you.'

Maybe camp life had broken him or maybe he was illiterate but words failed to come. I basically dictated a simple letter home, addressed to his mother in St Austell in Cornwall, and he seemed to cheer up a little.

The days at sea went slowly and my mind kept returning to the haunting memories of our POW existence. Playing quoits on deck could preoccupy me for only so long. My recurring nightmare of surrender at Fort Canning continued and the Black Prince, the Mad Mongrel, Hellfire Pass and the sinking of the hellship also began to haunt me. They continue to disturb me to this day.

We arrived at the port of Manila on 25 September 1945. Trucks ferried us to a military hospital, which was run by Americans but we were cared for by Filipino nurses who treated us very well. The eyes of the nurses welled up and many were reduced to tears when they saw the state of us. Seeing so many pitiful walking skeletons and so many men robbed of their youth was too much for the nurses to bear. They were more openly disturbed by our appearance than the Americans had been and their unconcealed emotion brought home just how malnourished and ill we were.

For two weeks we lay confined to our hospital beds. Occasionally I would get up and walk around the ward but it was not encouraged. The one upside for many of us was that the Filipino nurses were extremely beautiful, as well as dutiful and kind. One about my age took a particular shine to me, which cheered me up no end. She was very attractive, with flowing black hair that glistened like coal, and asked for my home address, vowing to write to me. I was wary that she wanted a Western husband but maybe I was too harsh on her, for when I arrived home there was indeed a very sweet letter waiting, wishing me well and saying how much of a pleasure it was meeting me.

We bade farewell to the lovely nurses of Manila and clambered back on board the USS *Tryon*. Ten days later on 19 October we arrived at Honolulu, the capital of the far-flung US state of Hawaii. As the ship berthed in the now rebuilt Pearl Harbor, a tannoy announced that any men who wished to could go on deck, where on the starboard side a traditional welcoming ceremony would be performed for us.

I raced upstairs, bounding two at a time, elbowing others out of my way. This sounded too good to miss. It was a balmy evening bathed in moonlight that shimmered off the calm water in the harbour. We waited in an expectant silence that was broken by a jaunty ukulele tune that got louder and louder. As a fleet of small wooden canoes came into sight from the bow the sky filled with glorious female voices singing strange songs that I took for indigenous classics. As the occupants of the guitar-playing and angel-voiced canoes came into the light the men erupted into cheers and clapping. Buxom Hawaiian lassies with bright flowers around their necks and grass skirts wiggling were waving, smiling and still performing, putting on a real show. Seeing the women perform the hula-hula dance and hearing the upbeat music brought tears to many a hardened eye. We felt like returning heroes yet it would be the first and last time that I would have that feeling. I didn't realise it at the time but this was the best homecoming I would receive.

We stayed overnight to refuel and I cabled home. I wrote in longhand, 'Am well. Hope to be home soon. Safe in Hawaii. Love Alistair', and gave the message to the ship's purser who arranged for it to be wired.

Six days later on 26 October we arrived at San

Francisco, sailing under the magnificent Golden Gate Bridge, completed just eight years before in a Herculean engineering feat. Setting foot on American soil was nearly as emotional as the Hawaiian welcoming party, just without the fanfare. The sensation of being safe was more tangible – being in a Western country where people looked and dressed the same, had much the same sensibilities and ate the same food just felt right. It was probably an unwarranted sensation but even so it was how I felt.

A lorry took us to another military hospital on the suburban outskirts of the hilly city. Now feeling slightly better with every day, the thought of lying in a hospital bed for another period of weeks sucked a lot of energy from me. I was becoming more and more frustrated that it was taking so long to get home. At first I had imagined that we would be taken to an air-base and flown home immediately, possibly first-class after what we had endured.

A British Red Cross telegram from my parents sat waiting for me at the San Francisco hospital. It read, 'Cables received. All well. Hope see you soon – Urquhart.' Hearing from the clan, knowing they were well and that they knew *I* was well, was enough to encourage a long and unbroken sleep. In the morning I felt as fresh as a Yankee soldier's T-shirt and probably better than I had felt in years. Around mid-morning, while I was following one of the orderlies on his rounds, trying to pick up some tips, the head nurse came in with a visitor. She was introduced as 'Miss Ash', an elderly lady who ran a rehabilitation centre near by. The head nurse told us that

Miss Ash wanted to know if any of us would like to join her for a day out of the hospital. The offer was met with virtual silence until I piped up, 'I'll go.'

Miss Ash reminded me of my mother; she looked similar and even shared the same 'bun' hairstyle. She was delighted that someone had taken up her offer. No doubt half of the other men would have agreed if she had been thirty years younger and blonde but I was simply keen to get out of the hospital. I had been cooped up too long.

She led me to her car, a bright blue land-whale so immense I could hardly believe she was about to get behind the wheel. Before we left the hospital car park, she turned to me and asked in her highly refined American manner, 'Where would you like to go?'

I considered her question for a moment before realising that I had no clue what was near by. I didn't even have any money, not a dime.

'You choose,' I said.

We went through the streets of San Francisco, a booming town full of sailors, soldiers and tramcars similar to those in Aberdeen but that went up and down steep hills later to become famous in Hollywood car chases. We bounced along in the huge Pontiac past rows of wooden two-storey houses gaily painted in pastels, and across the Bay Bridge into the spectacular Californian countryside. On that first day Miss Ash drove for hours, taking me to see the giant redwood forests, trees that reached into the heavens, dizzying my disbelieving head. She spoke incessantly, asking all about me. She was especially keen to hear all about the POW camps, the Death Railway and the hellships. Despite her tears and my sentences that tailed off like the tarmac in her rear-view mirror, she ploughed on. I had no qualms at that time talking about my experiences to her and relayed them as accurately as I could.

After driving around all day Miss Ash dropped me back at the hospital shortly before dusk. I thanked her and as I stepped out of the car she said, 'See you tomorrow. We'll go up the Big Sur. It's beautiful this time of the year.'

'You don't have to, Miss Ash. I've had a lovely day, and you must be awfully busy.'

'Nonsense,' she said. 'I'll pick you up after breakfast.'

And so began a most enjoyable stay. Miss Ash and I drove all over California – the Golden State stretches for 160,000 square miles, over five times the size of Scotland. She took me to parties with her friends at which I met several ex-patriots from Scotland. We went on long drives along the coast and enjoyed picnics in the woods. It was one of the most pleasant experiences I had ever had. She even took me to Los Angeles, paying for us to stay at a hotel just off Hollywood Boulevard. We took in the Walk of Fame, the Chinese Theatre, Venice Beach and everything in between. Miss Ash knew I had no money and she paid for everything without ever making a fuss. She was a life-long spinster and I became something of a son to her. It was the start of a close friendship that lasted for many years and involved her coming to visit me and my family back in Scotland, and a huge hamper sent across the Atlantic every Christmas.

Every night I when returned to the hospital the boys would be waiting to ask where I had been that day. I relished filling them in in great detail – they were hugely envious. I always came back bearing stacks of fruit, cake and sweets for general distribution that eased their envy somewhat. I just thanked my lucky stars that I had volunteered that day to go with this remarkable, kind and charismatic woman.

One evening Miss Ash invited me to a Halloween party at the convalescent home where she lived. In a grand mansion tucked away in acres of bushy shrubs, cultivated lawns, paved areas and waterfalls, Miss Ash gave me the honour of wheeling in a ninety-nine-year-old lady in a wheelchair for dinner, after 'dooking for apples' and 'feeding the baby' with the sick and recovering children. I met a lovely girl, who was about twenty-one, paralysed and in a wheelchair. I took an interest, wheeling her about, trying to help her, and make her evening a memorable one. Miss Ash commented that the girl's eyes followed me around the room. At least it appeared that I had made somebody at the party as happy as I was.

Sadly the time came for us to leave San Fran and my new-found but short-lived life. On 2 November 1945 we were taken to the train station, where first-class Pullmans and dining cars awaited us, and a six-day journey to New York, spanning the three-thousand-mile girth of America. Miss Ash, thoughtful and generous as ever, showed up at the station with a large hamper brimming with goodies, including fruit, chocolate and cigarettes for the lads.

Another tearful farewell, and I waved goodbye to Miss Ash and went to find my seat. Before I sat down I noticed that an elderly couple were without a seat and I nudged a fellow Scot already sitting and staring out the window. Seeing the couple he got up without thinking and I ushered them over, offering our seats. To our great surprise they were extremely grateful for our generosity, exclaiming that they had never heard of such gentlemanly courtesy. Before long the whole cabin heard of our 'remarkable good manners' and we swelled with pride. At least some of our pride in our country and where we came from was still there.

The trip, although long, was not one I would have missed. The ushers treated us like royalty, pulling down our beds in the evening and waiting on us hand and foot. I spent most of the journey sipping tea and staring out of the window. The countryside changed so much, from the fertile coastal lands through to cactus-clad deserts, where I saw my first-ever 'proper' cowboys just like the ones from the silver screen, grisly gents on horseback wearing Stetsons and spurs. Arriving at Chicago train station was something spectacular even though we never got off and sat there for three hours – just taking in the sublime architecture of the station and its bustling inhabitants was enough for us 'former' POWs, who had suffered from sensory deprivation for so long.

Despite being at liberty we still needed telling what to do. None of us had money for food, beds or activities so when we got to New York City on 7 November we were still at the mercy of Army logistics. They put us into another hospital but this time allowed us out and about, with Army guides to show us the sights. Being a freshly liberated POW did as it happened have some benefits.

When we arrived at the base of the mighty Empire State Building at the intersection of Fifth Avenue and West 34th Street, we found ourselves ushered to the front of the snaking queue. With several elevators freed exclusively for our use the rest of the building was cleared. We had the run of what was then the tallest building on the planet. Once at the top we giggled like schoolgirls as we clambered to the side to take in the scenery. Yellow taxis crawled like maggots down below and the rush-hour foot traffic appeared no more than a fumbling army of dots. Sadly it was rather smoggy and our vista was clouded out but we could still see as far as the Hudson River, the Statue of Liberty and Central Park, as well as take in the fresh air of freedom.

The next day we went to see the world-famous Norwegian ice skater Sonja Henie perform her show. As a keen dancer I was staggered by her speed, grace and showmanship and clapped rapturously, until my bony hands hurt. We had no time for shopping – and still didn't possess a dime between us – but New York was a wonderful city to wander around. Inhaling its colourful mix of creeds, cultures and commerce temporarily relegated the horrors of the last few years to the back of my mind.

The respite was brief and after five pleasant days we were ready to sail back to the United Kingdom on 12 November on the *Queen Mary*, once a luxury liner, now converted into a less than luxurious troop ship. It had once carried British Prime Minister Winston Churchill across the Atlantic for crunch talks with fellow allied forces officials. When we boarded at New York it was crammed with hundreds if not thousands of other soldiers all gleefully bound on the last leg across the Atlantic for home.

Five days at sea, sleeping on the floor of a former lounge, unable to move about because of the sheer volume of passengers, I was glad to enter Southampton harbour. We had been well looked after, with exceptional care taken to provide us with the best food. But I was probably one of the poorest eaters on board. I still couldn't face eating anything substantial and stuck to bowls of cold custard or soup. To watch others gorge themselves made me nauseous.

I had been counting the hours. The thought of arriving home was mind-boggling to me. It felt like visiting a strange land for the first time, one I had only read about in books. It was like when you go on holiday to somewhere new and you know it won't resemble the picture you've built up in your mind, but that is all you have to go with so you succumb to it. That is how I felt, and I tried to limit my expectations and shun thoughts of what I would do once I got back to Aberdeen. I banished thoughts of gaining new employment and readjusting to society.

Despite my low expectations nothing could have prepared me for the disappointment of arriving in dismal Southampton. No quayside band, no media or fanfare awaited us. And most importantly, no family. I had fully expected to see Mum and Dad, Auntie Dossie, maybe even Bill and Rhoda, but there was nobody, just a handful of industrious dockworkers. All of the men felt devastated, as if a light had been snuffed out in our souls.

Feelings of disappointment, irritation and dread of travelling to the north of Scotland by train outweighed any anger on my behalf. That would come later though, when I fully realised how disgracefully the British government was treating its returning heroes. Despite dying in our thousands, sacrificing honest, hard-working and ordinary lives for the greater good, liberty and justice, we found they shunned us, forgot about us, brushed us under the political carpet. I was sure that my three-month journey home by the most circuitous route had been a deliberate political ploy by the government. I felt that they wanted us to recuperate on the way home to shield the British public from the state we were in and allow for the development of future good trading relations with Japan.

I sent a cable home from Southampton rail station saying, 'Home tomorrow', and obtained a rail warrant. I caught a commuter train to London, where I hopped off at Victoria Station. Disorientated and bewildered I bungled my way across London asking strangers for directions to King's Cross, where my last train awaited.

At King's Cross Station a couple of military police officers accosted me. 'Are you going to Aberdeen, lad?' one of them asked in a cockney accent. He must have heard me asking for my ticket.

'Yes, why?'

'Come with me.'

Wondering what I had done wrong this time, I followed him to an office. A ghostly-looking chap sat on a chair rocking back and forth in front of a paper-strewn desk.

He looked up at me and said bleakly, 'They're out to get me.'

I looked at the Red Caps, who shrugged. Not caring that the poor chap could hear them they told me he was 'away with the fairies'. He had been a regular in the Gordons and had been captured in Singapore. He was a complete wreck and had obviously suffered horrendously at the hands of the Japanese but all they could elicit from him was that his name was Hugh and he was from Inverurie in Aberdeenshire. Despite the fact that he was extremely depressed and mentally ill they put me in charge of him for the journey home, with strict instructions not to let him out of sight and to hand him over to some Red Caps at Aberdeen Station. I reluctantly agreed, thinking that it would at least keep my mind off other things.

We got a second-class seat and I plonked him by the window, hoping the passing countryside would placate him. He had a wild look in his eyes and jabbered nonsense constantly. I had the feeling that he could become aggressive at any time so I treated him good-naturedly and tried to calm him with soothing words.

The journey was a nightmare. Hugh was a handful and I spent most of my time apologising to others for his loud outbursts, which were frequent and disturbing. Seeing him in that state really got to me. I prayed that I wouldn't descend back down the same dark path.

I tried to convince him that he was back in Britain and would be safe now. Nobody was coming to get him. As we pulled into Aberdeen Joint Station at 6 a.m. on

18 November 1945, I told him to look out the window, hoping he would recognise the view as we crossed the River Dee. I left him with the Red Caps in much the same state as when I first met him, bidding him farewell and wishing him luck, though I'm not sure he heard.

Once I knew Hugh was safely in their hands I ventured to the main entrance, where I knew the family would be waiting. I spotted Mum first, her distinctive hair and height gave her away. I walked up to Mum, Dad, Dossie, Rhoda and a young chap I didn't recognise. I hugged Mum and I shall never forget the look in her eyes. She was so shocked and upset, probably by my skin-and-bone appearance and lack of hair. I hugged Dossie, Dad and Rhoda and the tears could no longer be held back. Both my mother and father had aged far beyond their years. My ordeal had taken a toll on them as well as myself.

I turned to the young chap and said, 'Are you Rhoda's boyfriend?'

Eyebrows raised, he said, 'No, you bloody fool! I am your brother Bill.'

It just went to show what six years of war could do – to him and me. Also there was Doug's new wife Cicely, from Oxfordshire, and she introduced me to their new baby boy born just a few months before. They had named him Alistair in my honour. Then it emerged that they had all thought I had been killed. None of the half-dozen cards or so that I had sent from the camps had ever arrived in Aberdeen. I was back from the dead.

On the tram journey home to Seafield Drive I asked where Douglas was. They told me that he was 'abroad' working for the Foreign Office but nobody had heard from him in months. He had been in the Army's glider regiment. He had broken both of his ankles during a mission into occupied France and reinvented himself as a war correspondent in the Middle East. Before the war he could speak French and German from his school days and had subsequently learned four more languages, which suited the Foreign Office, and they had signed him up. I wouldn't see him again until the following Christmas, when he returned as a shattered wreck, barely alive, looking as if he himself had been a POW and confined to the black hole for several months. He had disappeared on some cloak and dagger mission, abandoning his new wife and baby boy for more than a year. On his bizarre return he refused to tell anybody where he had been and was very nearly a broken man.

So by the time we reached home I was already feeling panicky. Everyone had so many questions; sometimes it felt as if they were all asking at once. This was not how I had thought I would feel on my homecoming. So much had changed. Mum had prepared a lavish breakfast for my return and the table was laid out when we got back home shortly after 7 a.m. We sat down for a family meal with everyone on their best behaviour – even Father was keen to dote on me. Mum served up tattie scones, sausages, eggs, the real works. But despite much encouragement and insistence I could only pick at my food. I asked about Hazel and without looking at me Mum said she had married during the war and moved to Canada. I was not upset; in fact I was glad that she had moved on and seemed happy.

Then Mum cleared her throat and told me nervously, 'You should also know, Alistair, that your friend Eric didn't make it.'

I felt ill. I could barely lift my head and the conversation buzzed around me. The words became jumbled and I could no longer make them out, as the kitchen walls seemed to close in. It was like a bout of cholera, the claustrophobia enhanced by the cramped kitchen and the desperate shows of love and affection my poor family poured on me.

'He was killed on his first mission over Europe,' Dad said. 'He was a rear gunner, a real brave soul.'

It was all too much, yet another kick in the face. Even though I had been around so much death, lived it and breathed it, nothing prepared me for the loss of such a close friend. All I could think was, Why then am I still alive? By what miracle had I returned home? Suddenly I snapped. I slammed my fork down on Mum's finest crockery plate and stood up, the chair screeching on the wooden floor. The room fell silent. It was so unlike me to make a scene, completely out of character. I knew they were trying to help but I just couldn't stand it.

'I'm going out,' I announced. I was already half out the door when a chorus of 'I'll come with you' and 'Come back, Alistair' rang out.

But I was off. I needed to be alone. My head felt like it was going to pop and fresh air seemed the only answer.

I walked and walked. Past the Co-op and up Auchinyell Brae, I hardly broke stride. Before long I was miles from home, walking with purpose but without forethought or direction. Aberdeen could not possibly have physically changed much during the war years but somehow I failed to recognise any of the surroundings. It all felt surreal and nothing seemed familiar. God knows where I walked but I kept on going, strolling without respite. Even when it got dark I kept on going and going, step after step, on my own enforced route march.

I did not return home until around five o'clock the next morning. My parents were still up, obviously worried sick. As I crawled up the stairs to find a bed to lie down in, utterly exhausted, they asked where I had been.

'We've been out looking for you,' Mum pleaded, begging for information.

'And all night,' Dad chimed in. 'We even called the police. What have you to say for yourself, son? It's freezing outside.'

I hated myself. I knew they were trying to be there for me but I just wanted to be on my own. I had lived a solitary and sorry life for so long that love only suffocated me. In many respects my family felt like strangers. How does one describe the feelings of a person who has been through something like we had, something no one could ever have envisaged? They could never comprehend the depths of man's inhumanity to man or the awfulness of an existence that consisted of surviving one day at a time.

I flopped down on my old bed in the room that I had helped build with my father all those years ago and slept all day and the next night. The recurring nightmares of the railway came again, leaving me afraid to lie down.

When I went downstairs the next day I ate a quick and light breakfast before promptly disappearing again. For the next few months my daily routine consisted of long and pointless walks. After a while I started looking at people's faces trying to spot anybody I knew from before the war but I never did. Not in the whole town. But I did purposely avoid my old haunts, especially the plumbers' merchants, Duthie Park and the dance halls.

I created mayhem at home, where I was morose, rude and short on patience. My sister Rhoda, God bless her, was so supportive and in many ways eased the situation, although I cannot ever remember thanking her, such was the state of my mind. I was irrational and unable to control my actions. I wanted only to be on my own, outside the four walls, wandering aimlessly in and around the streets of Aberdeen.

After a few weeks pounding the strange streets of my home town my body began to fall apart. I started to suffer with pains from beriberi, which attacked my legs, back and arms, and the cold winter air did not help. When my bowels started playing up as well I decided it was time to visit my local GP, Dr Rice.

I told him that I had amoebic dysentery while incarcerated so he put me on a course of inter-muscular injections. He injected my left arm but the skin began to tighten and then swell and became incredibly painful, so he went for the other, which did the same thing. After that I couldn't lie on my back or sides, couldn't bear sheets or clothing to touch them. Life was pretty bad despite the relative luxury I was afforded.

I still could not eat properly. I left untouched all of my old favourites, which Mum loved preparing for me. Much to my surprise I craved rice, the lousy stuff that we had all hated so much. The aptly named Dr Rice arranged for me to attend Stracathro Hospital – a large country house near Brechin in the neighbouring county of Angus that had been converted into a military hospital.

They did all of their tests and suggested different foods but I was still unable to take anything except fluids. My health suffered accordingly and I became weaker by the day.

I stayed there for several weeks. I could go home at the weekends but I had little money and nobody in the family had a car, so it was not an option. Mum and Dossie started out one Saturday but got on the wrong bus and never arrived at the hospital.

One day a baffled doctor visited my bedside and said he couldn't understand why I couldn't take food. I told him, 'If you had to survive on nothing else but rice and water for three and a half years, then maybe you could understand!'

'Yes, perhaps you are right. We just don't know what else to do for you,' he said rather ashamedly.

'Maybe my body is craving rice,' I suggested in a less defensive tone.

'We could try it.'

It seemed logical and perhaps not surprisingly it worked. My body responded to the rice and seemed to relax. My throat opened up and my bowels went from a stormy sea to a millpond. I ate rice pudding every day for several weeks – and relished it too! After a while I was put on to tripe, which did me the world of good, and then on to some white fish.

After three months and a final prognosis of having suffered from a duodenal ulcer, I came out of hospital armed with instructions for my mum on how to cook tripe, which she despised. She cooked fish, poached in milk, and servings of rice, as exotic as it got in those days. To this day I still have to eat rice two or three times a week, with some fish or chicken. Anything else causes havoc with my insides. One of my favourite dishes in Singapore had been a curry but never again. Even an onion is enough to set me off. The diet courtesy of the Emperor's Imperial Army, along with years of dysentery, had destroyed the linings in my stomach and done irreparable damage.

Thanks to my new diet and more rest and recuperation at home – where I hardly had to lift a finger – my body, mind and soul began to recover. I wrote to the Royal Army Pay Corps headquarters, gave them my rank and number, and asked for payments because I was still unfit for work. They tallied up my pay for my time as a POW and after deductions for 'subsistence' I received the grand sum of £434.00 – for the period from 15 February 1942 to 18 November 1945.

The charge for 'subsistence' infuriated me – they were making us pay for those handfuls of maggoty rice. Yet it was standard practice and applied to all returning prisoners. It is a miracle that they did not charge me for the loss of my rifle, as they did some men.

Early in 1946 and still a de facto member of the British Army, I was summoned to appear in front of a medical board at Woodend Hospital, Aberdeen. The board comprised four well-fed and comfortable-looking officers sitting behind a desk. They told me that the conditions of my military discharge hinged on my producing my Army 'records' and that unless I could produce records of all the diseases that beset me in the POW camps, they were not able to consider my situation.

I was stunned. I sat in an awkward silence trying to compose my thoughts and control my rage, before speaking.

'Sirs,' I said. 'Have you any conception of conditions in the Japanese prison camps?'

They did not reply so I went on. 'There were no pencils, pens, paper, aye, no toilet paper, drugs, toiletries, soap or water to wash! Never mind keeping records of each POW in many, many camps, certainly not in Kanyu or the Hellfire Pass camps. Just how much recording the Japanese kept is very little, as my Japanese Record Card shows!'

The chairman broke the silence that followed, saying, 'Then we are sorry, we are unable to help.'

This then was the sort of treatment meted out by the Army. It took another three or four meetings with various medical boards before they offered me demobilisation – but only if I agreed to pass myself as A1, which foolishly I did. I was so fed up of being downtrodden by the Army but I had let them off the hook of having to pay me any kind of disability war pension – it was a dirty trick played on many of the returning Far Eastern prisoners of war.

Two days later I went on my way down south for an official discharge and was issued with a brown-checked demobbing suit and hat, the usual Army fitting, and a pair of shoes. Hurrah, free of the Army at last.

By February 1946 I thought it was time to take a chance and try dancing again. I dusted off an old pair of dancing shoes with leather soles (my good pair had been abandoned back in Singapore) and shined them up. As I nuggeted them and buffed up a reasonable shine I was surprised at how unsteady my hands were. I was nervous. While dancing had always come very easily and naturally to me, it felt like starting afresh. It had been so long since I had allowed myself any luxurious thoughts of quick-steps or the tidal rise and fall of the waltz. But above all else, returning to social circles, dealing and talking with strangers, horrified me.

I decided to go to the Palais de Dance, the classier of the halls, on a quiet Wednesday night. I wore my uniform, which fitted only where it touched my still skeletal frame, and was pleased to see a lot of military people milling around outside. I recognised no faces, however. Inside the band started up and men at once crossed the floor, seemingly as fraught with danger as no man's land or the mine-ridden seas of the Indian Ocean, and asked women to dance. I stood there for a long time, probably an hour, before I approached a girl. I had noticed she could dance and looked assured yet kind. I 'tipped' her dance partner, the polite way of 'cutting in', and got the chance for a quickstep double novelty dance. The first thing she said to me was, 'So you can dance! Why did you stand for so long?'

I smiled and swung her around, delighted to be back in the saddle, so to speak. I only got halfway around the floor when I was tipped by a woman, who could also dance. Before I knew it I was back in my element. I tried to remember the female faces so I could get another dance with them later.

At the end of the night on my way out, with the smile still plastered on my face, one of the women collared me to say, 'I hope you come back, as I enjoyed dancing with you.'

That broke the ice and I went back two days later for the big Friday night dance. My legs were still aching from all of the unexpected exercise, using different muscles, and muscles that still needed to be built up, but nothing would stop me now. Early in the evening I met a woman called Mary Milne who was wearing a Women's Auxiliary Air Force uniform. She was a local lassie, three years younger than me, and a very good dancer. I had seen her earlier and she had caught my eye, so I made sure I tipped in later on and we got on well immediately.

'Will you be going to the dance tomorrow?' she asked, as we tapped out a slow fox-trot.

'Most certainly,' I said, hardly able to control my delight.

Dancing was the best rehabilitation I could have asked for, and it was also crucial to my reintegration to society. I slowly came out of my shell and thanks in no small part to Mary. She didn't ask me any questions and I liked it that way. I told her I had been a prisoner of the Japanese but that was as much detail as I gave. It turned out that in previous years she had courted someone who had been a prisoner of the Germans – so she sure could pick 'em!

Before long we were 'walking out', and seeing each other as much as possible. One of our favourite things was a stroll along the beach. On one such occasion, memorable for its cloudless sky, I took an attack of malaria. It came on quickly, forcing me to sit on a bench, sending me into hot, sweaty shivers. Mary was terrified as she did not know what was happening, and when I went into a tense rigor she helped me to a taxi and we rushed home. Dr Rice came, with his quinine, and gave me a dose in bed, which sorted me out. But it took me a fortnight to recover because of an enlarged spleen. I considered it a minor setback and got back to the dancing straight away, though by now struggling to breathe through my nose properly – it had been broken so often during all of those beatings on the railway. I went in for an operation to have a hole bored through my nose bone, and while I was in I took another malaria attack, which laid me out again, this time for a month.

As a couple Mary and I soon made friends at the various dance places. One of Mary's best friends and her boyfriend often joined us to make up a foursome. I enjoyed getting out but I must have been awkward and possibly miserable company. In reality I had little or no conversation. I did not wish to talk about my six and a half years in the Far East, especially as the others had not been abroad or on active service. If someone asked about my time in the war, I regurgitated my stock answer of, 'It was so bad that I don't want to talk about it.' If the war came up in conversation, I would keep quiet or steer the topic elsewhere. At the outbreak of the war Mary and her pal had gone to Glasgow to enlist and got caught in the blitz on Clydeside. They had been in the thick of it and while physically unharmed, they were mentally shaken. We just wanted to move on from the war.

Still painfully thin and very unfit I was unable to keep up with my new-found friends, especially in the dance halls, which put me at a disadvantage as Mary was pursued by several rivals. One particularly keen would-be suitor, who had been in a reserved occupation in Aberdeen and had never suffered during the war, really annoyed me. I became defensive and jealous. I suppose that being very self-conscious about my frail appearance and the fact that I was not earning did not help either. However, Mary and I still went out together; perhaps she sensed there was an ember smouldering within and at some stage it would turn to flame – I really do not know. I felt happy in her company because only then did I find some peace of mind.

No one other than one of us POWs could imagine the turmoil of the recurring nightmares that so many of us suffered. It seemed that every time I shut my eyes I was back in the camps. It all came back to life so vividly that my body would suddenly pour with sweat and fear. I was always glad when the morning light came.

During that period I was very pleased to hear of justice being meted out to some of the worst Japanese war criminals. The Japanese press lionised General Yamashita as 'The Tiger of Malaya' but he should have been known as 'The Butcher of Malaya'. He was hanged after a lengthy trial. Major General Shimpei Fukuye, the architect of the Selarang Incident, went on trial and was subsequently taken to the same spot where he had brutally executed the four escaped prisoners and shot. Disgracefully, General Takuma Nishimura, who had ordered the massacre of the Australian wounded at Parit Sulong, received only ten years imprisonment from the British. Later he would be arrested by the Australians in Hong Kong as he travelled home after completing his sentence. He was subsequently tried by an Australian military court and hanged.

As the trials went on it became obvious just how much bunkum all of the bushido code had been. The so-called 'Way of the Warrior' precluded capture yet so many of these ring leaders *had* been captured – the shame that to them had made us so despicable now seemed bearable and certainly preferable to the ordained hara-kiri.

Happily among the 256 Japanese war criminals to be executed were a loathsome duo from the Death Railway. The Black Prince had failed to fall on his samurai sword and revealed himself to be the coward that most swaggering bullies are. He was hanged, as was the Mad Mongrel. Inexplicably, Dr Death received only ten years.

One day in July 1946 there came a knock at the door and Dossie shouted on to me to get up and come down as I had visitors. I came downstairs, opened the door and almost fell over. Freddie Brind stood there, with his trademark grin and his ever-present buddy, brother Jim. It was just great to see them. I hadn't heard of them since leaving Chungkai on the other side of the world. Until they had turned up I didn't even know if they had made it.

We shook hands and embraced. In the finest British tradition I asked them in for a cup of tea. As Jim stayed silent Freddie recounted their story. After their father had been taken prisoner by the Japanese and taken to Changi at around the same time as us, they hadn't seen him. He was kept in the prison where he had previously been a warden. Freddie remained stoutly calm as he said that his father died there in that jail. He had never spoken about the man much. His mother, who had escaped, was obviously much closer to the brothers.

I refilled the teapot and Freddie continued updating me in great detail. He was now working as a plumber's mate. Jim had a job at the Selo film factory in Brentwood, which he would work at all his days.

After a while Freddie got around to why they were in Aberdeen. They had arrived for a reunion of the Gordon Highlanders. Once he raised that topic he wanted to talk only about the prison camps. No matter how I tried to divert the subject he would always bring it back, recalling his comical moments, the characters and the scams, but also the horrors and the unspeakable. It was as if he were trying to make sense of it. I got the impression that he was also struggling to readjust to civilian or British life. In the camps we all knew him as a man, or boy really, who could acquire things, get things done. But back in Blighty he was just another veteran despite being still in his teens. In his own eyes he wasn't special any more.

I invited them to stay with the family while they were in Aberdeen but they insisted that they would not impose and had booked digs in Crown Street. The next day I went with them to the reunion at the Station Hotel in Aberdeen. It was an emotional affair but one that indeed was necessary. I relaxed finally in the company of others who had suffered as much as I had. They knew my pain. They didn't ask awkward questions or stare at me as if I were a leper

For the rest of his life Freddie would phone me every night, no matter what was happening in either of our lives. He just wanted to talk – always about the camps, which had left a fatal impression on him. He had to be checked in to Roehampton hospital several times, for a month or more at a time, and had even been granted a twenty-four-hour telephone line to a psychologist. Yet he preferred to phone me and chew my ear for an hour every night, sometimes two hours at a time.

He got married to an Essex girl, Nora, whom he met through his church. But Freddie never came out of the camps. And he drank heavily to forget. Given his experience and his character it should not have been a shock that he became an alcoholic. Despite the love he received from his wife, his family, and me and my family, he would die within ten years of returning to the UK of cirrhosis of the liver – still a young man.

The reunion had been a cathartic experience for me and by August 1946 I felt fitter both mentally and physically. My thoughts returned to work. I could still hear Mr

Grassie in his inimitable tone saying he would always have a job for me, one of 'his boys'. But I knew that I would never manage the physical job I had done before the war. I paid him a visit anyway.

At Lawson Turnbull & Co. Ltd's reception desk a stranger was on duty. I asked to see Mr Grassie and she lifted the phone and dialled his room. Within seconds the old Great War veteran appeared from his office off the main reception area. He ushered me inside and closed the door behind us. I stood, waiting to be seated in front of his large desk that commanded the immaculately tidy room. Before he sat he eyed me up and down, taken aback by my appearance. Mr Grassie wasn't one to show his feelings at all but I swear that in that instant, for just a fleeting moment, he shed a tear.

'It's grand to see you,' he choked. 'None of us thought we would ever see you again.'

He called for tea and biscuits to be sent in, as if trying to divert attention from his emotions. I explained to Mr Grassie that I needed to start work again, although my health was not good, which of course he could see for himself.

'You can start back whenever you feel able, Alistair. We'll find a job for you.'

Mr Grassie never asked about the war.

I reported for work in early September 1946 and Mr Grassie assigned me to the office section, where I got a job estimating, controlling contracts and customer services. I was back at work. But life could never get back to normal.

*

My experiences at the hands of the Japanese continued to haunt me both physically and mentally – as they still do all of these years later. Even after I married, life could be hell. To this day I suffer pain and the nightmares can be so bad that I fight sleep for fear of the dreams that come with it.

Yet I owed it to myself and to the others who never made it back to make the most of my life. I threw myself into a career and worked my way up to become managing director of another plumbing supplies business, making health and safety a priority for the staff – after what I had witnessed on the Death Railway. I enjoyed the work.

My two children grew and I took great pleasure from their success, as I did when my grandchildren came along – and when they went to university!

Life continued to throw up challenges. After my wife Mary suffered a stroke, losing the power of speech, I nursed her for twelve and a half years during which she was wheelchair-bound. I think that the experiences I had on the railway and the inspirational example of our medics helped me to cope during that difficult period.

At the age of seventy-five, after Mary's death, I briefly emigrated to Canada to be close to my daughter, yet I found myself lonely and isolated in a strange country. I decided to return to Scotland. Through all of this my sufferings as a prisoner taught me to be resilient, to appreciate life and all it has to offer.

Back in Scotland I quickly made new friends in the world of my lifelong passion, ballroom dancing – and at ninety years of age I am still working on my slow fox-trot.

I dance an average of five times a week and organise two weekly tea dances. I campaign for the residents of my sheltered housing complex and have managed to persuade the council to give us funds for computer, painting and t'ai chi classes to keep us active. I am pleased to say that the council also came off worse in my battle to have our grass and hedges cut. In recent years my charity fund-raising activities for the complex have raised hundreds of pounds to fund our activities.

I am a proud member of the Far East Prisoner of War Association (FEPOW) and regularly answer the queries of families anxious to know how their grandfathers and fathers were treated. On behalf of FEPOW I am very pleased to speak to schoolchildren about our experiences.

My life has been long, rich and rewarding but always, always, the ghosts of the river Kwai have remained with me. The cruel faces of the Black Prince, Dr Death and the Mad Mongrel have stalked my dreams for more than six decades now. And in my thoughts and prayers I will never forget the faces of all those young men who died looking like old men, those prisoners who endured terrible deaths in a distant land.

Acknowledgements

I would like to thank Kurt Bayer of Scottish News Agency who spent many hours quarrying my memory to make this book possible. Thanks are also due to Graham Ogilvy, our editor at Scottish News Agency, and to 'Stan', our agent at Jenny Brown Associates. I am indebted also to Richard Beswick at Little, Brown who recognised the potential of my story.

The Australian War Memorial and David Martin of Fotopress assisted with photographs. Leslie Bates generously supplied still photographs of the rescue of torpedoed survivors taken by her father Mr Joe Bates, an officer aboard USS *Sealion II*.

A number of individuals have done so much to keep alive the memory of what we suffered in the Far East. They include: Ron Taylor and Keith Andrews of the Far East Prisoner of War Association; Roger Mansell in San Francisco, who maintains and updates an excellent website that is invaluable for research; and Rod Beattie, who deserves recognition for his sterling efforts in developing the work of the Burma Thailand Railway Memorial Association. US Navy veteran Sid Mouser helped contact the Bates family and hosts moving film of the rescue of the torpedoed survivors on his SubRescue channel on YouTube.

The Gordon Highlanders Museum has also been very supportive and helpful.

My daughter, Joyce, and son, Philip, have been a great encouragement and my dear friend Helen Scroggie has been a pillar of strength during the writing of these memoirs. I would like to thank Meg Parkes of the Liverpool Hospital of Tropical Medicine. Last but not least, I would like to thank my consultant and friend Keith Baxby but for whose skill and dedication I would not be here today.

Index

Aberdeen, 11–12, 16–17, 155, 193, 205, 238–9, 278
  Alistair's return, 273, 283–90
  Bridge of Don barracks, 14, 19–20, 26, 52, 55, 85, 146, 164
  Capital Theatre, 136
  Highlanders' reunion, 299–300
  Palais de Dance, 23–4, 193, 294
  Woodend hospital, 292
Aden, 45–6
Afghanistan, 29
Albury, First Lieutenant Charles, 255
Alfie, Uncle, 166
Alice, Aunt, 166
Anderson, Sandy, 16
Arbroath, 31–2
Argyll and Sutherland Highlanders, 44, 63, 77, 89, 119
Ash, Miss, 277–80
Aso, Taro, 247–8
'atap stare', 157
atomic bombs, 255–8, 263–4
Auchinyell Brae, 239, 288
Australia, 110, 206
Australians, 77–8, 89–90, 177, 241
  and clandestine cigarettes, 201–2
  and cricket, 206

  and Parit Sulong massacre, 89, 298
  and Selarang Incident, 112–15

ballroom dancing, 5, 22–6, 70–6, 294–5, 302
Bam Pong, 129, 210
Bangkok, 144, 194, 204
banzai charges, 137
Barker, Tommy, 70–7, 79–80
Bataan Death March, 3
Battle of Britain, 64
Battle of the Somme, 13, 18–19
Bay of Bengal, 46
Beahan, Kermit, 256
bed bugs, 154, 215
Bedfordshire and Hertfordshire regiment, 167, 205
bicycles, 166
Bissett, Eric, 22–3, 25, 57, 108, 287
Black Watch, 63
Blackpool, 70, 75
Blakamati, 64
Bon Accord Swimming Club, 21, 208
Borneo, 214
Boy Scouts, 21–2, 26, 28, 142, 160, 191, 233
Bradman, Don, 206
Brechin, 291
Bren guns, 27–8
Brentwood, Essex, 87, 299